D0210903

PSYCHOTHERAPY

DIRECTIONS IN PSYCHIATRY
MONOGRAPH SERIES

A NORTON PROFESSIONAL BOOK

DIRECTIONS IN PSYCHIATRY
MONOGRAPH SERIES

PSYCHOTHERAPY

NUMBER 5

EDITED BY

Frederic Flach, M.D.

W·W· Norton & Company • New York • London

Copyright © 1989 by The Hatherleigh Co., Ltd.

Portions of this work copyright © 1981, 1982, 1983, 1984, 1985, 1986

All rights reserved.

Published simultaneously in Canada by Penguin Books Canada Ltd.,
2801 John Street, Markham, Ontario L3R 1B4.

Printed in the United States of America.

Library of Congress Cataloging-in-Publication Data

Psychotherapy.

   (Directions in psychiatry monograph series no. 5)
   "A Norton professional book" — Ser. t.p.
   Includes index.
   1. Psychotherapy. I. Flach, Frederic F. II. Series.
[DNLM: 1. Psychotherapy. W1 DI659D no. 5 /
WM 460.6 P9747]
RC480.P824 1989   616.89'14   88-31263

ISBN 0-393-70063-1

W. W. Norton & Company, 500 Fifth Avenue, New York, N. Y. 10110
W. W. Norton & Company Ltd., 34 Great Russell Street, London WC1B 3NU

1 2 3 4 5 6 7 8 9 0

Editor

FREDERIC FLACH, M.D., Adjunct Associate Professor of Psychiatry, Cornell University Medical College, and Attending Psychiatrist, The Payne Whitney Clinic of New York Hospital and St. Vincent's Hospital and Medical Center, New York.

Editorial Board

E. JAMES ANTHONY, M.D., F.R.C.PSY., Director of Child and Adolescent Psychotherapy, Chestnut Lodge, Rockville, MD.

ROSS J. BALDESSARINI, M.D., Professor of Psychiatry and Neuroscience, Harvard Medical School; Interim Director, Mailman Laboratories for Psychiatric Research, McLean Hospital, Belmont, MA.

JOEL ELKES, M.D., Professor of Psychiatry, University of Louisville; Distinguished Service Professor Emeritus, Johns Hopkins University, Baltimore.

JOSEPH T. ENGLISH, M.D., Director of Psychiatry, St. Vincent's Hospital and Medical Center, New York; Professor of Psychiatry, New York Medical College; Adjunct Professor of Psychiatry, Cornell University Medical College, New York.

SHERVERT H. FRAZIER, M.D., Professor of Psychiatry, Harvard Medical School; Psychiatrist-in-Chief, McLean Hospital, Belmont, MA.

CARL P. MALMQUIST, M.D., Professor of Psychiatry, Institute of Child Development; Professor of Law and Professor of Criminal Justice, University of Minnesota, Minneapolis.

TIMOTHY B. MORITZ, M.D., Staff Psychiatrist, Charter Hospital of Las Vegas.

HOWARD P. ROME, M.D., Professor of Psychiatry Emeritus, Mayo Graduate School of Medicine, Rochester, MN.

MICHAEL A. SCHWARTZ, M.D., Clinical Professor of Psychiatry, New York Medical College; Chief, Psychiatric Research, St. Vincent's Hospital and Medical Center, New York.

LOUIS JOLYON WEST, M.D., Professor and Chairman, Department of Psychiatry and Biobehavioral Sciences; Director, The Neuropsychiatric Institute, University of California, Los Angeles.

PETER C. WHYBROW, M.D., Professor and Chairman, Department of Psychiatry, University of Pennsylvania, Philadelphia.

ROBERT L. WILLIAMS, M.D., D.C. and Irene Ellwood Professor and Chairman of Psychiatry, Chief of Psychiatry Service, Baylor College of Medicine, Houston.

Contributors

Leopold Bellak, M.D.
>Emeritus Professor of Psychiatry, Albert Einstein College of Medicine/ Montefiore Medical Center; Clinical Professor of Psychology, Postdoctoral Program in Psychotherapy, New York University.

Ivor W. Browne, F.R.C.P.I., M.Sc. (Harv), F.R.C.Psych., D.P.M.
>Head, Department of Psychiatry, University College, Dublin, Ireland.

Hans W. Cohn, Ph.D.
>Member of the Group Analytic Society (London).

Sidney Crown, Ph.D., F.R.C.P., F.R.C.Psych.
>Consultant Psychiatrist, The London Hospital, Whitechapel, London, England.

Sol L. Garfield, Ph.D.
>Professor Emeritus of Psychology, Washington University, St. Louis, MO.

Vincent Kenny, M.A., M.S.
>Director, Psychotherapy Training, University College, Dublin, Ireland.

Carolin S. Keutzer, Ph.D.
>Associate Professor of Psychology, University of Oregon, Eugene.

Michael Joseph Miller, Ph.D.
>Attending Psychologist, Cabrini Medical Center; Clinical Instructor in Psychiatry, New York Medical College and the Psychiatric Residency Training Program of the Cabrini Medical Center of New York.

Leon Salzman, M.D.
>Clinical Professor of Psychiatry, Georgetown University Medical School, Washington, D.C.

Richard K. Sherlock, Ph.D.
>Associate Professor of Philosophy, Utah State University, Department of Languages and Philosophy, Logan, Utah.

Henry I. Spitz, M.D.
  Clinical Professor of Psychiatry, Columbia University, College of Physicians and Surgeons; Director, Group Psychotherapy Program, New York State Psychiatric Institute, New York.
Robert L. Stewart, M.D.
  Clinical Professor of Psychiatry, University of Cincinnati; Training and Supervising Analyst, Cincinnati Psychoanalytic Institute, Ohio.
Anthony Storr, F.R.C.P., F.R.C.Psych.
  Emeritus Fellow, Green College, Oxford, England; Honorary Consulting Psychiatrist, Oxford Health Authority.
Fraser N. Watts, Ph.D.
  Research Clinical Psychologist, Medical Research Council, Applied Psychology Unit, Cambridge, England.

Contents

Introduction

I came very close to abandoning my training in psychiatry and returning to a more tangible and defined form of medical practice by the end of my third week of residency.

Bewildered and overwhelmed, I went to the office of Dr. Oskar Diethelm, who was then Psychiatrist-In-Chief of the Payne Whitney Clinic in New York, for our weekly supervisory meeting. There weren't enough hours in the week to do this kind of work, I complained. I felt I just didn't have what the job required. I had twenty inpatients under my care. Following a set of self-imposed guidelines based on naive notions about traditional Freudian psychoanalysis, I saw each patient three times weekly for one hour. That accounted for sixty hours. Then I spent another ten hours writing up charts. Seventy hours. Morning staff conference, noon case conferences and lectures, and occasional seminars accounted for another sixteen hours, at least. I was working an average of twelve hours a day, seven days a week. What made it even more distressing was that I hadn't the foggiest notion of what I was doing. I sat there with patients, sometimes mostly listening, asking a few questions hesitantly lest I interfere with the spontaneous flow of free associations. At other times both the patient and I sat in total silence as the hour dragged painfully on.

Dr. Diethelm, who made rounds daily and was personally familiar with each and every one of the patients in the hospital, smiled. He asked for a roll call of those assigned to me. As I responded, our exchange went something like this:

"Mrs. Jones."

"Fifteen minutes every day."

"Mr. Smith."

"Two full hours a week, and five minutes on the days you don't have regular session."

"Miss O'Leary."

"Half an hour, three times a week."

He then went on to explain to me why each patient required a different time structure for psychotherapy. Mrs. Jones was receiving electric convulsive treatments and the purpose of my contact with her was to assess her progress and offer her reassurance. Mr. Smith had a long history of recurrent depressions; it was important to probe into his past to uncover experiences and correct attitudes that might make him more vulnerable to the return of his disabling moods. Miss O'Leary, a woman in her seventies who had suffered a series of mild strokes, needed my help to adjust to her illness and plan the kind of life she would be able to lead after her hospital discharge.

Therein I learned an invaluable lesson that has served me well indeed during the 35 years that have passed since then. *The psychotherapeutic approach to every patient a therapist sees should be individually shaped to conform to his or her unique personal, social, and psychopathological needs.* So that, in 1960, when Dr. Peter Regan and I wrote what was my first text, *Chemotherapy in Emotional Disorders*, one of our strongest messages was a warning against the dangers of therapeutic exclusiveness—the tendency of psychiatrists and all other mental health professionals to offer patients not so much what the patient required, but rather those special skills in which the therapist may have been trained, whether they be psychoanalytic psychotherapy, cognitive therapy, family systems approaches, or strictly biological and nonpsychotherapeutic.

I felt reassured by Dr. Diethelm's clarification. At the end of our session, I asked him how long he thought it would take me to become proficient at psychotherapy. Again he smiled.

"Ten years, perhaps. Perhaps longer."

Looking back, I think his estimate was rather optimistic. He might better have said: "A lifetime."

Learning to be an effective psychotherapist is a never ending process. Without a doubt, it is the most complex task which physicians and other professionals undertake. The talents required of a good psychotherapist are undoubtedly determined genetically and shaped by his or her own life experiences from childhood on, even as a proficient orthopedic surgeon must have an inborn gift for engineering. In my own opinion, *lack of psychotherapeutic talent cannot be compensated for by training any more than raw talent can be productively directed without proper education and an ongoing, open-minded commitment to learning.*

What kind of education does a psychotherapist require? I believe that *a solid foundation in the liberal arts and the humanities is essential.* Consider the elements that noted psychiatrist Jerome D. Frank considers the core of all psychotherapeutic approaches, regardless of their theoretical bases. Frank writes:

Psychotherapy is a process whereby a socially sanctioned healer seeks to help persons overcome psychologically caused distress and disability by a systematic procedure linked to a theory of the sources and nature of the sufferer's difficulties and how to alleviate them . . . The weight of evidence is that any form of psychotherapy yields significantly better results than the so-called spontaneous improvement rate.*

Frank feels that the restoration of morale is a critical feature of all successful therapy. He identifies four features common to all forms of psychotherapy which contribute to this goal. The first is a trusting, confiding, emotionally charged relationship between a patient seeking help and a therapist offering it. The second is the setting, a special place which possesses the aura of healing. The third is a rationale or conceptual scheme—a belief system—that explains what has happened and what will happen, one that is convincing to both the patient and the therapist and hence *linked to the dominant worldview of the culture.*

It is Frank's third point which I believe so clearly emphasizes the prospective therapist's need for a broad education in history, literature, art, philosophy, religion, and the other constituents of the traditional humanities curriculum *before embarking on the more specialized learning in the pursuit of a graduate degree in medicine, psychology, social work, or any other mental health discipline.*

His fourth ingredient in all psychotherapies is a procedure, a ritual that therapist and patient follow for the purpose of restoring health. Thereby

anxiety and other distressing emotions are neutralized through repeated exposure to anxiety-arousing stimuli in a supportive context . . . enabling the patient to become conscious of feelings or maladaptive behavior of which he had been unaware, and encouraging him to experiment with new responses.*

This is where specific training comes in, both with regard to theoretical models ranging from the ego-superego-id structure of personality to Pavlovian conditioning and systems theory, and tactics to translate these hypotheses into moment-to-moment action within the setting of each psychotherapeutic contact. The couch with the therapist out of sight and the patient free associating, encouraging the patient to expose himself to the specific objects of his phobic fears, giving him homework designed to enhance his sense of self-worth and stimulate positive thinking, maneuvers to shift the power center within the family group—each represents the evolution of techniques to implement a particular theoretical vision.

—Frederic Flach, M.D.

*Frank, JD: Psychotherapy: Restoration of morale. *Weekly Psychiatry Update Series*, 1:2, Biomedia, Inc, Princeton, NJ, 1976.

PSYCHOTHERAPY

1

How Does Psychotherapy Work?

Part I: The New Science Paradigm for Psychotherapy Theory

Ivor W. Browne and Vincent Kenny

EDITOR'S NOTE

In this chapter and the following the authors explore the question that recurrently haunts even the most experienced clinician: Does psychotherapy really work? Do the hours, weeks, and years we spend carrying out this modality really have a healing influence?

The approach they take is not, however, statistical. Rather, they emphasize that many of the traditional methods in research may be simply inadequate to the task for confirming—or denying—the importance of psychotherapy. They divide scientific endeavor into a past—dominated by Newtonian concepts that deal in measurable forces of cause and effect—and contemporary (and future), which began with Sadi Carnot's formulation of the second law of thermodynamics, to the effect that any isolated physical system will proceed spontaneously in the direction of ever increasing disorder. Darwin, de Chardin, and Einstein continued the evolution of vision and thought that moved away from the idea of the material world being a comfortably ticking clock to be repaired when out of order to an indeterminate interweaving of interdependent interrelationships.

Studies of psychotherapy following the Newtonian model have been singularly inconclusive. Some, such as those of Eysenck, suggest psychotherapy is totally

ineffectual; others give the appearance of proving the efficacy of one psychotherapeutic approach over all others; some suggest that every form of psychotherapy is
equally effective.

The authors offer a fresh, challenging view of psychotherapy and redefine the
nature of psychotherapy as a way to help patients who are in psychological distress
because their personal theory of reality has failed to reconstruct their view of the
world and consequently help them reorganize themselves in a new and different way.
The concept of open systems suggests an active principle emerging in matter characterized by change, instability, and continual fluctuation; at bifurcation points fluctuations destabilize the current organization of the system, which may then disintegrate into chaos or suddenly reorganize itself into a higher level of organization. The
purpose of psychotherapy is to facilitate a constructive outcome for such an event
when the individual cannot do so on his own.

Introduction

To find the answer to the question "How does psychotherapy work?" we
must first ask another question, viz., "Why, after more than half a century,
do we not have answer to the question 'How does psychotherapy work'?"
The answer to this question probably lies in the inappropriate application of
Newtonian science to the area of human experience. Part I of this chapter
explores the tacit assumptions and problems inherent in the old science and
outlines the essential ingredients of the new science paradigm. Part II outlines the application of the new science outlook to psychotherapeutic practice and attempts to illustrate how psychotherapy works within this framework. We will begin with a brief historical review of the major conceptual
landmarks on the way from Newtonian to systemic theory.

Galileo (1564–1642): The scientific revolution began with Nicholas Copernicus who first proposed that the earth was no longer the center of the
universe but merely one of a number of planets circling a star. This theory
was published in 1543, the year of his death. The real change in scientific
thinking, however, was ushered in by Galileo. He not only confirmed the
work of Copernicus but for the first time combined scientific experimentation with the language of mathematics. Galileo stated that science should
restrict itself to studying the essential properties of material bodies — shapes,
numbers, and movement, i.e., that which can be measured and quantified.
In doing this he was very aware that this did not represent all of reality and
that the science he suggested did not deal with other aspects such as experience, quality, or values. Nevertheless the views he put forward represented
the dominant features of science throughout the 17th century and still remain as important criteria in scientific work today.[1]

Francis Bacon (1561-1626): Classical Empiricism: Francis Bacon was the father of empiricism, a pragmatic view which has dominated the British tradition in science ever since. Bacon is also of particular interest in that he established the strongly masculine influence we associate with scientific endeavor. As Attorney General at the time of James I, Bacon had the task of conducting the trial of suspected witches. It is not surprising that, when addressing himself to nature which has always traditionally been considered female (e.g., Mother Earth), he used phrases such as "torture nature's secrets from her," or "to make a slave of nature." We see here the idea that we can interfere as we like with nature, make her do as we want, and we can see this influence still at work today in medicine and psychiatry and in the deterministic notion of "giving" a person a "course" of psychotherapy as if it were a form of medicine to make them do our bidding.[2]

Rene Descartes (1596-1650): Classical Rationalism: Both Bacon and Descartes split the person into a "higher" and "lower" self. Baconian observation and Cartesian intellect acted as the "higher" self which discerned truth, as opposed to our "lower" self (prejudiced, irrational) which promoted error. Descartes started from a position of doubting all things until he came to something he could not doubt — himself as a thinker. This gives rise to his famous phrase, "Cogito ergo sum" — "I think therefore I am." Here we have the separating of mind from matter. He said "there is nothing included in the concept of body that belongs to the mind; and there is nothing in that of mind that belongs to the body." This fundamental division between mind and matter has had an enormous effect on Western thought and plagues medical thinking to this day. More than anything else, this has made it difficult for us to think rationally about psychotherapy, and many Westerners think of their bodies simply as something which transports their "real" (thinking) self, i.e., their mind. Descartes's greatest contribution was probably the use of analytic method of reasoning. This was extremely valuable and underlay most of the advances in the development of scientific achievement for the next 300 years. Unfortunately, overemphasis on this Cartesian method has led to the ubiquitous attitude of reductionism in science, the idea that all natural phenomena can be understood by breaking them up into smaller parts. We have thus arrived at a view of causality that disturbance of the "whole" will always be explained by a malfunction in one of its parts. It is the model which is used in attempts to study and understand how psychotherapy works. Descartes's clockwork, a mechanistic model of nature, has had a major effect on biologists, physicians, and psychologists for the past 300 years, indeed right to the present day. Unfortunately the kind of illnesses and health problems affecting us in the late 20th century do not yield their secrets to this kind of reductionist thinking.[3]

Isaac Newton (1643-1727): The conceptual framework created by Galileo and Descartes was completed by Newton who developed a consistent mathematical formulation of the mechanistic view of nature. From the second half of the 17th century to the end of the 19th century the Newtonian, mechanistic model of the universe dominated all scientific thought. Newton created a new mathematical method (i.e., differential calculus) to describe the motion of solid bodies. He used this to formulate the exact laws of motion of all bodies under the influence of the force of gravity. The great significance of these laws lay in their universal application where the universe was seen as a vast machine operating according to exact mathematical laws. The unique importance of Newton's work was understood by his contemporaries. The natural sciences, as well as the humanities and social sciences, all accepted this mechanistic view of classical physics as the correct description of reality and modeled their own theories accordingly. Whenever psychologists, sociologists, or economists want to be scientific they always turn to the basic concepts of Newtonian physics and base their research on them.[4]

After Isaac Newton, scientists believed they had laid bare the laws governing the universe and that all happenings were understandable at last in terms of strictly determined laws of cause and effect. By identifying all of the "inputs" in any situation one could determine precisely the result which would follow. The existing uncertainties and areas of incomplete knowledge would be conquered by the steady growth of scientific knowledge. Our understanding of nature would be complete, including the complex area of human existence, the treatment of disease and the phenomena of madness.

Thermodynamics (1824): "The Science of Complexity": The formulation of the laws of thermodynamics constituted the first great break with the static, reversible world of Newton and classical dynamics. The first law is concerned with the conservation of energy. It states that the total energy involved in a process is always conserved. In 1824 Sadi Carnot formulated the second law of thermodynamics which stated that any isolated physical system will proceed spontaneously in the direction of ever increasing disorder. In the 1850s Rudolf Clausius introduced a new concept which he called "entropy" to measure the degree of evolution of a physical system. Thus entropy can be seen as a measure of disorder. Boltzmann developed this work further, demonstrating that irreversible thermodynamic change is a change towards states of increasing probability. This move to explain a physical concept in terms of statistical probability marks a sharp departure from Newton. With the help of probability theory the behavior of complex mechanical systems can be described in terms of statistical laws. Thus, in any isolated system made up of a large number of molecules, the entropy (or disorder) will keep increasing until the system reaches a state of maximum equilibrium. This introduced for the first time into science the notion of irreversibility and, as Eddington called it, "the arrow of time." Nothing could ever be the same again.[5]

Charles Darwin (1809-1882): Charles Darwin brought together an array of evidence to create a theory of evolution with a firm biological footing. Darwin's Origin of the Species had the same all-embracing effect on subsequent biological thought as Newton's Principia had earlier on astronomy and physics. Once again the concept of irreversibility and an "arrow of time" was emerging but now as an evolving and everchanging system in which complex forms of life developed from simpler structures. At first Newtonian scientists tried to dismiss this development as unimportant accidents and peculiarities of nature but by the end of the 19th century the classical dynamics of Newton were already losing their central role as the fundamental theory of natural phenomena.[6]

Pierre Teilhard de Chardin (1881-1955): Teilhard de Chardin's major work was in geology and paleontology. He tried to integrate his philosophical and scientific insights into a coherent world view. This view shows remarkable compatability with recent systems theory. He emphasized that evolution proceeds in the direction of increasing complexity with an attendant rise of consciousness. This he called the "Law of Complexity—Consciousness." He defined consciousness as "the specific effect of organized complexity," a view similar to that of Gregory Bateson. He also saw the manifestation of mind in larger systems and postulated that, as human evolution progresses, human beings "pressing up against" one another cover the planet with a web of ideas for which he coined the neologism "noosphere". He viewed the growing tensions between the physical and biological sciences as follows:

On the one hand, we have in physics a matter which slides irresistibly, following the line of least resistance, in the direction of the most probable forms of distribution; and, on the other hand, we have in biology the same matter drifting (no less irresistibly but in this case in a sort of "greater effort for survival") towards ever more improbable, because ever more complex, forms of arrangement.[7]

Albert Einstein and the Quantum Physicists: Albert Einstein produced two papers in 1905 which marked the beginning of 20th century scientific thought. One dealt with the theory of relativity and the other with a new way of looking at electromagnetic radiation which was to form the foundation of quantum theory. As Capra describes it, "The new physics necessitated profound changes in concepts of space, time, matter, object, and cause and effect: and because these concepts are so fundamental to our way of experiencing the world, their transformation came as a great shock."[8] The material world which had been viewed as a comfortably ticking clockwork mechanism, was now transformed into a complex and indeterminate interweaving of interdependent interrelationships.[9]

While psychologists were struggling to exclude consciousness from their fields of study, the quantum physicists such as Max Planck, Heisenberg, and Neils Bohr were eagerly building into their experiments the human relational features of consciousness, intentionality, and subjectivity. In experiments of subatomic particles it became clear that the answer, when obtained, depended critically on the initial conditions, the way the experimenter framed his question, and upon his position as a participant-observer. The human observer was now seen as being part of the observation process and of what he was observing. The world was now seen as sets of interrelations and not merely as static separate entities. It is only recently that such thinking has begun to appear in biological and applied sciences. These continue to be dominated by reductionistic thinking. In the psychotherapeutic literature, for example, we see how a rigid Newtonian view of linear causality is applied, fruitlessly, to the question of effectiveness in psychotherapy.

Ilya Prigogine (1917–   ): For the last two decades Prigogine and others have been bringing about the same kind of radical change in our thinking at the macroscopic level that the quantum physicists did during the early years of this century. In 1977 Prigogine was awarded the Nobel Prize for his work on the thermodynamics of nonequilibrium systems. In his work on the characteristics of self-organizing systems — which he calls irreversible, non-linear transformations under conditions far from equilibrium — he dealt very systematically with a complex interdependent holistic view of the universe. As Prigogine puts it, "Our vision of nature is undergoing a radical change toward the multiple, the temporal and the complex."[5] It would seem then that we are living in a pluralistic world and there is not simply one way of understanding reality. In some aspects of the universe we see processes which appear to operate like machines. These closed systems now appear to form only a small part of the physical universe. When we turn to open systems we find what appears to be an active principle emerging in matter which, far from being orderly and stable, is characterized by change, instability, and continual fluctuation. Such systems exchange energy or matter with their environment. When the principles underlying the second law of thermodynamics are extended to these systems a new set of properties emerges which was not formerly apparent. These new properties include capacity for "self-organization," i.e., for a spontaneous shift from a lower to a higher level of organizational complexity. Prigogine has named such self-organizing systems "dissipative structures." We can say that each such locally developing system achieves an increase in structural order and complexity only by "ingesting," "digesting," and "assimilating" the negative entropy (i.e., the orderliness previously possessed by the structure in its surrounding environment), and by "excreting" back into that environment "waste products" which are higher in positive entropy (i.e., disorderliness) than those which it has initially ingested. He has shown that as the input of energy into such a dissipative structure is increased, and as it moves further from equilibrium, it is likely to be characterized by continual fluctuation. This in turn can give rise to increasing turbulence and now and then cause a fluctuation so powerful that it destabilizes the preexisting organization. This is what Prigogine refers to as a "bifurcation point" at which time it is inherently impossible to determine in advance in which direction the change will move. The system may disintegrate into a chaotic state or suddenly reorganize itself into a quite fresh, more differentiated, higher level of order or organization which then takes on the characteristics of irreversibility. This process of order and organization arising spontaneously out of disorder and chaos, through a process of self-organization, has deep implications for the whole of psychotherapy and for personality change and development in relation to life crises.[10,11]

Humberto Maturana and Francisco Varela (1970): The Chilean biologists, Maturana and Varela, have asked the questions: "What is it to be alive?" "What is the essential difference between a machine and a living organism?" They have arrived at a similar formulation to that of Prigogine, stating that the essential characteristic of life is a state of self-organization. The term they coined for this is "autopoiesis" — "auto" meaning self, and "poiesis" (from the Greek root, poinein) meaning to produce, i.e., self-producing. According to this view, the essence of something which is living is that it actively maintains and produces itself, that its first priority is to maintain itself in existence. This is in contrast to other structures such as machines, which they term "allopoietic" meaning that they do or make things other than themselves, and are made by others. Maturana gives the example of a donkey as an autopoietic system which when harnessed to a cart becomes an allopoietic machine but which on being unharnessed becomes autopoietic once more. Essential to this notion of self-organization is the concept of boundedness. It is by virtue of our boundary that we can distinguish what is outside from what is inside, what is self from nonself. As Varela points out, an interesting characteristic which follows is that living creatures essentially relate to themselves. This is all the more true as the complexity of self-organization increases. At the human level we find a living system which is in an enormously complex state of communication with itself and hence manifests consciousness. Varela illustrates the operational closure of the living system as follows:

For example, if we were to travel with the nerve activity originating at the retina into the cortical area (of the occipital lobe), we would find that for each fiber from the retina entering this piece of cortex, 100 other fibers enter at the same spatial location from all over the brain (1). Thus the activity of the retina at best sculpts or modulates what is going on internally in the high interconnection of the neural layers and nuclei.

What this means quite simply is that if we ask the question "What causes a given activity in our nervous system or any action of the whole human being?", the answer is quite simply the nervous system and the human organism itself. No longer can we talk of some external input "causing" us to behave in a specific way. There are simply no direct linear correlations between the outside and the inside, between the inputs and the outputs. From this point of view, an input from the outside world can be no more than a perturbation, which meets a very complex world of communication busily creating its own reality. The most that can be achieved is for the input to perturb the equilibrium and the state of self-coherence of the organism so that it must readjust its state of self-organization, perhaps with the conclusion that it acts in a particular manner. Here is one aspect of indeterminacy in that the living organism relates to the outside world only indirectly through the altering of its own state of self-coherence. Thus the organism may completely ignore the input altogether.[12-14] This has obvious implications for research in psychotherapy, since it means that studies which ask questions from the viewpoint of linear causality can only arrive at meaningless results. This is not to say that the study of psychotherapy is impossible but rather that we will have to approach it from a completely different perspective, that of the constructivist philosophy which builds in probability theory and the uncertainty principle. In dealing with living creatures we are involved in a form of circularity where the organism essentially relates to itself, and where simplistic notions of causality must be abandoned.

The Psychotherapy Research Literature

Almost half a century of "scientific" research into psychotherapy has brought us no nearer to answering the question "How does psychotherapy work?" Research efforts have cast more confusion than clarity on the other fundamental question "Is psychotherapy effective?" In a review of psychotherapy research studies Eysenck[15] stated that there was no empirical evidence to demonstrate that psychotherapy had any significant effectiveness in treating patients. Since that time there have been numerous publications attempting to refute his claim: Meltzoff and Kornreich;[16] Bergin;[17] Luborsky, Singer and Luborsky;[18] Smith and Glass;[19] Bergin and Lambert;[20]

and Smith, Glass and Miller.[21] These studies have not managed to scientifically demonstrate the effectiveness of psychotherapy to a degree that would satisfy critics such as Eysenck,[22] Kazdin and Wilson,[23] and Rachman and Wilson.[24] The area is characterized by unseemly and unscientific internecine criticism and accusations, for example, of selective bias in studies chosen for analysis. There is a tendency for researchers with a behavior therapy bias to "prove" that behavior therapy is superior to psychodynamic and psychoanalytic therapy, e.g., Rachman.[25] On the other hand there is a tendency for the psychodynamically biased researchers to "prove" that psychodynamic therapies are indeed effective. There are many outright contradictions arising here partly from the "scientific" approach used and partly from the unacknowledged personal nature of "knowing" or "proving" anything. Thus we have Bachrach[26] asserting that psychoanalysis leads to psychotherapeutic benefits, while Garfield,[27] commenting on the research findings of behavior therapists such as Eysenck and Rachman, states, "With regard to psychoanalysis, they find no acceptable evidence to support it as an effective treatment, a conclusion that is difficult to refute." It is evident, 33 years after Eysenck's initial attack, that this area of research is a morass of unrecognized value system bias. As Rosenthal[28] demonstrated, experimenters will often find what they set out to find. It is also becoming apparent that psychodynamic psychotherapists cannot hope to find an answer from within the double bind that Eysenck put them in originally. His challenge is of the variety "Have you stopped beating your wife yet?" Eysenck demands an answer within his reductionistic and logical positivistic framework, and while this may suit the mechanistic behavior therapy approaches, this Newtonian view of science defeats the very subject matter attended to by psychodynamic therapists, for example, emotions, the mind, the unconscious, dreams, etc.

The Dodo Verdict: Many of the psychotherapy research studies which showed a high effectiveness rate: Meltzoff and Kornreich;[16] Luborsky, Singer and Luborsky;[18] and Bergin and Lambert[20] gave rise to feelings of unease when it began to appear that all psychotherapies seemed to be effective. Moreover, they appeared to be equally effective, and further, that it did not seem to matter what specific techniques were used, how often the treatment occurred, or even how well-trained or experienced the therapist was. In "Alice's Adventures in Wonderland" the Dodo, having presided over the chaotic Caucus-race, was unable to decide who had won and consequently concluded that "everybody has won, and all must have prizes." This statement provided an ironic subtitle to the paper written by Luborsky et al.[18] These findings, while cheering to practicing clinicians, have done nothing to alleviate doubts regarding the credibility of the psychotherapeutic enterprise.[29]

Many of these problems stem from attempts to apply an inappropriate mechanistic model of science to the subject matter of psychology and psychotherapy. In attempting to work within the Newtonian approach academic researchers have either completely excluded the most interesting and important aspects of human nature (e.g., the mind is systematically excluded by behaviorists) or they have attempted, vainly, to capture a reduced and often caricaturized version of important human experience within the mechanistic model, a task akin to that of trapping a flow of water in a fishing net. As Wittgenstein pointed out, " . . . the existence of the experimental method makes us think we have the means of solving the problems which trouble us; though problem and method pass one another by."[30] The absurdities of this type of research are such that it now takes an army of researchers and a vast amount of money and time to even begin to answer questions regarding the effectiveness of psychotherapy. In discussing the NIMH project to compare three different approaches to unipolar depression, Garfield comments that "This project in its first phase is estimated to cost $3 million. If we were to conduct such a study for the 200 different forms of psychotherapy with several of the major disorders, it would probably take hundreds of years as well as a good share of our federal research budget."[27]

Future research in psychotherapy must take place within the new science paradigm.[31] Only by a return to the experiential and essentially personal nature of psychotherapy can we hope to begin influencing clinical practice — which has largely continued to ignore the academic-scientific debate about psychotherapeutic effectiveness. As Smail points out, " . . . research in psychotherapy tends to destroy the significance of findings concerning the personal nature of the therapeutic relationship precisely through attempting to mechanise them."[32]

The Need to Change to a Constructivist Outlook

In discussing the philosophy of radical constructivism, Ernst von Glasersfeld[33] introduces the idea that the best we can ever hope to aspire to in our knowledge of the real world is to discover what the world is not. More succinctly, not only does the world not tell us what it is, neither does it tell us what it is not. It only reveals to us that certain aspects of our human endeavors are possible or viable. When we learn this, we are learning only about ourselves in the world, and not about the world we inhabit. Underlying this proposition are two further propositions, namely that (a) we cannot know the world directly and (b) that we personally construct our view of the world.

These statements are a radical shift away from the traditional realist epistemology which held the view that human knowledge of the world related to the actual world in a picturelike or representationalist correspondence (or match) between the two. As Glasersfeld puts it: "The metaphysical realist looks for knowledge that matches reality in the same sense as you might look for paint to match the color that is already on the wall you have to repair."[33] The constructivist epistemology, on the other hand, holds that the relation between human knowledge and the world is not that of matching but rather that of fitting. Glasersfeld uses the metaphor of a key fitting a lock. A key fits a lock if it serves to open it. Many different keys with alternative shapes can serve to open the same lock. Within this metaphor, the relationship between human knowledge and the world we live in is the same as that which exists between a burglar and a lock which he must open in order to proceed. As we have seen above, scientific theories are no longer regarded as "wrong" or "right" or "true" or "false" but rather as being useful, relevant, and viable or not.

George Kelly[34] proposed a theory of personality which viewed each person as if he were a scientist, constructing theories about the world and testing out such theories through his behavior. Each individual's personal theory of the world can be seen to fit the world to one degree or another, and to work usefully for the individual most of the time. Psychological disturbance can be defined within this view as when the person's theory no longer fits satisfactorily with "reality." The person's outlook or the conceptual "goggles" through which he views the world leads him into difficulties with the world. Things are not as he perceives them. Psychological distress is therefore a signal that his theory fails to make adequate sense of his world. Therapy consists in aiding the patient to actively reconstruct his view of the world thereby reorganizing himself in a different way.

That reality can disprove our theories is obvious. What is perhaps not so obvious is the fact that we cannot ever "prove" a theory.[35] What is often not fully appreciated is that having been informed by reality that our theories do not fit, we are no wiser as to what actually constitutes that reality as to what it is. Thus, each "breakthrough" in science, each "discovery" that is made does not actually push back the frontiers of reality but rather is a statement about the internal consistency and validity of the theories we have constructed in our attempts at explaining reality. Thus, while we may come to know what is not the case, our theories as to what is the case must remain forever mere conjecture.

Our theories of the world not only describe the world but also dictate how we will experience it. As Glasersfeld says: "The world we experience is, and must be, as it is because we have put it together in that way."[33] Just like any good burglar, this view of reality encourages one to carry many alternative "keys" about one's person to ensure that obstinate locks will yield to one's probings. At the heart of Kelly's[34] personal construct psychology we find the

philosophical notion of "constructive alternativism." This states that whatever exists may be reconstrued. It states that man does not have to be a
victim of his biography or his circumstances, but that he may enslave himself with his interpretation or his construction of his circumstances. Our
outlook on reality therefore may be liberating or imprisoning.

Summary

Classical science thought it had found eternal laws where all processes were
reversible and static, but what has now emerged as the dominant view
involves time and evolving systems. Where once there appeared to be a
universal symmetry, recent scientific developments have shown symmetry-
breaking processes at all levels from elementary particles up to biology and
ecology. Our outlook on nature is changing radically towards plurality, tem-
porality, and complexity. It would seem then that we are living in a world
where there cannot be simply one way of understanding reality. In a small
degree some aspects of the universe appear to operate as stable machines.
However, with open systems we find what appears to be an active principle
emerging in matter which is characterized by change, instability, and continual fluctuation. A bifurcation point is reached when fluctuations destabilize
the current organization of the system. Issues of "being" and "becoming"
are raised here in the context of the indeterminate nature of the "choice" of
direction the system will take. The system may disintegrate into chaos or
suddenly reorganize itself into a quite fresh, more differentiated, higher level
of organization which then takes up the characteristics of irreversibility.
These processes of increasing organization arising spontaneously out of
chaos through a process of self-organization have direct applicability to
human change processes, and are readily illustrated within the framework of
crisis theory.

Conclusion

There are a number of important questions raised by the foregoing, for
example how well do modern theories of psychiatry fit with human reality?
Ever since David Rosenhan's[36] study illustrated how the making of the psychiatric diagnosis invented, rather than described, a reality wherein any
patient behavior (even normal behavior) was seen as disturbed, many clinicians have begun to question the self-fulfilling nature of such diagnostic
practices. If we are concerned with constructing an alternative theory to fit

TABLE 1
Summary of the Dichotomies Between the Old and New Sciences

Epistemological Position

Old		New
Discover world	:	Invents world
Match	:	Fit
Absolute truth	:	Usefulness/viability
Accumulative fragmentalism	:	Alternate constructivism
Reductionism	:	Constructivism (Holism)
Reversibility	:	Irreversibility
No time	:	Time dimension
Verification	:	Falsification
Initial conditions specify outcome	:	Impossibility
Analysis	:	Synthesis
Symmetry	:	Asymmetry
Absolute knowledge	:	Uncertainty

Image of the Person

Old		New
Finished product	:	Process
Determined by inputs	:	Self-organization
Linear cause and effect	:	Boundedness and circularity
Object	:	Reflexive subject
Separate entity	:	Intersubjective process
Objective observer	:	Participant-observer (experiential)
'Value-free'	:	Value context
Man as machine	:	Man as scientist
Passive	:	Active
Mechanism	:	Humanism

reality better, then such a theory has to encompass many of the issues raised in the above discussion. Such a theory must encompass the view of the person as a process who exists in time and who is embedded in a causal, interactional, and intersubjective context within which he actively creates or invents his own world and his image of himself in that world. Such a theory must also be reflexive in that, since we are what we study, i.e., we are the same type of phenomenon as our patients, our theory must apply equally to ourselves as to our patients — rather than having a double standard where we use one theory to fit our patients and another to fit ourselves. Furthermore, any such theory must recursively explain itself. Since there is no one reality that we can find a "match" for, then we need to develop the discipline of theoretical plurality or what Kelly called constructive alternativism.[34]

References

1. Drake S: *Galileo Studies,* University of Michigan Press, Michigan, 1970.

2. Bacon F: *Philosophical Works,* Robertson JM (Ed.), Routledge, London, 1905.

3. Descartes R: *Philosophical Works,* Cambridge University Press, New York, 1931.

4. Newton I: *Isaac Newton's Philosophiae Naturalis Principia Mathematica,* London, 1687. Koyrae A, Cohen B (Eds.), Cambridge University Press, New York, 1972.

5. Prigogine I, Stengers I: *Order Out of Chaos,* William Heinemann, London, 1984.

6. Darwin C: *The Origin of Species,* Mentor, London, 1958.

7. Teilhard de Chardin P: *Activation of L'Energie,* Harcourt, Brace, Jovanovich, San Diego, Calif., 1963.

8. Capra F: *The Turning Point,* Flamingo, London, 1983.

9. Hoffman B, Dukas H: *Albert Einstein,* Viking Press, New York, 1972.

10. Prigogine I: *From Being to Becoming — Time and Complexity in the Physical Sciences,* Freeman & Company, San Francisco, 1980.

11. Nicolis G, Prigogine I: *Self-Organization in Nonequilibrium Systems,* John Wiley & Sons, New York, 1977.

12. Varela FJ: *Principles of Biological Autonomy,* Elsevier, New York, 1979.

13. Varela FJ, Maturana H: *Living Ways of Sense-making: A Middle Path for Neuroscience,* Paper presented at the International Symposium on Disorder and Order, Stanford University, Palo Alto, California, 1981.

14. Maturana H, Varela F: *Autopoiesis and Cognition,* Boston Studies in Philosophical Science, Volume 42, D. Reidel, Boston, 1980.

15. Eysenck H: The effects of psychotherapy: An evaluation. *J. Consult. Clin. Psychol.* 16:319–324, 1952.

16. Meltzoff J, Kornreich M: *Research in Psychotherapy,* Atherton Press, New York, 1970.

17. Bergin AE: The evaluation of therapeutic outcomes. In Bergin AE, Garfield SL (Eds.): *Handbook of Psychotherapy and Behavior Change,* John Wiley & Sons, New York, 1971.

18. Luborsky L, Singer B, Luborsky L: Comparative studies of psychotherapy: Is it true that "Everybody has won and all must have prizes?" *Arch. Gen. Psych.* 32:995–1088, 1975.

19. Smith M, Glass G: Meta-analysis of psychotherapy outcome studies. *Am. Psychol.* 32:752–760, 1977.

20. Bergin A, Lambert M: The evaluation of therapeutic outcomes. In Garfield S, Bergin A (Eds.): *Handbook of Psychotherapy and Behavior Change,* Second Edition, John Wiley & Sons, New York, 1978.

21. Smith M, Glass G, Miller T: *The Benefits of Psychotherapy,* Johns Hopkins University Press, Baltimore, Md., 1980.

22. Eysenck H: An exercise in mega-silliness. *Am. Psychol.* 33:517, 1978.

23. Kazdin A, Wilson G: *Evaluation of Behavior Therapy: Issues, Evidence and Research Studies,* Ballinger, Cambridge, Mass., 1978.

24. Rachman S, Wilson G: *The Effects of Psychological Therapy,* Second Edition, Pergamon Press, New York, 1980.

25. Rachman S: *The Effects of Psychotherapy,* Pergamon Press, New York, 1971.

26. Bachrach H: The efficacy of psychotherapy. Lesson 17 in *Directions in Psychiatry,* Volume 4, The Hatherleigh Co., Ltd., New York, 1984.

27. Garfield S: Effectiveness of Psychotherapy: The Perennial Controversy. *Professional Psychology: Research and Practice* 14(No.1):35–43, 1983.

28. Rosenthal R: *Experimental Effects in Behavior Research,* Appleton-Century-Crofts, New York, 1966.

29. Parloff M: Psychotherapy research and its incredible credibility crisis. *Clin. Psychol. Rev.* 4(No.1): 95–109, 1984.

30. Wittgenstein L: *Philosophical Investigations,* Blackwell, Oxford, 1968.

31. Reason P, Rowan J (Eds.): *Human Inquiry: A Sourcebook of New Paradigm Research,* John Wiley & Sons, Chichester, 1981.

32. Smail D: Learning in psychotherapy. In Salmon P (Ed.): *Coming To Know,* Routledge & Kegan Paul, London, 1980, p. 175.

33. von Glasersfeld E: An introduction to radical constructivism. In Watzlawick P (Ed.): *The Invented Reality,* Norton, New York, 1984.

34. Kelly G: *The Psychology of Personal Constructs,* 2 Volumes, Norton, New York, 1955.

35. Popper K: *The Logic of Scientific Discovery,* Hutchinson, London, 1972.

36. Rosenhan D: On being sane in insane places. *Science* 179:250–258, 1978.

2

How Does Psychotherapy Work?

Part II: A Systems Approach to Psychotherapy Practice

Vincent Kenny and Ivor W. Browne

A New Paradigm for Psychotherapy

The previous chapter raised the issue of what is reality and what is illusion. It was argued that there is a large gulf between the view of reality inherent in the Newtonian mechanical model on the one hand and the experience of reality as humans live it on the other. Psychotherapeutic research framed within the old physics model has failed completely to grasp the experiential richness of the psychotherapeutic venture as well as having failed to say anything sensible about the varieties of psychotherapy in practice. Living on the cutting edge of a new scientific paradigm is not a comfortable place to set up house. The attempts to date to transfer concepts such as homeostasis, equifinality, etc., have largely been "lipservice, rather than an actual development in theoretical elaboration."[1] Even the issue of deciding what constitutes the component units of a human system is a complex one. While there is a certain reluctance[1-3] to extrapolate from biological systems to human societies, Stafford Beer[4] leaves one in no doubt as to his conclusions:

I am quite sure of the answer; yes, human societies are biological systems. . . . Any cohesive social institution is an autopoietic system — because it survives, because its method of survival answers the autopoietic criteria, and because it may well change its entire appearance and its apparent purpose in the process. As examples I list:

16

firms and industries, schools and universities, clinics and hospitals, professional bodies, departments of state, and whole countries.

This chapter will attempt to spell out in some detail the implications of the new science paradigm for psychotherapy practice and how changes may be effected within the psychotherapeutic context. To begin this task we must spell out what it means to be a living system.

Definition of a Living System

The basic principle of a living system is that of self-organization. This means essentially that its order in structure and function is not imposed by the environment but is established by the system itself. Thus something can be held to be "alive," to be an "organism" if, and only if, it fulfills the following five conditions:

1. It contains a number of elements.
2. These elements are involved in a dynamic process of interaction and interrelationship.
3. It is separated from its environment by a boundary of its own elements such that it permits transactions of import and export across the boundary, i.e., it is an "open system."
4. It maintains and renews (regenerates) its own elements by its own internal processes. Living organisms continually renew themselves; cells breaking down and building up structures, tissues and organs replacing their cells in continual cycles of regeneration. Nevertheless the living system maintains its overall structure and integrity in space. Its components are continually renewed and recycled but the pattern of organization remains stable.
5. Living systems show a tendency to transcend themselves. As Capra says, "To reach out creatively beyond their boundaries and limitations to generate new structures and new forms of organization. This principle of self-transcendence manifests itself in the processes of learning, development and evolution."[5] Thus living systems not only tend to change and adapt but also to reproduce themselves and thus to ensure the survival and evolution of the species.

If these are the essential characteristics which describe what it is to be alive then they must apply to every living being whether plant, animal, or human. But it is important here to note the interesting characteristics of living systems, i.e., that they tend to form a hierarchical order of one living system within another. Thus the basic living system out of which all superordinate systems are constructed is the cell. The most common form of life on this planet is still the unicellular organism or amoeba, but over the long course of evolution nature has found ways for cells to combine to form new multicellular living systems such as a bee, an ant, a baboon, or a human being.

In Kelly's *The Psychology of Personal Constructs*[6] this superordinate hierarchical arrangement is replicated within each person's system of constructs or theory of the world. The way we think about the world is conceptually organized in a hierarchical manner so that certain constructs or concepts are superordinate to (i.e., control) other constructs which are subordinate. The superordinate constructs of the system tend to be those core constructs concerned with the maintenance of the "self." The criteria for a living system obviously applies to one's personal construct system, since in Bruner's[7] terms, "You are your constructs." Thus, properly speaking, we do not "have" a theory or map of the world with which we try to fit, rather we *are* our map, we *constitute* our theory, or our theory constitutes us. It is *we* who fit the world or not. Therefore, taking a closer look at the psychological (construct) system which we constitute in terms of the five criteria of the living system we find the following:

1. The construct system contains a number of components. We have thousands of verbal labels within our communication and labeling system.
2. Constructs are interrelated and intercorrelated to one degree or another. Thus whenever we describe somebody as sincere, we also imply that the person is likable, trustworthy, worth knowing, etc. Our abstract (verbal) system of anticipation hangs together in an intercorrelated pattern.
3. The construct system has a semipermeable boundary so that we are variously open to the validational experiences of the environment. However, sometimes we can act in a hostile[6] manner whereby we attempt to force reality to conform to our expectations of it. Such a person has a poor fit with the world. Since they do not fit it, they try to force it to fit them.
4. The construct system maintains and regenerates itself by its own internal processes, by redefining itself more clearly, by engaging in "fine tuning," by improving prediction of events.
5. The living construct system has a tendency to transcend itself. As Epting puts it, "In construing one must reach out beyond what exists at present to that which is emerging and becoming."[8] Kelly's psychology of constructivism encourages one to transcend the obvious and to come to grips with the unknown.[9]

If we keep in mind the criteria of a living system it can be seen that they have a wide range of applicability. Throughout nature many examples of a third order of living system can be found. The most highly organized examples of these exist among the social insects — the termite mound, ant heap, or the beehive. The important thing to note here is that these third order systems fulfill the definition of a living system just as completely as do the individual bees or ants of which they are composed and it has therefore increasingly been accepted by entomologists that, for example, a beehive or termite mound must truly be classed as a living creature in its own right.[10] In a similar way, although the process has not as yet developed so highly, various birds, fishes, and mammalian groups can also be recognized as forming third order systems such as a colony of baboons, a gorilla or human family, or a human village. These too may be understood as separate living beings. Beyond this, further superordinate living systems can be discerned: ecosystems and, finally, the living envelope covering the surface of the entire planet — the biosphere, maintaining itself (until recently at any rate) as a delicately balanced self-referential living system.

In all of these situations where we find one living system existing within another, as in the case of the cell within our own bodies, or where a third order is involved — the cell within the body of a bee, the bee within the body of the beehive — we find the superordinate system is in a position of influence over the primary or secondary systems of which it is constituted. Each system retains its proper integrity as a living system on its own level but nevertheless its autopoiesis is depressed and transmission and exchange across its boundary are increased to a significant degree under the influence of the superordinate system. An important point should be clarified here in considering superordinate human living systems. The fact that one as a human individual may be under the influence of a superordinate group system should not in any way be taken to mean that the superordinate system is necessarily more developed or more conscious than the individual living system of which it is constituted. On the contrary, all the evidence would suggest that the individual human person is by far the most complex and highly developed form of life of which we have any knowledge on this planet. Most human systems are by comparison primitive, largely unconscious, and comparatively simple in their range of behaviors; nevertheless they do have a powerful superordinate influence on the human individual in them. As Stafford Beer remarks:[4] It means that every social institution (in several of which any one individual is embedded at the intersect) is embedded in a larger social institution, and so on recursively — and that all of them are autopoietic. This immediately explains why the process of change at any level of recursion (from the individual to the state) is not only difficult to accomplish but actually impossible — in the full sense of the intention: "I am going completely to change myself". The reason is that the "I," that self-contained autopoietic "it," is a component of another autopoietic system.

To say how psychotherapy works, we must take into account the criteria for a living system not only in relation to the interpersonal/social interfaces within which the individual system exists, but also in relation to the intrapersonal system through which the individual interprets and constructs the meaning of the perturbations arising from his interrelationships.

Definition of the Therapeutic System

Different levels of living systems are involved in the psychotherapeutic enterprise. Each clinician must deal with systems from the cellular-biological level, through the personal-psychological level, to the psychosocial and sociocultural levels. These systems are organized hierarchically with lines of influence moving up and down the total hierarchy. We cannot deal with an individual in isolation from the systems in which he is embedded contextually. Each individual joins his family and grows up within a family context coevolving with the other family members. The family system coevolves within the context of other neighborhood family systems within a community/cultural/national identity, etc.

Even were we to "completely" remove the individual from his living context we still could not treat him in isolation since, firstly, he carries within himself the coherence of his coevolved self-organization. The holographic conceptualization of the family or group implies that the whole family has its "existence" within each person. Thus, even when dealing with an "individual" we may be working with the representation in that person of the total historical family constellation. Secondly, the therapist necessarily forms a relational dyad, or a new system within which both will coevolve a new coherence together.

Just as the client brings a context with him, so too does the therapist who lives within similar systems. Furthermore, the therapist is influenced by the immediate work hierarchy of the clinic wherein the consultations take place. This in turn must exist within other umbrellas, the parent hospital, the culture of the medical profession, the overall Department of Health structures, policies, etc.

Maturana[11] describes these interactions between different systems as "structural coupling." This will occur between any two systems over a period of time. This can be seen every time a newly born infant is brought home to join his older siblings. There follows a time of turbulence after which a new family coherence is achieved. Bateson also referred to this movement toward internal consistency as "self-healing tautology."[12]

Consider individual therapy from this new standpoint. It can now be seen that what is involved in setting up a therapeutic relationship is indeed the creation of a new living system, within which the individual boundaries are lowered and both exchange and change are now possible under the influence of the superordinate system, i.e., a group of two. This is all the more true if one member of the new system is skilled in and not threatened by the task of lowering the individual boundary and allowing projections and introjections to flow across from one person to the other — to empathize and make conscious for both what is hidden and unconscious.

One of the primary questions for the therapist in each new case is "At which of these possible levels will it be most effective for me to join and influence this system?" For a variety of therapists who have a specific commitment to particular therapeutic strategies this question is answered all too automatically. For example, the family therapists tend to see the most appropriate level to join as being the "family." In psychoanalysis and behavior therapy the level of joining dictated by the approach is largely that of the "isolated" individual. For marital therapists the selected system level is the "couple," and so on.

The manner in which we define what constitutes a "system" at the different levels is purely theoretical. Our theory may fit effectively or not. If we find our efforts are unsuccessful we should seriously question the manner in which we decide that this particular segment of reality (e.g., defining the family systems as "those members who live in the same house") is an effective way to define the going "system." Where therapists are over-committed to one view, one theory, one set of tactics, then they are unlikely to question their basic approach which sees them working at the same level of "system" all the time.

Interpersonal and Intrapersonal Systems

A main point of discontinuity in defining levels of system can be found with the "individual system" on one side of the divide and couples, families, groups, etc., on the other side. This is a major dividing line between those biological/psychological approaches which are intrapersonal and those which are interpersonal. In systems terms the main difference lies in the type of components which go to make up the system. At the individual level the components are various theoretical constructs postulated to describe and explain psychological functioning. Thus we have terms such as "cells," "organs," "neural connections," "ego," "needs," "personal constructs," etc. On the other side of the divide the components are whole individuals who make up a family, etc. Family therapists attempt to change the family system by influencing the actions of individual members, while intraindividual therapists attempt to change the person's self-organization by dealing with his personal constructions, meanings, etc. Both endeavors are similar in that they may attempt to promote change in the overall organization of the system by changing the structural components. Both may work equally on the whole in order to have a recursive impact on the components. Both tend to precipitate the system (individual or family) into a state of flux or disorganization as a prelude to emergent change in the form of a new state of self-organization. Both recognize the hierarchical lines of influence in attempting to restructure the whole by working on the parts, or change the parts by working on the whole. In this way the overall level of coherence of the system is altered. "Coherence simply implies a congruent interdependence in functioning whereby all the aspects of the system fit together."[13] In any given situation it may be more appropriate to work with individual, couple, or family. In a given case at various times we may choose to work with different levels of these systems in sequence or concomitantly.

The Problem of Fit

In what way must the epistemological position of "fit" influence clinical practice? The answer, as we shall see, is that the concept has extensive implications for etiology, diagnosis, and treatment. Shotter[14] outlines three major areas of "fit" which must be considered, viz., (i) mind-to-world fit, (ii) world-to-mind fit, and (iii) mind-to-mind fit. To avoid any mind-body duality we must simply substitute the word "person" for the word "mind" in the above.

These three areas cover the realms of anticipation, feedback, and communication. Psychotherapy involves all three at many different levels. Etiology may be viewed as the story of where the person's beliefs or anticipations (person-to-world fit) broke down. Diagnosis (and much else in psychotherapy) depends on the level of communication between therapist and patient (person-to-person fit). Treatment involves evoking reality-contact and facing the vicissitudes of invalidation from reality experience (world-to-person fit).

Suicide can be seen to involve all three types of fit. One form of suicide occurs in the context of personal confusion about the world (poor person-to-world fit). The person experiences invalidation and absence of gratification (world-to-person fit). Finally the person is isolated from anyone whom he feels could understand him (person-to-person fit), and so he decides to kill himself.

How Do Symptoms "Fit"

From an etiological point of view, it is important to consider the role of symptoms as an attempt to personally organize oneself or reach a state of coherence. It is notable that many patients arrive in a state of relative incoherence. The individual must "fit in" with his family. When his person-to-world fit breaks down and symptoms develop we must consider how his symptoms (as new person-to-world projects) help him to make better sense than did his old outlook. It is also important to ask what type of (family or other) reality is he failing to fit? Do his symptoms raise particular questions about the form of reality he is attempting to make sense of? In other words, his symptoms are "symptoms of" the difficult reality to which he is trying to fit himself, or to which he is attempting to join himself as a complementary piece of the overall family jigsaw. In this sense, his symptoms may point to the elusive nature of the family reality he is attempting to predict and fit. This is commonly seen in the case of pathological communication systems which use the double-bind.[15] No matter what the patient attempts, he finds his fit is "wrong" even when it seems to be "right." However, the person never gives up the attempt to reach a coevolved coherence, and in pursuing the search for meaning may strike upon certain unusual theories or outlooks which seem to him to fit the family facts. Such theories are commonly diagnosed as "delusions," "hallucinations," "madness," etc.

Watzlawick[16] quotes a number of noncontingency experiments (i.e., where the subject's behavior in attempting to solve a task has no connection with the feedback he receives) to illustrate the human struggle to make sense of events when our person-to-world fit has no symmetry with the world-to-person fit. Consequently the person must develop a rather idiosyncratic and sometimes bizarre outlook in order to encompass the noncontingency feedback. Watzlawick states, " . . . once we have arrived at a solution—and in the process of getting there, have paid a fairly high price in terms of anxiety and expectation—our investment in this solution becomes so great that we may prefer to distort reality to fit our solution than sacrifice the solution."[16] Thus the subject's new person-to-reality fit becomes rhetorical and encapsulated. Every therapist is familiar with the apparently incorrigible nature of certain delusions. This coherence reached by the patient becomes more so with practice.

Coherence evolves in the direction of that to which we must relate. The system can in one sense be seen as a specialization of interaction. The more one repetitively practices, the more coherent one becomes. Thus, the family doctor tends to develop a very ossified and stereotyped consultation pattern[17] using the same phrases and sequences of clinical interpersonal behavior. Those who repetitively practice sports develop a coherence in relation to the behavior sequences needed. The anorexic develops her speciality in relation to food and weight. Psychotherapists who specialize in treating psychotic patients tend to develop an obvious coherence in that direction (H. S. Sullivan; Fromm-Reichmann; R. D. Laing). Many clinicians who feel that the person-to-person fitting required in treating psychotics is impossible to achieve are criticized by Fromm-Reichmann where she says that the fault lies in the therapist's personality, not in the schizophrenic's.[18]

Playing an effective role in relation to another person is defined by Kelly[6] in person-to-person fit terms. He says that to the degree that we can accurately construe the other person's constructions about us we can play a role in relation to him. Even if we disagree with the other person's outlook (e.g., a particular delusion) we may evolve a complementary fit with the other person and be able to effectively communicate and develop a relationship with him.

"Too Close a Fit"

The fear which many clinicians experience in this area is that of being "sucked into" the patient's madness. In the nonpsychotic sphere the family therapist fears being "enmeshed" in the family system to the point where he becomes neutralized by the family and then acts merely as an additional component. He has become part of the problem instead of part of the solution. The therapist has coevolved a coherence with the family system rendering him therapeutically neutral. An image we may use from lower down the system hierarchy is that of the action of phagocytosis occurring at the cellular level. When a phagocytic cell encounters some foreign matter it quickly engulfs, breaks down, neutralizes, and incorporates the foreign substance within itself. Thus, the therapist can no longer create "inputs" or perturbations from the outside since he is now firmly placed inside the family cell. The therapist's system has become "at one" with his environment. He now fits the family.

This phenomenon explains why family therapists like to work in teams[19] (where certain members are "isolated" from the family system acting as supervisors-from-a-distance) and why Tavistock group methods insist that the therapist "sits on the boundary" of the group[20] — a form of therapeutically "sitting on the fence."

The Issue of Change: How to Precipitate It?

Another implication of these views is that the patient is not necessarily seen as a "victim" and the family as a "procrustean bed" upon which unwitting victims are "stretched to fit." Rather the whole family is a mutually determined coherence of all the individual parts. Each individual fits with the family reality to one degree or another. As Neils Bohr's principle of complementarity obviated the arguments as to which view of light (wave versus particle theory) was "correct," so we must view the complementarity of relationships within the family and avoid the attribution of "blame." The family does not "cause" an individual to become schizophrenic. Many clinicians still think in causal terms in relation to psychological processes.[13] For example, a patient is obsessive "because" he fixated at the anal stage of development. A young girl is anorexic "in order to" bring her parents closer together. A child is acting out "because" his mother does not love him, and so on. It is clear that such attributions of "cause" or "purpose" are in the eyes of the beholder. It is this form of causal thinking that leads to convictions that one person more than another is "to blame" for psychopathology. Consequently, interventions are often directed more towards such a "causal figure" than others.

Reflexively, we must apply the same type of analysis to our own interventions. Rejecting the linear causal view we must admit that psychotherapy is not something that you can do to someone else. It is not a mechanical skill that can be reliably "applied to" psychopathology. Rather it must involve coevolving a coherence with the patient in such a way that we provide an experimental context within which he may begin to alter his current level of self-organization. To this end the therapist will spend a lot of time extricating himself from the patient's attempts to coevolve a coherence that is similar to one already existing in his life.

The issue of transference relates centrally here. If the patient can set up a relationship with the therapist on the basis of his existing self-organization, then he has little need to revise his system or to change it in any way. One of the first perturbations provided by the therapist is, therefore, that of being elusive, or "difficult to pin down." Within this model one would rarely discuss food intake with an anorexic since she has already evolved a "starvation coherence." Speaking to her within her reduced frame of reference is merely helping her practice "more of the same."[21] We have all seen cases of "borderline" anorexia being admitted to an anorexic ward and emerging several weeks later as a fully committed anorexic, i.e., one whose system has reached a new level of coherence oriented around food and weight.

The theory of learning implicit here is that "you become what you do." We have seen how this works for producing psychopathology, but the same principle applies to relearning more "adaptive" or "fitting" behavior. One of the main roles of the therapist is to persuade the patient into taking novel actions through which he may transform himself. Since novelty is a spontaneous experience, and since we cannot intend to be spontaneous, we can see once again how the causal model of "doing" therapy to the patient breaks down. This is one of the junctures in psychotherapy where the risk factor enters since for the patient it is a case of "leap before you look." To aid this process the therapist must engage in a type of "instruction" which Vygotsky[22] defines as "that which marches ahead of development and leads it; it must be aimed not so much at the ripe as at the ripening functions." This is not to say that the therapist must give instructions in the form of directives or advice but rather—from the Latin instruere meaning to build up—to structure a context for the patient's self-experimentation. Such personal experimentation often provides the bifurcation points for self-reorganization.

Destabilization

Having accurately subsumed and understood the complex self-organizational style of the patient and the consequent significance of the symptoms used, we must then decide how to destabilize his current organization. This consideration applies equally to individuals, couples, or families. There are many techniques evolving especially in certain schools of family therapy[19,23] which aim to destabilize the going system with the hope that it will reorganize itself in an alternative manner. At a less haphazard level, Milton Erickson[24] specialized in framing a destabilization in such a manner that the patient moved through an oscillation to a more predictable but still indeterminate bifurcation.

Thus the perturbation put into the system by the therapist must take cognizance of (a) the current state of self-organization, i.e., the construction style of the contract system; (b) the intensity of destabilization needed; (c) likely construction the person will make of the perturbation from the therapist; (d) the possibilities of perturbations arising from inside the construct system itself.

It is here that the concept of crisis enters the therapeutic arena. Crises can be precipitated by sudden change in the external world, such as sudden death of a dear one (as described by G. Caplan), or through a developmental change affecting the internal state of coherence as in pregnancy, childbirth, or adolescence—the developmental crises emphasized by Erik Erikson. In both of these types of crises a destabilization occurs spontaneously without any influence from a therapist. The concept of crisis intervention is to avail of this state of fluctuation and the approach of a bifurcation point when the system (person, family, etc.) is in a chaotic state, to try to move it (influence it) towards a better (higher) state of self-organization. These are the times when a person is in a receptive state to accept help and is open to the possibility of change in the state of self-coherence. Thus the possibility of therapeutic intervention is enhanced.

It should be remembered that the system is in a continual process of flux and of self-perpetuation and self-organization. It is not a fixed frozen entity but rather a living organism. Again this applies as much to a family group as to an individual. Here we can see that the old idea of direct causality is no longer present. This assumption of causality is still very prevalent in psychiatry where we see attempts to change the biochemical balance of the system or where ECT is used as a direct shocking perturbation as if this could somehow determine that the system would realign itself in a "proper balance." This assumes again that there is an absolute whereby one can tell what a proper balance consists of, and that a direct linear causality can be appealed to. In criticizing technical approaches to therapy that emphasize control and the use of technique, Keeney[25] states that "a therapist who sees himself as a unilateral powerbroker or manipulator is dealing with partial arcs of cybernetic systems. Such a position threatens the recursively structured biological world in which we live. Only wisdom, that is, 'a sense or recognition of the fact of circuitry' (Bateson, 1972, p. 146), can safely and effectively deal with ecosystems."

Summary

The object of psychotherapy is to precipitate new movement in the patient and in his life. New movement will be carried forward by changing the person's inner self-organization. It is the new organization that will take the person forward to his future rather than entrap him in the endless present of his psychopathology. In order to begin this process we must first accurately subsume the complex state of the person's current level of self-organization. Very frequently we see that patients have organized their lives around the practice of a particular symptom, for example "doing" anorexia or "doing" hypertension. One of the important changes in our thinking as clinicians must be that of moving from the use of static nouns to action verbs. Thus it is becoming popular in family medicine to think of a patient as not "having" hypertension but rather to be "hypertensing." Similarly in psychiatry we must begin to see patients actively doing their pathology as opposed to being victims of socioculture sanctions on the one hand or genetic/biochemical accidents on the other. From the Kellian point of view, the most important human task is that of making sense of one's world.[6] Very often, the sense one makes is that he is "unable to cope"; that he is "mad"; that he is "depressed," etc. Thomas Szasz has described professional activities in relation to life problems as merely sanctioning a way for the person to escape his responsibilities.[26] Within the proposed model such therapist-patient collusion is understood as a particular type of coevolved coherence which "makes sense."

Apart from changing our thinking from using nouns to verbs, and to seeing the intrinsic sense-making of a patient's symptoms — for example, Haley discusses the symptom as a strategy[27] — there are other changes in conceptualization and approach that are important to achieve if the new science clinician is to reflect the implications arising from the systems view of the world. What are these other pragmatic/conceptual changes? In the first place our view of diagnosis ceases to be something that is a fixed reality. Diagnosis becomes instead a fluid way of planning treatment rather than a static "pigeon-holing" of a person. It has been shown that the diagnostic label a patient receives on entering an institution is not the same diagnostic label he will hold some years later.[28] Thus even within the unchanging world of an institution, somehow the quasiscientific diagnostic category manages to shift over time. The one thing we do know about human beings is that they change over time often despite themselves. We must learn to see the person plotted along a time-line of personal history and extending along the same arrow of time into the future. As clinicians we are therefore concerned with the pathways which the patient may have available to take him into his future. Much of George Kelly's work focused on this issue.[6] The philosophy of constructive alternativism tells us that any construction we make of reality (e.g., a diagnosis of a patient) is only one view or opinion on the matter. Other diagnosticians may well, and very often do, diagnose the person differently. We must reconstruct our diagnostic language so that it is constituted by a more fluid process-oriented language which can allow the person to move and change within the categories we prescribe. We must be prepared to see when our diagnosis does not fit the reality of the patient. The way we invent reality in the form of our constructions of patients must be seen as just that, an invention rather than a fact.

References

1. Elkaim M et al.: Openness: A round-table discussion. *Fam. Process* 21(No. 1):57–70, 1982.

2. Maturana H, Varela F: Autopoiesis and cognition, *Boston Studies in Philosophical Science*, Vol. 42, D. Reidel, Boston, 1980.

3. Maturana H: The biology of cognition. In Maturana and Varela, Op. Cit.

4. Beer S: Preface to Maturana H, Varela F, Op. Cit.

5. Capra F: *The Turning Point*, Flamingo, London, 1983.

6. Kelly G: *The Psychology of Personal Constructs*, Norton, New York, 1955.

7. Bruner J: You are your constructs. *Contemp. Psychol.* 1:355–356, 1956.

8. Epting F: *Personal Construct Counseling and Psychotherapy*, John Wiley & Sons, Chichester, 1984.

9. Kelly G: The psychology of the unknown. In Bannister D (Ed.): *New Perspectives in Personal Construct Theory*, Academic Press, London, 1977.

10. Chauvin R: *Animal Societies*, First Edition, Sphere Books, London, 1971.

11. Maturana H: Biology of language: The epistemology of reality. In Miller G, Lenneberg E (Eds.): *Psychology and Biology of Language and Thought*, Academic Press, New York, 1978.

12. Bateson G: *Mind and Nature: A Necessary Unity*, Dutton, New York, 1979.

13. Dell P: Beyond homeostasis: Toward a concept of coherence. *Fam. Process* 21(No. 1):21–41, 1982.

14. Shotter J: Understanding how to be a person. In Shepherd E, Watson JP (Eds.): *Personal Meanings*, John Wiley & Sons, London, 1982.

15. Bateson G et al.: Towards a theory of schizophrenia. In Bateson G (Ed.): *Steps to an Ecology of Mind*, Granada, London, 1978.

16. Watzlawick P: *How Real is Real? Confusion, Disinformation, Communication*, Vintage Books, New York, 1977, p. 54.

17. Byrne P, Long B: *Doctors Talking to Patients*, Her Majesty's Stationery Office, London, 1976.

18. Fromm-Reichmann F: *Psychoanalysis and Psychotherapy: Selected Papers*, University of Chicago Press, Chicago, 1959, p. 177.

19. Hoffman L: *Foundations of Family Therapy*, Basic Books, New York, 1981.

20. Rice AK: *Learning for Leadership: Interpersonal and Intergroup Relations*, Tavistock, London, 1965.

21. Watzlawick P, Weakland J, Fisch R: *Change: Principles of Problem Formation and Problem Resolution*, Norton, New York, 1974.

22. Vygotsky LS: *Thought and Language*, The M.I.T. Press, Cambridge, 1972, p. 104.

23. Selvini-Palazzoli M et al.: *Paradox and Counterparadox*, Jason Aronson, New York, 1981.

24. Haley J (Ed.): *Advanced Techniques of Hypnosis and Therapy: The Selected Papers of Milton R. Erickson, M.D.*, Grune & Stratton, New York, 1967.

25. Keeney B: *Aesthetics of Change*, Guilford Press, New York, 1983.

26. Szasz T: *The Myth of Mental Illness: Foundations for a Theory of Personal Conduct*, Hoeber and Harper, New York, 1961.

27. Haley J: *Strategies of Psychotherapy*, Grune and Stratton, New York, 1963.

28. Coulter J: *Approaches to Insanity: A Philosophical and Sociological Study*, Martin Robertson, London, 1973.

3

The Prediction
of Outcome
in Psychotherapy
Sol L. Garfield

EDITOR'S NOTE

Innumerable controversies surround the issue of whether psychotherapy is or is not effective, although for most clinicians this activity consumes most of their professional time. Although efforts have been made to define the nature of psychotherapy more concisely and to set up reasonably well-controlled studies to ascertain its value, the vast number of variables ranging from the personality structure of the patient and his environment to the personality makeup of the therapist and his particular training bias have made objective evaluations nearly impossible.

In this chapter, the author cites the various factors which have been selected for such studies and raises a number of critical questions. For example, how should one evaluate the large number of patients who drop out of therapy after a few visits where no follow up is possible? In general, the more education the patient has, particularly if he is from an upper socioeconomic group, the more likely he will be to continue in therapy. The same dimensions, however, do not seem to have any bearing on outcome. There is a suggestion that the more disturbed the patient is at the onset of treatment — particularly if this is a problem with feelings rather than behavior — the greater the eventual improvement will be. At the same time, many factors that are not related to "illness," such as intelligence, environmental support systems and the like, undoubtedly influence the results.

While most therapists have little doubt that psychotherapy makes a difference, proving this is not easy. On the other hand, lack of scientific proof does not mean that psychotherapy is without effect — only that research efforts must continue and perhaps employ heretofore unused methodologies and hypotheses.

The problem of predicting outcome in psychotherapy is one that has interested researchers in this area for some time.[1] However, like other problems in the area of psychotherapy, it is a complex one with many potentially interacting variables. Among the most important variables to be considered are the patient, the therapist, the type of psychotherapy, the patient-therapist interaction, and the criteria of outcome used.

Introduction and Overview

The Psychotherapy Patient: Psychotherapy patients come in all sizes and colors, they vary in age and belong to both sexes, and they seek help with a variety of problems and disorders. They also differ greatly in intelligence and verbal ability, in personality, in socioeconomic status, and in their motivation and desire for psychotherapeutic treatment. All these attributes of patients could influence the outcome of psychotherapy, and a number of them have been investigated as possible correlates of successful outcome in psychotherapy. We shall review some of this work shortly.

The Psychotherapist: Just as patients differ widely, so do psychotherapists—and they vary on many of the same dimensions as those already mentioned for patients (e.g., age, sex, education, personality, and problems). Psychotherapists also differ in a number of other characteristics that theoretically may be of some importance with regard to the process of psychotherapy. They come from different educational and professional backgrounds, they vary in terms of experience, and they do not all practice the same type of therapy. Again, these differences have been thought to be of potential importance in terms of the outcome of psychotherapy.

The Type of Psychotherapy: Since not all psychotherapists practice the same type of psychotherapy, this variable would also have to be considered in predicting the outcome of psychotherapy. Some therapies are long, some are brief, some are conducted on a couch, and some are conducted in groups. This is perhaps a more complicated problem today than it was some years ago because of the tremendous proliferation of psychotherapies.[2]

The Patient-Therapist Interaction: Although the patient and the therapist have rightly been considered important variables by themselves, we also must consider the possible effects of the combination of particular patient-therapist dyads. Some patients may do better with certain therapists than with others, and vice versa. Consequently, looking at patients or therapists separately as predictors of outcome may not be adequate.

Criteria of Outcome: Most psychotherapists generally will acknowledge the potential importance of the previously mentioned variables in influencing outcome. However, they usually are less sensitive to the problems involved in evaluating outcome. Since the criteria used may lead to varying judgments concerning the efficacy of the psychotherapy offered, one cannot disregard this variable.

The Patient as a Variable

Ever since the time of Freud, therapists have offered pronouncements concerning prognosis for psychotherapy. Psychoanalysts generally have stated that patients who do well in psychoanalysis are well educated, are fairly well integrated, are uncomfortable enough to seek treatment and sufficiently motivated to continue treatment, and can withstand the rigors and demands of the treatment. Freud also believed that persons over 50 years of age were probably too rigid and their defenses too fixed to be good candidates for therapy.

Psychodynamic therapists, for the most part, have tended to take a similar view, and, except when economic circumstances demand it, they have been somewhat selective in their choice of patients. This has led one observer to state that the ideal patient is one who is young, attractive, verbal, intelligent, and successful—the YAVIS syndrome.[3] With patients like this, it would seem that the therapist has a higher probability of success. Behavior therapists, on the other hand, have not been so selective and have worked with a number of severe problems that have tended to be avoided by therapists of other persuasions.[4,5] Before we attempt to draw any conclusions, we will want to inspect some representative findings from the research literature. However, before we examine studies specifically devoted to the evaluation of outcome, it is important to examine one particular and related problem: premature termination.

Premature Termination

It is an interesting fact that a large number of patients who commence psychotherapy in outpatient clinics drop out of therapy prematurely—that is, before the therapist has decided that treatment has been completed. This even occurs when the treatment is free.[6] Two problems arise from this occurrence. One is that it is wasteful of the therapist's time to have the treatment interrupted in the middle, and since this occurs with some frequency, it is a problem of some magnitude. The second problem pertains more directly to our concerns with evaluating outcome. How are we to evaluate such cases? Should we disregard them, or should we consider them treatment failures or treatment successes? Although there is no readily acceptable answer to these questions, probably a majority of those who have studied this problem would not view premature termination as a successful outcome. In fact, dropping out of treatment has been viewed as a problem, and considerable research has been devoted to it.[7] Since this may be seen as one potential outcome of psychotherapy, let us briefly review some of the existing research.

Frequency of Premature Termination: A large number of studies have indicated that many patients drop out of therapy very early in the process. For example, in one Veterans Administration outpatient clinic, half of the patients terminated their psychotherapy by the third interview.[8] Median lengths of treatment ranging from four to six sessions were reported for other VA clinics.[6,9,10] Recent studies of community mental-health clinics have secured even more striking results. A study of three urban mental-health centers indicated that 37–45% of adult outpatients terminated therapy after the first or second session.[11] In another report of 400 clinic patients, 45% were seen for less than five interviews.[12] A majority of them simply dropped out — a pattern noted frequently in the research literature.[7]

Patient Variables and Premature Termination: Although a large number of variables have been studied, only a few really reliable findings have been made. One would expect personality characteristics to be of some importance. However, personality attributes are not always well defined and tend to be evaluated in a number of ways. Consequently, the results are frequently conflicting or inconclusive. The same can be said for a number of other variables. For example, motivation for psychotherapy is held by many therapists to be an important factor in both continuation and outcome of therapy. However, what research has been done is inconclusive, largely because motivation for therapy is defined or appraised in different ways. Thus, although a positive relationship between motivation and continuation in therapy has been reported,[13] other studies have not secured such results.[14,16]

Social-class Variables and Premature Termination: Social-class variables have shown some moderately consistent relationship to premature termination. In general, patients of lower socio-economic status have been more prone to terminate their psychotherapy prematurely than have upper-class patients.[7] Education has also shown a positive relationship to continuation in a majority of the studies reported. Some of the differences in findings are probably due to differences in the patient samples accepted for psychother-

apy. Patients accepted for psychoanalysis, for example, have to meet higher
selection standards and tend to be drawn from the higher social strata in our
society. It is also likely that patients from the lower social classes have less
positive views of "talking therapies" and would prefer quick and relatively
directed treatments. Finally, it can be noted that such variables as age, sex,
and psychiatric diagnosis have for the most part not been found to be
related to continuation in psychotherapy.[7]

Outcome in Psychotherapy

A great many studies have been conducted on patient characteristics and
outcome. Again, because of difference in patient samples, therapists, and
techniques of appraisal, clear-cut findings and conclusions are hard to come
by. Nevertheless, it is worth reviewing some of this work.

Social Class and Related Variables: In contrast to the findings on premature termination, there does not appear to be a consistent relationship between social-class variables and outcome.[17,18] Lower-class patients who remain in therapy generally do as well as the other patients who continue in
therapy. However, age and sex again show no significant relation to outcome. We should note, though, that the problems of evaluating outcome are
more complex than those of continuation. When a patient drops out of
therapy, there is no ambiguity in the number of sessions of therapy he or she
has received. With the diverse criteria of outcome, however, the issue is more
complicated. Different methods of evaluating outcome may influence the
results obtained, as we shall see later.

Personality Variables and Outcome: The research literature on patients'
personality and outcome is quite heterogeneous and quite difficult to sum-
marize in brief fashion. For example, an early study of 40 patients based on
several psychological tests concluded that successful patients were of superi-
or intelligence, were not rigid, had a wide range of interests, and were
sensitive to the environment. However, other studies using some of the same
tests have been unable to obtain similar results. Some studies have found a
relationship between degree of initial disturbance and outcome,[19] whereas
others have not.[20] Truax and Carkhuff[21] hypothesized that patients with the
greatest personal "felt disturbance" and the least behavioral disturbance
showed the largest improvement in psychotherapy. However, conclusive evidence for this hypothesis has yet to be provided.

  Some interesting results were obtained in a study comparing two different
types of psychotherapy.[22] The less disturbed patients (as measured by the

MMPI) had better outcomes with analytically oriented therapy, but behavior therapy produced positive treatment results regardless of the patients' degree of disturbance. In a study of long-term therapy conducted at the Menninger Clinic, clinical appraisals of ego strengths correlated 0.35 with a measure of global improvement.[23] However, these appraisals were relative to the particular population studied, and the correlation is rather modest.

Anxiety and Outcome: Several investigators have mentioned that the presence of anxiety is a positive indicator of outcome. Frank,[24] in reviewing the results of 25 years of research, noted that the symptoms of anxiety and depression were relieved the most, whereas less positive results were secured with somatic complaints. However, the type of anxiety and the patient's coping capacity must also be considered. Patients who show anxiety to current stress appear to have more favorable outcomes.[25] However, chronic and severe anxiety may not indicate very favorable prognoses.

Patients' Expectations and Outcome: Patient's expectations about psychotherapy also have received attention from researchers. In some earlier studies, expectations of improvement were correlated with positive outcome, but these promising findings were not always supported by later investigations.[7] Nevertheless, in spite of conflicting results and methodological limitations, a number of investigators have stressed the potential importance of patients' expectations concerning psychotherapy.[26,27]

Undoubtedly, the construct "expectancy" has been treated in a fairly loose manner and includes a variety of expectations, ranging from those concerning outcome to those pertaining to therapeutic procedures and length of therapy. Although it would be desirable to specify the type of expectancies being investigated, it must also be remembered that the expectations a patient brings to therapy are not isolated traits but interact with other features of the patient as well as those of the therapist. Nevertheless, we believe that patient expectancies are of some consequence for continuation and outcome in psychotherapy, and these should be evaluated early in therapy.[28]

Other Patient Attributes: A number of other patient attributes have received at least some attention as possible indicators of outcome. Such characteristics as patient attractiveness, likability, relatability, similarity to the therapist, and internal-external frame of reference have been among those investigated. However, the findings are too limited to be viewed as anything more than suggestive.[7]

In general, we have not been very successful in terms of actually being able to predict outcome on the basis of pretherapy evaluations. However, it does appear that changes early in therapy may be predictive of subsequent outcome. At least, this was an observation reported in two studies of behavioral therapy.[29,30]

The Therapist as a Variable in Outcome

Very few would disagree with the statement that the therapist plays at least some role in the outcomes secured in psychotherapy. However, it is interesting that although there are a number of studies comparing different forms of psychotherapy, very few investigations have appraised the relative effectiveness of different therapists. Rather, group studies have been made of such general attributes as the age, sex, experience, or orientation of therapists.

Therapist Experience: One of the obvious assumptions is that a therapist's amount of experience should influence the kind of outcome obtained. Several past reviews of psychotherapy research have appeared generally to agree with this assumption.[31-33] Two more-recent reviews of this literature, however, are both rather critical of the earlier research, stating that the expected positive effects of amount of therapist experience have not been clearly demonstrated.[34,35] There are methodological deficiencies in many of the studies, and thus definitive conclusions cannot be drawn.

Other Therapist Attributes: The literature on the effect of the current life adjustment of the therapist on patient improvement, although far from being extensive, does suggest that there is a positive relationship. There is considerable literature on the therapeutic value of empathy, nonpossessive warmth, and genuineness or congruence. Earlier research by Rogers and his followers indicated a relationship between high levels of these elements and a successful outcome in therapy. More recent research has, for the most part, been less supportive of this connection.[35] This does not mean that such variables as empathy and genuineness are of no concern in psychotherapy; rather, it indicates that the methods used to appraise them may be limited and the problem more complex.

Therapist and Patient Variables in Combination

The preceding section dealt with studies of therapist characteristics and outcome. The present section will look at therapist and patient variables in combination.

Congruence of Expectations: Although studies have shown little relationship between congruence of patient and therapist expectations and outcome, studies in which attempts have been made to prepare patients for the kind of therapy they are to receive have shown some positive effects on both attrition and outcome.[1,33]

Demographic Variables: Like much of the other related literature in this area, the findings on the matching of therapists and patients in terms of social class, race, or sex are far from conclusive. A major reason for this is that there have actually been very few studies designed specifically to appraise the influence of these variables on outcome.[36] Clinicians and some researchers believe that experience with particular groups of patients and dealing early with therapist-patient differences are important, although adequate studies have not been done. However, attitudes and biases of the therapist may influence the outcome of therapy more than demographic factors per se.[35]

Personality Variables: As might be anticipated, this is a highly complex area. Although most psychotherapists would tend to emphasize the importance of personality variables for progress in psychotherapy, the problems in defining and measuring the selected personality constructs make research difficult. As Parloff et al.[35] concluded: "Only suggestive evidence is found for the usefulness of establishing compatible therapist-patient dyads on the basis of personality dimensions, and it is not clear which dimensions are most important for effective compatibility" (p. 273).

Cognitive Complexity and Values: Another variable that has received only modest investigation is that of cognitive similarity between patient and therapist. Nevertheless, it has been hypothesized that such similarity may be important in terms of the communication between the participants in psychotherapy. Although the studies vary in procedure, one hypothesis is that therapy may be more productive if there is similarity in the complexity of cognitive structure. However, dissimilarity in cognitive content may facilitate change by indicating directions in which the patient needs to move. Further, judged improvement may be related to an increased similarity in patient and therapist values.[35]

Criteria of Outcome

As indicated earlier, one of the factors that needs to be considered in research on outcome in psychotherapy is the type of measurement or criteria used to evaluate outcome. Different criteria may lead to different judgments concerning outcome. We will now examine some of the commonly used procedures.

Ratings by Therapists: Probably the most commonly employed measure of outcome in the past consisted of ratings or judgments of outcome made by the therapist. The therapist is supposedly the person most knowledgeable about what has taken place in therapy and thus is in a good position to provide an evaluation of outcome. At the same time, however, it is recognized that the therapist is not a truly objective observer. Consequently, his evaluations could be more positive than other means of appraising outcome, and this has been supported by results from several studies.[22,37]

Ratings by Patients: Another source of data on outcome has been ratings provided by patients. Again, since patients are the ones who have received the treatment, their appraisals would appear to be meaningful ones. However, they also are not objective and may react to variables other than the extent of change resulting from therapy—e.g., the personality or sincerity of the therapists or the need to justify the expenditure of time and money. Nevertheless, in several studies, their ratings correlated more highly with those of objective observers than did those of therapists.[22] Also, therapists' and patients' ratings of outcome generally are not correlated very highly.[28]

Ratings by Objective Judges: For the reasons mentioned above, there has been a definite trend in more recent studies to utilize clinicians or other noninvolved observers to make independent judgments based on interviews with patients before and after treatment. Although this removes the potential bias of involvement in the therapy, the clinicians' ratings are limited to some extent by the information provided by the patients and by the observations possible during the interview.

Psychological Tests: Another means of appraising outcome is by administering standard psychological tests before and after treatment. There are both advantages and disadvantages in this procedure. Psychological tests may be relatively objective and reliable. Also, the difference in the pre- and post therapy scores may reflect change more adequately than ratings performed at the end of therapy, which may be unduly influenced by the overall level of the patient's adjustment. However, some tests may not be appropriate for certain kinds of problems—e.g., removal of specific symptoms. In addition, there are some technical statistical issues operant when the patients evaluated have very different scores at the start of the therapy. Patients who are very mildly disturbed have less chance to show large changes than those who are more seriously disturbed. However, there are statistical procedures that allow one to correct for problems of this sort.

Behavioral Measures: With the recent popularity of the behavioral thera-pies, there has been a somewhat greater emphasis on behavioral measures of outcome. If, for example, a person is afraid to leave his home or go on an airplane, the most appropriate measure of improvement is performance. If the person can actually perform behaviors that he or she could not before therapy, this is an observable indication of improved behavior.

Standard Battery Versus Individualized Measures: Some researchers be-lieve that the use of a standard battery of instruments for appraising out-come would advance the field, since there would be a greater chance of comparing and replicating results from different centers.[38] Others, however, believe that patients vary greatly and that measures have to be individual-ized. Each of these points of view has merit; however, the use of diverse and unreliable measures has clearly kept us from having more definite knowl-edge regarding the prediction of outcome.

The Use of Multi-Measures of Outcome: For a variety of reasons, a number of investigators also believe that more than one measure of outcome is desirable. Strupp and Hadley,[39] for example, have proposed a tripartite scheme that emphasizes three vantage points—the patient's, the mental-health professional's, and society's. The patient would report on his subjec-tive feelings of well-being and self-esteem, whereas the mental-health profes-sional would utilize observations, tests, and clinical judgment. Society would focus on the observations of the individual's behavior in relation to social norms. The rationale for this scheme is that more than one perspec-tive is required in order to evaluate psychotherapy. Although this seems reasonable, there do not appear to be easy solutions for resolving differences among the various vantage points.

Discussion

We have discussed a number of the problems and variables that must be considered before we will be able to predict outcome in psychotherapy with any degree of clinical adequacy. This kind of background was deemed essen-tial for interpreting the frequently conflicting and disappointing results in this area. As has been noted, several variables may affect the results secured and lead to failures in replication of the results of others. The use of limited criteria of outcome has been a particular problem in the past, but it is not the only problem.

Actually, true prediction studies have been quite rare. Rather, many of the studies have been correlational and exploratory in terms of ascertaining potential predictors of outcome. Even here, however, the results are very modest. As indicated in a recent report[40] of two relatively large investigations: "In sum, for patients who start psychotherapy, predictions of benefits achieved by the end of treatment are only minimally accurate; at best they account for 5%–10% of the variance in outcome" (p. 473). Unfortunately, this is a reasonable appraisal of the situation as it now exists.

References

1. Garfield SL, Bergin AE (eds): *Handbook of Psychotherapy and Behavior Change*, Second Edition, John Wiley & Sons, New York, 1978.
2. Herink R (ed): *The Psychotherapy Handbook: The A to Z Guide to More Than 250 Different Therapies in Use Today*, New American Library, New York, 1980.
3. Schofield W: *Psychotherapy, the Purchase of Friendship*, Prentice-Hall, Englewood Cliffs, N.J., 1964.
4. Kazdin AE: The application of operant techniques in treatment, rehabilitation and education. In Garfield, SL, Bergin, AE, (eds): *Handbook of Psychotherapy and Behavior Change*, Second Edition, John Wiley & Sons, New York, 1978.
5. Ross AO: Behavior therapy with children. In Garfield, SL, Bergin AE (eds): *Handbook of Psychotherapy and Behavior Change*, Second Edition, John Wiley & Sons, New York, 1978.
6. Garfield SL, Kurz, M: Evaluation of treatment and related procedures in 1216 cases referred to a mental hygiene clinic. *Psychiatr. Q.* 26:414–424, 1952.
7. Garfield SL: Research on client variables in psychotherapy. In Garfield, SL, Bergin, AE (eds): *Handbook of Psychotherapy and Behavior Change*, Second Edition, John Wiley & Sons, New York, 1978.
8. Affleck DC, Mednick, SA: The use of the Rorschach Test in the prediction of the abrupt terminator in individual psychotherapy. *J. Consult. Psychol.* 23:125–128, 1959.
9. Blackman N: Psychotherapy in a Veterans Administration mental hygiene clinic. *Psychiatr. Q.* 22:89–102, 1948.
10. Kurland SH: Length of treatment in a mental hygiene clinic. *Psychiatr. Q. (Suppl.)* 30:83–90, 1956.
11. Fiester AR, Rudestam KE: A multivariate analysis of the early dropout process. *J. Consult. Clin. Psychol.* 43:528–535, 1975.
12. Gabby JI, Leavitt A: Providing low cost psychotherapy to middle income patients. *Community Ment. Health J.* 6:210–214, 1970.
13. McNair DM, Lorr M, Callahan DM: Patient and therapist influences on quitting psychotherapy. *J. Consult. Psychol.* 27:10–17, 1963.
14. Affeck DC, Garfield SL: Predictive judgments of therapists and duration of stay in psychotherapy. *J. Clin. Psychol.* 17:134–137, 1961.
15. Garfield SL, Affleck DC, Muffley RA: A study of psychotherapy interaction and continuation in psychotherapy. *J. Clin. Psychol.* 19:473–478, 1963.

16. Siegel N, Fink M: Motivation for psychotherapy. *Compr. Psychiatry* 3:170–173, 1962.

17. Lorion RP: Socioeconomic status and traditional treatment approaches reconsidered. *Psychol. Bull.* 79:263–270, 1973.

18. Lorion RP: Research on psychotherapy and behavior change with the disadvantaged. In Garfield SL, Bergin AE (eds): *Handbook of Psychotherapy and Behavior Change*, Second Edition, John Wiley & Sons, New York, 1978.

19. Stone AR, Frank JD, Nash EH, Imber SD: An intensive five-year follow-up study of treated psychiatric outpatients. *J. Nerv. Ment. Dis.* 133:410–422, 1961.

20. Prager RA, Garfield SL: Client initial disturbance and outcome in psychotherapy. *J. Consult. Clin. Psychol.* 38:112–117, 1972.

21. Truax CB, Carkhuff RR: *Toward Effective Counseling and Psychotherapy*, Aldine, Chicago, 1967.

22. Sloane RB, Staples FR, Cristol AH, Yorkston NJ, Whipple K: *Psychotherapy Versus Behavior Therapy*, Harvard University Press, Cambridge, Mass., 1975.

23. Kernberg OF, Bernstein CS, Coyne R, Appelbaum DA, Horwitz H, Voth TJ: Psychotherapy and psychoanalysis: Final report of the Menninger Foundation's psychotherapy research project. *Bull. Menninger Clin.* 36:1–276, 1972.

24. Frank JD: Therapeutic components of psychotherapy: A 25-year progress report of research. *J. Nerv. Ment. Dis.* 159:325–342, 1974.

25. Smith GJW, Sjoholm L, Nielzen S: Individual factors affecting the improvement of anxiety during a therapeutic period of 1½ to 2 years. *Acta Psychiatr. Scand.* 52:7–22, 1975.

26. Kazdin AE, Wilcoxon LA: Systematic desensitization and nonspecific treatment effects: A methodological evaluation. *Psychol. Bull.* 83:729–758, 1976.

27. Lick J, Bootzin R: Expectancy factors in the treatment of fear. Methodological and theoretical issues. *Psychol. Bull.* 82:917–931, 1975.

28. Garfield SL: *Psychotherapy: An Eclectic Approach*, John Wiley & Sons, New York, 1980.

29. Bandura A, Jeffrey RW, Wright CL: Efficacy of participant modeling as a function of response induction aids. *J. Abnorm. Psychol.* 83:56–64, 1974.

30. Mathews AM, Johnston DW, Shaw PM, Gelder MG: Process variables and the prediction of outcome in behaviour therapy. *Br. J. Psychiatry* 125:256–264, 1974.

31. Bergin AE: The evaluation of therapeutic outcomes. In Bergin AE, Garfield SL (eds): *Handbook of Psychotherapy and Behavior Change*, John Wiley & Sons, New York, 1971.

32. Luborsky L, Chandler M, Auerbach AH, Cohen J, Bachrach HM: Factors influencing the outcome of psychotherapy. *Psychol. Bull.* 75:145–185, 1971.

33. Meltzoff J, Kornriech M: *Research in Psychotherapy*, Atherton Press, New York, 1970.

34. Auerbach AH, Johnson M: Research on the therapist's level of experience. In Gurman AS, Razin AM (eds): *Effective Psychotherapy: A Handbook of Research*, Pergamon Press, Oxford, 1977.

35. Parloff MB, Waskow IE, Wolfe BE: Research on therapist variables in relation to process and outcome. In Garfield SL, Bergin AE (eds): *Handbook of P   -*

chotherapy and Behavior Change, Second Edition, John Wiley & Sons, New York, 1978.

36. Berzins JI: Therapist-patient matching. In Gurman AS, Razin AM (eds): *Effective Psychotherapy: A Handbook of Research*, Pergamon Press, Oxford, 1977, pp. 222–251.

37. Garfield SL, Prager RA, Bergin AE: Evaluation of outcome in psychotherapy. *J. Consult. Clin. Psychol.* 37:307–313, 1971.

38. Waskow IE, Parloff MB (eds): *Psychotherapy Change Measures*, National Institute of Mental Health, Rockville, Md., 1975.

39. Strupp HH, Hadley SW: A tripartite model of mental health and therapeutic outcomes: With special reference to negative effects in psychotherapy. *Am. Psychol.* 32:187–196, 1977.

40. Luborsky L, Minta J, Christoph P: Are psychotherapeutic changes predictable? Comparison of a Chicago Counseling Center project with a Penn. psychotherapy project. *J. Consult. Clin. Psychol.* 47:469–473, 1979.

4

Values in Psychotherapy
Richard K. Sherlock

EDITOR'S NOTE

No psychotherapist with years of experience would question the probability that his or her own, personal value structure influences the treatment of patients. It seems apparent that the psychotherapist does have his/her own vision of reality, a variety of values he/she holds central to how he/she lives, and expectations of what will help others to lead healthier lives is inescapable, and that these communicate themselves to patients in one way or another.

In this chapter, the author explores more systematic efforts to define the role of values in psychotherapy. On the whole, most investigations have been diffuse and inadequate. Some professional writers have insisted that successful intervention depends on modifying the values patients have lived by; perhaps the most obvious example of this is the development of a sense of moral responsibility in sociopathic patients.

"Congruence" is a term used to describe the phenomenon of the patient coming to accept and incorporate values of the therapist. Although studies have supported the positive effect of congruence on therapeutic outcome, none has defined exactly what is measured or how to measure it.

The author concludes: "Psychotherapy is one of the most ambiguous therapeutic relationships," one that must remain open-ended, in which the patient will exercise his power of refusal and the therapist his need for restraint. Although much may take place that has to do with values and every effort should be made to identify what is really happening, the moral autonomy of patient and psychiatrist alike should be preserved.

Introduction

The role of moral beliefs and values in psychotherapy has been of continuing interest. Though Freud himself was a very stern moralist, as was seen in his views of homosexuality, classical psychoanalysis presupposed the neutrality of the analyst vis-à-vis the moral beliefs and values of the patient/client. After World War II, other forms of therapy that also stressed the moral

43

neutrality of the therapist were developed, such as Rogers' famous "client-centered therapy." These new modalities brought the question to the fore in professional literature.[1,2] In the intervening years there has been continuing discussion of these questions in the literature: Is such neutrality possible? Is it desirable? If it is neither possible nor desirable to remain neutral, then how should the moral convictions of the therapist and the patient enter into the therapeutic process?[3-5]

The discussion has not abated; if anything, it has intensified. It now seems appropriate to review and analyze this literature. I think this can be especially helpful from the perspective of someone whose primary discipline is the study of ethics and values as applied to health care questions. Much of the literature makes patently moral assertions and raises patently moral concerns, such as paternalism on the part of therapists or claims about the importance of various moral systems in the lives of individuals.

What we shall see is the enormous complexity of the questions themselves and the confusion that exists in much of the discussions about them.

The General Importance of Values in Therapy

Much of the early literature simply challenged what was perceived to be an impossible claim of strict neutrality on the part of the therapist. Two criticisms regarding the supposition of strict neutrality appeared in the literature. First, it was claimed that, whether he wishes it or not, the therapist's moral convictions do enter into and influence the course of therapy.[6-15] A typical expression of this point was Murphy's claim that the therapist " . . . cannot help conveying directly or indirectly to every client what he himself sees and feels and the perspective in which his own life is lived."[16] More direct and challenging was London's view that the question of the goals of psychotherapy was always answered by each therapist in terms of his own vision of the good life for human beings as such:

Perhaps the most general and accurate answer that sensitive and self conscious therapists could offer to the question of their goals could be put so: "I want to reshape this person's existence so that he will emulate values which I cherish for myself, aspire to what I wish humanity to be, fulfill my need for the best of all possible worlds and human conditions."[17]

Secondly, it was claimed that the therapist cannot remain neutral when the patient brings up matters of moral or valuational content, such as the patient's report of his or her chronic shoplifting for which no guilt is felt. Neither of these claims seems particularly surprising.

Such uneventful claims about the importance of moral convictions in therapy, however, were not what many critics were addressing. Their target was broader and their conclusions were substantially more challenging. Fundamentally, they held that the supposed neutrality of the therapist with regard to the moral beliefs and values of the patient was not only impossible but also wrong. Not only will the therapist communicate moral beliefs and commitments to the patient/client, but he must do so. In other words, the therapist must become a sort of moral counselor to the patient.[18-24] Typical of this literature was Samler's argument that intervention in the values of the patient was a "necessary part of the process" of psychotherapy. He further asserted that by drawing on our knowledge of the "mature personality," we could develop and refine various values and constellations of values that should be supported in therapy.[25] Even more strongly, Ellis constructed his "rational-emotive therapy," based on his belief that most of the emotional difficulties encountered in therapy are caused and maintained by faulty and self-defeating values and moral beliefs, and that the essential task of therapy is to "induce the patient to internalize a rational philosophy of life."[26]

Empirical Studies: Review and Analysis

Such conclusions regarding therapy as an exercise in moral teaching were buttressed in a number of ways. Most significant in this regard has been a developing body of empirical work which has supposedly demonstrated the importance of the therapist's role as a moral counselor. At first glance this would appear to be a relatively easy matter to study empirically, but it has actually been very difficult to examine in any exact fashion. This is especially true given the continuing debate about what constitutes a moral belief or moral value and how to measure the adherence to any specific values on the part of therapists and patients.

An examination of the relevant literature shows that a number of studies, especially recent ones, have supposedly found improvement by the patient in psychotherapy to correlate with the patient's coming to accept or internalize what the researcher defines as the values or moral beliefs of the therapist. This phenomenon, termed "congruence" by some authors, was first discussed in a study by Rosenthal.[27]

As can be seen in Table 1, the early work in this area was unimpressive in its findings. Rosenthal's study did show a correlation between "congruence" and success in therapy, but other studies either failed to show the phenomenon at all or did so with so few patients or in such a statistically insignificant fashion that the results did not really confirm the importance of the congruence phenomenon in therapy.

Since the mid-1960s another group of studies has appeared that offers the best substantiation to date of the importance of congruence. These studies

TABLE 1

Study	N's	Congruence Finding	Instrument
Rosenthal[27]	12	positive	SOV/MVQ
Parloff et al.[28]	2	positive	
Farson[29]	18	positive	B-H
Nawas and Landfield[30]	20	negative	RCRT
Nawas and Landfield[31]	36	positive	RCRT
Petoney[32]	23	positive	
Welkowitz et al.[33]	44	positive	WTL/SVIB
Beutler[34]	65	negative	Rokeach/MVQ
Beutler et al.[35]	34	positive	Rokeach/MVQ
Beutler[36]	97	positive	SAI
Beutler et al.[37]	13	positive	Rokeach/MVQ

SOV: Study of Values instrument
B-H: Butler-Haigh instrument
RCRT: Role Construct Repertory Test
Rokeach/MVQ: moral values Q sample constructed following Rokeach
SAI: Situational Appraisal Inventory
SVIB: Strong Vocational Interest Blank
WTL: Ways to Live Scale

are based on sufficient numbers of patients and have found congruence important to a statistically significant degree. Unfortunately, all of these studies suffer serious problems in defining what is measured and the means of measuring it. Each study used instruments that are so different and that imply such different definitions of values and moral beliefs that they cannot really be thought of as comparable. It may be that a phenomenon resembling congruence is being measured, but from the available data one cannot say much about the form that congruence takes. Therefore, we will have difficulty in offering any solid explanation for it.

Theoretically, one might wish to examine four distinct types of moral congruence in the process of psychotherapy.

Narrative: In the narrative type, one examines the vision or story the patient/client holds as to how human beings should live. This will, of course, involve a ranking of specific values or virtues as well as a view of what are right acts. However, it will also involve something else—something more diffuse and holistic as is captured by novelists when they describe the beliefs, actions, hopes, etc., of a central character. A number of contemporary writers in ethics have been exploring this much-neglected part of the moral life.[38,39]

Axiological: The term axiology is derived from the Greek word axios, meaning worth. It is the study of that which is worthy or valuable. In the study of ethics, it is used to denote the examination of what is good and bad in human life as distinct from the analysis of what specific acts are right or wrong. In the current context, we use it to refer to an examination of what things the patient believes are good, how he ranks various good things, and what values he attaches to things that may be worthwhile. For example, does he or she place a high value on life itself or on some qualities of living? Does he or she value family life or independence, commitment, or freedom, etcetera?[40]

Normative: Alongside considerations of the goods, the study of morality has been traditionally concerned with the study of the kinds of human acts that are right or wrong and the principle or principles by which right acts are deemed right. Is it a situational principle, such as "Maximize the beneficent outcome of each situation?" Or is it a more rigorous principle like, "Always tell the truth," or "Never kill an innocent human being?"[41]

Developmental: In addition to the previous types of moral convictions which deal explicitly with the content of moral belief, one might also want to study congruence in the context of theories of moral development. One such theory, proposed by Kohlberg, focuses on the form of moral reasoning, not its content.[42]

Unfortunately, the studies themselves differ widely with respect to what is being measured, and they are in fact quite unclear as to just what the object of study is and the instruments with which it is best studied. Table 1 illustrates this problem. Each of the studies employs a different instrument, measuring widely divergent concepts. The only one that examines our commonsense understanding of morality to be a concern with what is right or wrong as discussed above in the normative level, is the Situational Appraisal Inventory (SAI).[43] It asks the respondent to determine the "wrongness" of a person's behavior in discreet situations of choice. For example: "John finds a wallet containing a few dollars lying on the sidewalk. Since no one is in sight he pockets the money and leaves the wallet where he found it."

This sort of test does examine something of moral import, and if a sufficient number of questions are asked, grouped around various themes such as honesty or promise-keeping, one can see important moral patterns in the outlooks of the respondents. Unfortunately, of all the instruments used in this research, this one is the most clearly focused on moral content, and it was only used once.

Another instrument used only once but which also seems to focus clearly on moral content is Morris's Ways to Live scale.[44] In this instrument the respondent is presented with 13 paragraph-length descriptions of "ways to live," each of which describes in some detail a life lived in accord with certain central tenets. For example, one paragraph begins, "Self control should be the keynote of life, not the easy self control which retreats from the world but the vigilant, stern, manly control of a self which lives in the world." The subject is asked to respond to each by indicating along a seven-point scale how much he likes or dislikes it. This type of instrument seems to focus on something that is clearly morally important, including portions of the narrative and axiological levels discussed above. However much this instrument focuses on something of moral import, it is not the same focus as that of the SAI. In this respect, the results simply cannot be compared as replications of the same study.

An instrument that may focus on something of moral import is that used in various ways by Rosenthal and Beutler. In this instrument the respondent is presented with a series of statements about several different topics. The topics are selected to represent three levels of centrality to the belief structure and self-image of the respondent, along lines described by Rokeach.[45] For each topic the statements are arranged in a continuum from very positive to very negative. The patient/client is asked to designate his preferred statement, other acceptable statements, and those that are unacceptable, or he may simply be asked to agree or disagree. As an example, in one study the topics were: the need for approval, the threatening nature of the world, the existence of God, Karl Marx, Jesus Christ, premarital sex, and the need for laws. It seems clear that something of moral significance is being examined here, but the focus is still very blurred. We range from that which is not morally significant at all except in a motivational way (the need for approval) to that which is plainly normative (premarital sex), or highly significant in a narrative way (theism). Furthermore, statements about Jesus and Marx may be important in understanding a person's beliefs or fears but it seems plainly wrong to say that a response to the statement "Marx is a great economic theorist" is even close to the same thing morally as a response to the statement "Premarital sex hurts a later marital relationship."

Somewhat more tenuously connected to any of the levels noted above is the Allport-Vernon-Lindzey Study of Values instrument. This instrument purports to measure values, and in a sense it does so, but its focus is really on "dominant personality interest."[46] Questions are asked in two parts that are scored around six ideal types of "dominant personality interest" such as the aesthetic, in which harmony and enjoyment of the moment are dominant interests. The questions are either of the ranking type (e.g., "Would you rather be a minister, salesman, mathematician, or politician?") or of the dichotomous type (e.g., "Which field of study do you believe will benefit man the most, mathematics or theology?"). Some of these ideal types do reflect axiological choices or commitments, but some seem to be loosely related to anything of axiological or normative import. The questions themselves are, in some cases, even less clearly related to anything of moral import than are the idea types around which they scored. For example, in the occupational ranking above, the respondent might ideally wish he were a minister, but he might know that ministers are poorly paid and he might then rank other choices higher. This hardly seems to be the same as someone selecting "politician" because of a commitment to an ideal of public service.

Even less related to the moral categories noted above are the results of the Role Construct Reperatory Test.[47] In this instrument the respondent is first asked to list by name the persons with whom he is expected to be familiar; e.g., his wife or closest girlfriend. Afterward, he is asked to say how two of the people listed are similar to each other and different from a third. This sort of examination, of course, may be important in understanding how an individual views his world and the people in it. But none of this seems to focus on anything of moral import.

Finally, the Butler-Haigh Q instrument used in some of these studies seems not to measure anything resembling any of the moral beliefs noted above.[48] In this instrument the respondent is asked to sort 100 self-referential items (such as "I am punctual") in two sortings. The first describes the person, and the other describes his ideal self. Again, this may help us understand the person better, but one cannot seriously maintain that this is similar to material in the situational appraisal inventory.

What, then, has been measured in these studies? The only truthful answer is: a very diverse collection of attitudes about self and world, evaluative beliefs, and moral convictions. Some of these are morally significant and some are not. Some of the results may be important in personality assessment, but not as measures of moral convictions or values.[49-50] In general, we can distinguish among these instruments and the questions they ask in three ways.

The first is a distinction between questions that ask about moral beliefs or values and those that ask about some other phenomenon. Somewhat provisionally, this distinction may be made about qualities of human persons and their acts, and qualities of inanimate objects or human biological processes. For example, the statement, "This is a good man or woman," seems different than the statement, "This is a well-functioning heart," or "This is a good car." The former seems to be a moral judgment about which the congruence phenomenon should be concerned, while the latter is not. If the central concerns raised by the congruence phenomenon are those of therapeutic paternalism in telling others how to live, then we ought to be much more concerned with an individual's view of how he and others ought to live than questions about non-normal goods or values.

A second distinction may be made by comparing the degree to which these instruments ask about specific moral responses to discreet acts, such as premarital sex or student cheating. In some instruments or sections of instruments, the focus is on specific acts or moral norms. In others, specific character traits or virtues are in view, and in still others broad evaluative attitudes or philosophies of life are in focus. Each of these is important but each is also very different from the others.

Thirdly, following Rokeach, we might distinguish between levels of "centrality" in the moral beliefs examined. Some beliefs will be central to a moral outlook or a person's view of himself. Such seems likely to be the case with a belief that man's happiness is found in obedience to God or a belief in human equality. Other beliefs may be morally significant but not central, such as views about student cheating in various situations.

Given the range of moral and non-moral phenomena examined in these studies, it appears incorrect to conclude that the studies are all looking at the same phenomenon, or are achieving results that replicate earlier findings that lend credibility to a single result. Something significant is probably going on here, but we simply do not know what it is and how best to view it from the available data, as diverse and incomplete as they are.

What Changes in Successful Psychotherapy

If we grant, as many do, that congruence is a part of successful psychotherapy, we are faced with an important set of questions concerning the kinds of moral values and convictions that can be expected to change and the direction in which these changes ought to occur. Among the very wide range of beliefs, values, and attitudes that the various studies purport to measure, are some more resistant to change and others less so? Are some such changes more important in successful therapy and others not? Only one study has made any attempt to measure such questions, and its methods and results are unsatisfactory.[35]

In a study using a Rokeach-type instrument, it was found that beliefs of "medium centrality" were more likely to change in therapy, as predicted by the congruence thesis, than were beliefs regarded as either more or less central. In this study, beliefs of "medium centrality" were studied in terms of statements about Karl Marx and Jesus, grouped around a nine-point positive/negative continuum for each figure. But just why these should be counted as medium centrality beliefs, as opposed to those designated as more central (for example, the existence of God) or less central (such as premarital sex) is never made clear. I submit that one can easily suppose that, for some devout Christians, statements about Jesus may be as absolutely central as those about God, while statements about Marx may be less so. It seems reasonable to suppose that some beliefs may be more amenable to change than others, and this may explain some of the differences in the empirical findings. But which beliefs these may be is a very difficult matter to assess, and the shortcomings of the available studies on these issues leave us without solid answers to these questions.

As might be expected, the values and beliefs to which the therapist ought to guide the client are a matter of deep controversy. As such, we can only call attention to such differences here, perhaps best represented in a recent spirited exchange between two leaders of American psychology, Allan Bergin, a theist and conservative moralist, and Albert Ellis, best known as an atheist and situation ethicist.[51,52] My point is not to decide here between these divergent sets of moral beliefs. Rather, I believe that we simply do not know enough — and perhaps never will — to choose between them in any definitive manner for all human beings. Furthermore, statements about a "mature" or "healthy" personality,[53] do not solve the difficulties unless we can show concretely how these terms are to be defined in terms of specific beliefs and values. We do not know what changes occur or what changes ought to occur in successful therapy.

Explanatory Models

If we assume that the moral convictions of the therapist must play an important role in therapy, we can explain this importance in a variety of ways, some of which are relevant to the congruence phenomenon and some of which are not. In some versions, the actual fact of congruence is not relevant and may be counterproductive. What may be important is the fact that the therapist has moral convictions that he shares openly with the patient. In Lederer's model, for example, the therapist fills the role of an absent father for those patients who lack the moral control imposed by the superego which, hopefully, was developed under the influence of real fathers in most persons. In some patients part of the failure of their proper psychological functioning stems from this failure to develop a superego as a control on their impulses. Hence, they need to be confronted with the sense of moral conviction by the therapist so that they can learn it is "all right" to develop their own convictions and standards, not necessarily those of the therapist.[54]

This model, of course, explains the importance of explicit statements of moral conviction in therapy but it does not explain the congruence phenomenon. Two broad categories of explanations that deal directly with the congruence phenomenon may be noted in the literature: 1) those that focus on the unconscious or silent features of the therapeutic relationship, and 2) those that explain congruence as the result of a conscious process of persuasion on the part of the therapist. Those in the former category, of course, are based largely on versions of the transference phenomenon in which the patient comes to admire and depend on the therapist and then to emulate the beliefs and behaviors that he admires in the therapist. This sort of transference can occur without the conscious awareness of or manipulation by the therapist. In other words, the therapist need not view himself as moral counselor in order for congruence to work in this fashion in successful therapy.[55]

A second set of explanatory models views congruence as the result of deliberate activity on the part of the therapist. These models explicitly state that the therapist must "persuade" the patient to adopt a more "mature" or "healthy" set of values and beliefs, but they do so in different ways with very different moral implications. Social acceptance theory supposes that persuasion will be successful if the patient perceives the convictions of the therapist to be within his "latitude of acceptance." Empirically, acceptance theory would predict that a similarity of moral outlook on the part of the therapist and the patient will correlate with congruence.[34,56] To date, however, no such finding has been demonstrated in any of the relevant studies. If congruence is found in any of the studies, it has been associated with discrepancy in beliefs and attitudes, not similarity.

The model for which the best empirical support can be found is the dissonance model developed by Beutler on the basis of Festinger's theory of cognitive dissonance.[57] In this view, cognitive dissonance engenders change in the direction of similarity since the individual does not want to exist in a dissonant state. Thus, part of the task of the therapist would be to engender "maximal attitude discrepancy" between therapist and patient. This, according to dissonance theory, would lead to change on the part of the patient toward the values of the therapist. In this view, it is not the values of the beliefs of the therapist that are essential in starting and continuing therapy but the credibility of the therapist or his "acceptance" by the patient. Empirically, the dissonance theory would predict that attitude discrepancy and perceived credibility of the therapist would correlate with successful therapy, both of which have been found in studies noted above.

Though this is clearly a recipe for moral confrontation in therapy, where the authority of the therapist is used to produce dissonance and change, it is not a recipe that stands alone. A number of other writers have been moving in the same direction. Perhaps the most trenchant recent version is found in Hoffman's book, in which the problems of the patient are linked to unresolved guilt with which the therapist must confront the patient by challenging him on the basis of accepted social morality.[58] This framework is much like that put forth in earlier work by Mowrer.[59,60]

Congruence, Psychotherapy, and Paternalism

However it is to be explained, the body of opinion and data that we have examined has proven to be a source of serious concern to many therapists because of its supposedly paternalistic implications. Paternalism has been a subject of much discussion in clinical and ethical literature in recent years.[61-63] While the technical aspects of this discussion need not concern us here, we can note a broad agreement in the literature on a definition such as that offered by Childress in his recent extensive discussion: "Paternalism may be defined as a refusal to accept or acquiesce in another person's wishes, choices and actions for that person's own benefit."[64]

Taking Childress's definition as a starting point, we can easily see that some of the data and technical formulations we have reviewed would generate concerns of paternalism. This is especially true of the dissonance model. If successful therapy requires dissonance, then the conclusions seem to be that the therapist must actively challenge the beliefs of the patient and seek to change his ranking of values to agree with that which the therapist believes is best. This certainly seems to fit Childress's definition of paternalism in which the therapist deliberately refuses to acquiesce in the patient's view of how he ought to live.

Yet, I submit that—even granting the most severe claims of the literature that we have examined—it seems intuitively obvious that we do not find anything approaching the classical forms of paternalism in psychotherapy. Consider, for example, such classical cases of paternalism as physicians deceiving patients about the nature of their illness or judges ordering welfare mothers to submit to sterilization as a condition of probation. The differences between such actions that seem clearly paternalistic and the case of psychotherapy seems obvious, even though the difference is not captured in the standard definitions of paternalism.

The most helpful framework in which to view these matters is not the standard language of paternalism but the language of intervention and restraint. What strikes us as morally problematic in any human relation is not the failure of one person to accept or acquiesce to another's concept of the good and the right, nor even his readiness to challenge the moral outlook that he finds wrong. Rather, it is the willingness to intervene in another's life. The real problem is not that I act toward you as a parent toward a child, rather it is that I am doing what a parent sometimes does—intervening in your life. It is the absence of that sort of intervention in psychotherapy and its presence in the cases just noted that seems to be an important difference between these cases and one that we can intuitively recognize.

What restrains us from going further is the sense that, for all its inherently moral nature, psychotherapy is one of the most ambiguous therapeutic relationships. It is a tentative enterprise, lacking even the fixed certainties of pharmacotherapy in overtly psychotic patients. As other branches of medicine are just discovering, the "therapy of the word" is a crucial part of the healing art. But it remains that, an art, the practice of which cannot be based on fixed knowledge of how people ought to live.

Therapy will and must remain an open-ended enterprise, one in which the patient/client will exercise his power of refusal and the therapist his need for restraint. In this manner, the moral autonomy of both is preserved and the possibility of therapy in an ongoing, richly developed life is maintained without the redressing of a mannequin that some of the literature we have reviewed seems to imply.

References

1. Rogers C: *Client-Centered Therapy*, Houghton Mifflin, Boston, 1951.

2. Perls F et al.: *Gestalt Therapy*, Julian Press, New York, 1951.

3. Kessel P, McBrearaty JF: Values and psychotherapy: A review of the literature. *Percept. Mot. Skills* 25:669–690, 1967.

4. Dukes WF: Psychological studies of values. *Psycholo. Bull*. 52:669–690, 1955.

5. Erlich D, Weiner D: The measurement of values in psychotherapeutic settings. *J. Gen. Psychol*. 64:359–372, 1961.

6. Buhler C: *Values in Psychotherapy*, Free Press, New York, 1962.

7. Burgum M: Values and some technical problems in psychotherapy. *Am. J. Orthopsychiatry* 27:338–348, 1957.

8. Lowe C: Value orientations: An ethical dilemma. *Am. Psychol*. 14:687–693, 1959.

9. Lowe C: *Value Orientations in Counseling*, Carrol Press, Cranston, R.I., 1976.

10. Meehl P: Some technical and axiological problems in the handling of religious and valuational material. *J. Counseling Psychol*. 6:25–259, 1959.

11. Glad DD: *Operational Values in Psychotherapy*, Oxford University Press, New York, 1959.

12. Smith MB: Mental health reconsidered: A special case of the problems of values in psychotherapy. *Am. Psychol*. 16:299–306, 1961.

13. Segal S et al.: Religious factors and values in counseling: A symposium. *J. Counseling Psychol*. 6:255–272, 1959.

14. Lovinger R: Therapeutic strategies with religious resistances. *Psychotherapy: Theory, Research and Practice* 16:419–427, 1979.

15. Masserman J (Ed.): *Psychoanalysis and Human Values*, Grune and Stratton, New York, 1960.

16. Murphy G: The cultural context of guidance. *Personnel and Guidance J*. 34:3–9, 1955.

17. London P: *Modes and Morals of Psychotherapy*, Holt, Rinehart, New York, 1964.

18. Driekurs R: Psychotherapy as the correction of faulty social values. *J. Individ. Psychol.* 13:150–158, 1957.

19. Williamson E: Value orientations in counseling. *Personnel and Guidance J.* 36:520–528, 1958.

20. Callahan R: Value orientation and psychotherapy. *Am. Psychol.* 15:269–270, 1960.

21. Reid J: Psychotherapy and values. In Salzman L, Masserman J (Eds.): *Modern Concepts of Psychoanalysis*, Citadel Press, New York, 1962, pp. 21–43.

22. Wolff W: Fact and value in psychotherapy. *Am. J. Psychother.* 8:466–486, 1959.

23. Pepinsky H, Karst T: Convergence: A phenomenon in psychotherapy. *Am. Psychol.* 19:333–338, 1964.

24. Beutler L: Values, beliefs, religion and the persuasive influence of psychotherapy. *Psychotherapy: Theory, Research and Practice* 16:432–440, 1979.

25. Samler J: Changes in values: A goal in counseling. *J. Counseling Psychol.* 7:32–39, 1960.

26. Ellis A: *Humanistic Psychotherapy*, Julian Press, New York, 1973.

27. Rosenthal D: Changes in some moral values following psychotherapy. *J. Consult. Psych.* 19:431–436, 1955.

28. Parloff M et al.: Communication of therapy values between therapist and schizophrenic patients. *J. Nerv. Ment. Dis.* 130:193–199, 1960.

29. Farson RE: Introjection in the psychotherapeutic relationship. *J. Counseling Psychol.* 8:337–343, 1961.

30. Nawas M, Landfield A: Improvement in psychotherapy and adoption of the therapists meaning system. *Psychol. Rep.* 13:97–98, 1963.

31. Nawas M, Landfield A: Psychotherapeutic improvement as a function of the adoption of therapist values. *J. Counseling Psychol.* 11:336–341, 1964.

32. Petoney P: Value change in psychotherapy. *Hum. Relations* 19:39–45, 1966.

33. Welkowitz J et al.: Value system similarity: Investigation of patient-therapist dyads. *J. Consult. Psychol.* 31:48–55, 1967.

34. Beutler L: Predicting outcomes in psychotherapy. *J. Consult. Clin. Psychol.* 37:411–416, 1971.

35. Beutler L et al.: Outcomes in group psychotherapy. *J. Consult. Clin. Psychol.* 42:547–553, 1974.

36. Beutler L et al.: Attitude similarity and therapist credibility as predictors in success in therapy. *J. Consult. Clin. Psychol.* 43:90–91, 1975.

37. Beutler L et al.: Acceptance: Values and therapeutic changes. *J. Consult. Clin. Psychol.* 46:198–199, 1978.

38. Macintyre A: *After Value*, Notre Dame University Press, South Bend, Ind., 1978.

39. Hauerwas S, Burrell D: From system to story: An alternative pattern for rationality in ethics. In Englehardt T, Callahan D (Eds.): *Knowledge Value and Belief*, Hastings Center, New York, 1977.

40. Findlay J: *Axiological Ethics*, Macmillan, New York, 1975.

41. Frankenna W: *Ethics*, 2nd Ed., Prentice Hall, New York, 1975.

42. Kohlberg L: *Essays on Moral Development*, Harper and Row, San Francisco, 1981.

43. Pittel S, Mendlesohn G: The development and validation of a measure of evaluative attitudes. *J. Consult. Clin. Psychol.* 33:396–405, 1969.

44. Morris C: *Varieties of Human Values*, University of Chicago Press, Chicago, 1956.

45. Rokeach M: *The Nature of Human Values*, The Free Press, New York, 1973.

46. Allport G et al.: *Study of Values*, Knopf, New York, 1962.

47. Kelly GA: *The Psychology of Personal Constructs*, Norton, New York, 1955.

48. Butler J, Haigh M: The relationship between self concepts and ideal concepts consequent upon client centered counseling. In Rogers C, Dymond R (Eds.): *Psychotherapy and Personality Change*, University of Chicago Press, Chicago, 1954, pp. 55–75.

49. Handy R: *The Measurement of Values*, Warren Green, St. Louis, 1970.

50. Strunk O: Personal values and self theory. In Canning J (Ed.): *Problems of Values*, Charles Merrill, Columbus, OH, pp. 67–83, 1970.

51. Bergin A: Psychotherapy and religious values. *J. Consult. Clin. Psychol.* 48:95–105, 1980.

52. Ellis A: Psychotherapy and atheistic values: A response to Bergin. *J. Consult. Clin. Psychol.* 48:635–639, 1980.

53. Jahoda M: *Current Concepts of Positive Mental Health*, Basic Books, New York, 1959.

54. Lederer W: Value oriented psychotherapy. *J. Humanistic Psychol.* 2:401–406, 1962.

55. Gear MC et al.: *Patients and Agents: Transference and Countertransference in Therapy*, Jason Aronson, New York, 1983.

56. Sheriff C et al.: *Attitude and Attitude Change*, W. B. Saunders, Philadelphia, 1965.

57. Beutler L: Interpersonal persuasion and psychotherapy. In Beutler L, Greene RR (Eds.): *Special Problems in Child and Adolescent Behavior*, Technomic Publishing Co., Westport, Conn., 1978, pp. 119–159.

58. Hoffman J: *Ethical Confrontation in Counseling*, University of Chicago Press, Chicago, 1983.

59. Mowrer O: *The Crisis in Psychiatry and Religion*, Van Nostrand, Princeton, 1961.

60. Mowrer O: Some constructive features of the concept of sin. In Ard B (Ed.): *Counseling and Psychotherapy*, Science and Behavior, Palo Alto, 1966, pp. 217–222.

61. Karasu TB: Ethics of psychotherapy. *Am. J. Psychiatry* 137:1503–1512, 1980.

62. Levine M: *Psychiatry and Ethics*, George Braziller, New York, 1972.

63. Goldberg C: *Therapeutic Partnerships: Ethical Concerns in Psychotherapy*, Springer Verlag, New York, 1977.

64. Childress J: *Who Decides: Paternalism in Health Case*, Oxford University Press, New York, 1982.

5

Current Status of Classical Freudian Psychoanalysis
Leopold Bellak

EDITOR'S NOTE

Although the majority of psychiatrists in the United States are not psychoanalysts, psychoanalytic theory and practice have contributed substantially to the shape of a variety of psychotherapeutic modalities. In practice, such concepts as transference, countertransference, the balance between consciousness and the unconscious, and the importance of childhood developmental experiences in the etiology of adult psychopathological problems—universalities in everyday practice—derive, in no small measure, from early psychoanalytic explorations.

However, as society has changed and the nature of psychiatric treatment has become more holistic—in the sense that the practitioner considers not only the patient's psychological structure but also the environmental and biological correlates of his adaptive mechanisms—questions arise. Has psychoanalytic practice become obsolete? Is the theoretical basis of psychoanalysis still relevant? Does psychoanalytic thinking, which so dominated the psychiatric scene in the 1950s, still retain any significant influence now?

Here the author briefly traces the evolution of psychoanalysis from its beginnings to the contemporary scene, in which personality disorders, such as the borderline state, have overshadowed traditional neuroses and in which object-relations theory seems to have set the stage for new psychoanalytic approaches to treatment.

Object-relations theory attributes the origins of adult behavioral problems to conflicts originating in that phase of childhood development called pre-oedipal. Two of the original writers on this subject were Edith Jacobson, drawing on her extensive

I am indebted to Marlene Kolbert for editorial assistance and to Peri Faithorn M.D. and Saul Scheidlinger Ph.D. for their critical reading of and constructive suggestions for the manuscript.

57

work with depressed patients, and Margaret Mahler, who intensively studied infants, particularly those with autistic problems. They placed special emphasis on the role of separation and individuation in personality development. More recently, Kohut and Kernberg have elaborated somewhat differing approaches to understanding object-relations theory and self-psychology, the former moving away from the classical psychoanalytic model, the latter incorporating his thinking more within its framework. This work remains quite controversial. As the author points out, the language in which it has been expressed can be exceedingly difficult to fathom, and he advises us to introduce ourselves to these ideas "through interpreters."

Finally, the author explores certain other features of current psychoanalytic technique, including dream analysis and positions psychoanalysis, in the United States and in Europe, within the framework of today's broad biopsychosocial approach to human behavior in health and illness.

Introduction

When reading my account of the current status of classical Freudian psychoanalysis, the reader must be warned to take what I have to say with a large grain of salt. This assessment is *my* idea of the current status of psychoanalysis, with no guarantee that it is also anyone else's conception. One possible support for my ideas is the fact that I have been acquainted with psychoanalysis for over 40 years, and can appraise whatever I know of contemporary analysis in terms of this perspective. In fact, I started my own training analysis in Vienna in 1935 and, as a young medical student, was permitted to take my first courses at the Vienna Psychoanalytic Institute at that time. I have not been out of contact with psychoanalysis since.

In speaking of the current status of psychoanalysis, one has to keep in mind that there are vast fluctuations in theory and practice from country to country and, for that matter, among individual analysts. At best, my account should be viewed as trying to approach a mean. I will make a few comments on the status of psychoanalysis in different countries but, for the most part, will limit my discussion to the United States.

Psychoanalysis, like many a science, has passed through some characteristic phases. With Freud's *The Interpretation of Dreams* in 1900 until sometime in the '30s, it underwent its first and what might be called heroic phase. This initial stage was characterized by startling and exhilarating discoveries, often not sufficiently tempered by caution or qualifications — and certainly not by scientific and experimental proof.

The initial phase of relatively basic and sometimes unsophisticated notions came to an end in the late 1930s. The new era was initiated by Freud himself and then carried forward by Anna Freud's monograph *The Ego and the Mechanism of Defense* and by Hartmann's volume *Ego Psychology and the Problems of Adaptation.* Both Anna Freud and Hartmann elaborated on and refined the importance of the ego and its many functions in organizing psychic processes.

At almost the same time as their publications, the advent of the Nazis interrupted the growth of psychoanalysis not only by forcing Freud to flee Vienna but also by dispersing most of his immediate and closest collaborators all over the world, many of them to America. This led to a cessation of psychoanalytic development until new ground was found for it, primarily in the United States. The Nazi ideology and the war blighted any development of psychoanalysis in Europe at that time. It was proscribed by the Nazi as a "Jewish science" — notwithstanding the fact that there were a fair number of non-Jewish analysts, some of whom even tried to make an accommodation with the Nazis. Books were burned and associations dissolved.

The next flowering of psychoanalysis took place in the psychoanalytic institutes of the United States. A foundation for this development was laid during World War II by the application of psychoanalytic principles to psychiatric practice in the Armed Forces. As a result of the utilization of psychoanalytic psychotherapy during the war, a tremendous enthusiasm, widespread use, and a very esteemed status for psychoanalytic institutes sprang up all over the United States; candidates flocked to them, and it was unlikely that anyone could become chairman of a department of psychiatry if he was not a psychoanalyst. Some of those who did were obliged, often at considerable inconvenience, to become psychoanalytically trained *a posteriori*. This state of affairs lasted roughly until 1960. Until then, psychoanalysis had also inspired intensive psychotherapy for psychoses — schizophrenia especially — taking off from Freud's Schreber case and the early work of Federn, Tausk, and others. Bychowski, John Rosen, and Eissler treated schizophrenia within the orthodox Freudian framework, and Sullivan and Frieda Fromm-Reichmann developed a neo-Freudian frame of reference for the application of psychoanalytic principles to the treatment of psychotics.

The popular appeal of psychoanalysis in the immediate postwar period also manifested itself in such offshoots as Eric Berne's transactional analysis and such California fringe phenomena as Scientology, primal-scream therapy, and EST.

Pharmacotherapy and Community Psychiatry

A major change that occurred in psychiatry in the mid '50s was the introduction of thorazine (and, for a while, reserpine), to be followed soon by a tremendous number of other psychotropic drugs. A switch of interest from psychotherapy to pharmacotherapy — and eventually to biochemical theories, such as the dopamine hypothesis and the catecholamine hypothesis—took place. Parallel to this, in the early '60s, community psychiatry came to play a prominent role in mental health. Its spawning had also taken place, to a considerable extent, in the Armed Forces, when it was found that psychiatric patients could be treated in general hospitals. An enlightened approach based on psychoanalysis, combined with chemical control by psychotropic drugs and an emphasis on civil rights, furthered the cause of community psychiatry.

The net result of the development of pharmacotherapy and community psychiatry was that psychoanalysis as a method of therapy went into a measure of decline. One objective criterion is that the number of applicants to psychoanalytic institutes in the United States fell sharply. Less clearly demonstrable is the fact that fewer patients went into psychoanalysis or psychoanalytic psychotherapy, fewer residents had a primary interest in this field, and a general feeling of unrest seemed to pervade the profession. Indeed, at the 1975 meeting of the International Psychoanalytic Association in London, Anna Freud voiced the frustration and stagnation in the field. Her suggested remedy was that psychoanalysis again narrow its scope and do what it had always done best—namely, treat classical psychoneurosis. It was her belief that the psychoanalytic doldrums were due to overextension. This "overextension," which took place in the 1960s, referred to "the broadening of scope of psychoanalysis" to include the application of its treatment technique to character disorders, borderline states, and psychoses. As a matter of fact, some decline of psychoanalysis may also have been attributable, Anna Freud convincingly suggested, to the Vietnam spirit, which made many people outer-directed and concerned with politics rather than inner-directed and psychologically minded.

It was probably also at that congress that the adherents of classical orthodox psychoanalysis and those who wanted to introduce some changes—specifically, object-relations theorists—had their most dramatic clash.

From that point on, however, object-relations theory, which had already flourished in a variety of forms in England and South America—starting with Melanie Klein and including Fairbairn, Bion, Guntrip, and others—increasingly found a place in American psychiatry.

The two main figures among the ranks of classical psychoanalysis who played a role in the inclusion of object-relations theory within their discipline were Edith Jacobson (with her volumes on depression and with her work *The Self and Reality*) and Margaret Mahler (with her studies on infants, autism, and early object relations). Predicated on their work, as well as on that of some of the British school, Otto Kernberg became one of the main spokesmen of object-relations theory in the United States. Heinz Kohut also attracted many followers to his rather different "self-psychology."

Some of the main events in contemporary psychoanalysis in the past five years involved a dialogue between classical and "neo-classical" Freudians and the followers of Kohut and Kernberg. At the present time, some mutual integration of originally highly conflicting ideas has taken place. To a certain extent, this has occurred on account of Kernberg's increasingly stating his concepts within the structural theory of classical psychoanalysis. On the other hand, a good many classical psychoanalysts have found some of the concepts of object-relations theory, of one origin or another, conceptually useful and technically valid for therapeutic technique. Kohut's position has remained somewhat more of an independent development, further enlarged on by his followers.

A brief discussion of these two main lines of thought and their integration into the current status of psychoanalysis is appropriate.

At present, it is very likely that a typically dialectic process has been virtually completed: object-relations therapy rose in antithesis to "classical" psychoanalysis but now synthesis utilizing the best of both fields is under way.

Object-Relations Theory and Self-Psychology

The changes in psychoanalytic interests, theory, and techniques occurred in relation both to the internal development of psychoanalysis as a body of knowledge and to the social milieu. In the 1960s, the age of the "counterculture," communes, alternative life-styles, and the permissive society, psychoanalysts noted that psychoneurosis per se — such as obsessive-compulsive, hysterical, and phobic disorders — seemed to decrease sharply. It seemed that in the presence of a permissive society, superego formation was weak and inconsistent.[1]

At the same time, increased social and geographic mobility, the luxurious living of the affluent society, and the great increase in the divorce rate weakened other structures of the personality. The ego ideal, the concept of the self, became fuzzy, the identification figures blurred. Instead of repression and psychoneurosis, lack of organization and a feeling of emptiness were the chief complaints. Anhedonia, the simple absence of pleasure, prevailed. Drugs, from marijuana to a long list of "uppers" and "downers," and the loud music of the discothèques were used in an attempt to fill the void.

Object relations — internalized as well as externalized — were indeed poor, and in some ways this development was quite in keeping with some predictions of mine years before.[2] The classical analytic technique, with its heavy emphasis on the transference neurosis as the therapeutic vehicle, could not deal with these conditions in patients who did not have enough object relations in the classical sense to form a transference neurosis.

At this point, a tremendous interest in borderline states developed, and nearly a dozen monographs on that topic appeared. The difference between borderline states and another burgeoning concept, that of character disorder, was often blurred: character disorders, in distinction to psychoneurosis, were seen as such largely narcissistic disorders as to overlap into schizophrenia.[3]

In this social context, object relations and self-psychology developed — from different roots, in different ways.

Two outstanding figures in this field came from within the strictest classical bounds of psychoanalytic theory and professional allegiance — namely, Edith Jacobson and Margaret Mahler, both leading teachers at the New York Psychoanalytic Institute. Jacobson carefully developed her concepts concerning identification, the fate of introjects and of object relations, and the self from her decades of work with the depressed.[4] In her volume *The Self and the Object World*,[6] Jacobson extrapolated and elaborated into a cohesive theory what she had learned in her treatment of depression, as reviewed extensively by Bellak and Antell.[7] Mahler arrived at her contributions from the observation of infants — the study of autistic infants in particular, with special emphasis on the vicissitudes of separation and individuation and the development of object relations.[5]

Into this melee came Kohut,[8] a Vienna-born and -trained psychoanalyst working in Chicago, who eventually developed a theory emphasizing that narcissism goes through various states, parallel to the stages of libidinal development as postulated by classical psychoanalysis. This led him to a change in technique and to an emphasis on the psychology of the self, as distinct from classical tripartite theory (id, ego, superego).

Kernberg, on the other hand, formulated his own brand of object-relations theory with ideas about the self and borderline conditions. He based his conceptions on those of several British Kleinian psychoanalysts, as well as on those of Mahler and Jacobson.

A good many of the seemingly novel ideas actually were not original with either Kernberg or Kohut, or even with Mahler or Jacobson or the British school. It is often not realized that the concept of "splitting" as a defense was discussed earlier, and was actually the title and the subject of one of the last papers of Freud.[9] The concept of self-representations and object representations was discussed in a basic paper by Hartmann[10] as well as by Freud.

Surprisingly, one of the concepts of self-psychology and object-relations theory was anticipated (in somewhat different form) by Reik,[11] who spoke of the repeated mirroring of the analyst and his problems in those of his patients.

A Definition of the Theory

In essence, object-relations theory postulates and emphasizes "structural" aspects of psychoanalysis in the earliest years of life—i.e., the development of the structure of the self. It generally points up the importance of the pre-oedipal events as compared to the primary concern with oedipal problems in classical analysis. Certainly, interest in and the importance of pre-oedipal and oedipal events should not be seen as mutually exclusive by either group.

A more latent but hardly less important theoretical difference between object-relations theory, especially as derived from Melanie Klein and her close followers, and Freudian theory lies in moving away from conflict theory generally and substituting a defect theory—structural defect of the ego. In this theoretical development, part of this position of object-relations theory became a tendency to downgrade the concept of instinctual, libidinal energy and to upgrade the importance of aggression. Rage plays a major role, from Klein's "bad breast" concept to the infantile omnipotent rage in other authors' concepts.

"Object-relations theory" is a somewhat misleading term if it is to indicate something different and new, because the nature of object relations was one of the main concerns of Freud. What Melanie Klein first contributed was the belief that the infant can have a variety of object relations in the earliest days of life and that, for instance, the early conception of a "bad" breast and a "good" breast could have a structuring influence on later apperceptions of object relations and internalization of part object representation, part self-representation.

Mahler has contributed observations on the process of separation and individuation of the infant from the mother, and the various ways in which that individuation and separation may fail and then lead to a variety of disorders of self. Jacobson, especially in studying the depressed,[4] depicted the vicissitudes of introjects and their relationship to the formation of the self. To be sure, even the fragmented development of the ego has classical forerunners—for instance, in Edward Glover's theory of ego nuclei,[12] which dealt with stages of development of the different parts of the ego and discussed the vicissitudes of synthesis of these various "ego nuclei" or the pathology resulting from their failure to merge.

Psychoanalytic theory, broadly speaking, involves a drive theory (libido theory) and a structural theory (id, ego, superego). One must understand the contributions of object-relations theory as being extensions of the structural theory. Object-relations theorists believe that certain structures—namely, self-perceptions and object perceptions—and their internalization occur earlier in the infant's life than classical analysis posited and that they have a greater influence on personality formation than they did in classical analysis, which considered the Oedipus complex and its manifestation as the most crucial aspect. There need not be any controversy, of course, since it seems plausible that disturbances of the earlier structure formations would lead to more profound pathology than of the oedipal ones, the latter leading primarily to a classical psychoneurosis that in some ways is more benign than character disorders and borderline conditions.

The Accumulation of Perceptions

The language of the various theorists is often very obscure and confusing, but the basic facts can be made clear enough and are consistent with what other science has to teach us.*

From earliest age on, everyone accumulates perceptions and sees, for instance, mother as a good person, a feeling person, a punishing person, and also perceives an aunt or a teacher or sibling in similar fashion. To oversimplify, personality and character are the anlage of biological substrata plus the sum total of perceptual experience of different kinds.

We perceive contemporary figures as if through the accumulation of past perceptions, so that a man's perception of his wife might well be critically influenced by his perception of his mother, sister, teachers, and a variety of other people.

As long ago as 1954,[16] I discussed these phenomena as a theory of apperceptive distortions, contending that contemporary perception is influenced and more or less critically distorted by past perception. This whole picture is complicated by the fact that, as in a kaleidoscope, the different perceptual transparencies are overlaid and form new Gestalten, thus also organizing

---

*Bellak and Smith[13] and Bellak (in Spence's edition of Bellak's papers[14]) present some possibilities of exploring psychoanalytic concepts experimentally, within the psychoanalytic situation. The basic concepts are that early perception plays a structuring role in personality formation. What we are struggling with is to understand and formulate the many factors that affect "structural" aspects of the development of the personality.

I would once have entirely ruled out Melanie Klein's conceptions of early perception, because I could not believe that the neurological apparatus was ready for the complex assumptions that she makes. My skepticism is somewhat undermined by the ecologists, who observed and developed the concept of imprinting as some neurological process that takes place (at least in the flatbilled ducks soon after birth) and seems to have a regnant influence throughout life. On the other hand, some of Freud's thoughts, as well as Gestalt psychology and the developments in "cognitive science,"[15] stress that the idea of simple learning by conditioning is not at all consistent with the best data from information theory. Genetics makes clear that we apparently must also reckon with *innate* structures, which determine, in part by genetic code, the development of certain personality characteristics.

Findings in cognitive science also suggest that complex processes, including some that resemble a quantum leap, are involved in thought processes. These developments necessitate something more sophisticated than a simple associationism or a conditioned-response theory and, at least in part, are likely to demonstrate the importance of Gestalt principles. With all these strictures on the one hand and giving considerable benefit of the doubt, I find it unlikely that barely newborn infants would not only be neurologically capable of the complex perceptions Melanie Klein posits, but also engage in the symbolic thinking expected in her theory.

perceptions that never had any counterpart in reality but are derived from structural interaction. Clinically, object-relationship theorists have noted that there may be introjects that, per se, never had a counterpart in reality, but they have failed to give a plausible explanation for this finding, which I believe Gestalt psychology can provide.

As a matter of fact, the two most widely used personality tests, the TAT (Thematic Apperception Test) and the Rorschach, consist, respectively, of a number of pictures or blots to which subjects are asked to relate ideas. We make diagnostic inferences from the individual differences in responses to pictures or blots: the pictures of the TAT or the blots of the Rorschach are perceived differently by different people, depending on their past apperceptions and their cognitive style.

To get back to the defenses: Sometimes perceptions are distorted so as not to disturb the personality organization more than absolutely necessary — that is, defensively. A very simple mechanism accomplishing this is denial, or the blotting out of certain realities. In the TAT, this happens again and again. People with conflicts about sex do not see the woman in picture 2 as pregnant. There are many other defensive organizations of perception. Projection is a basic one that I investigated with the help of the TAT in a paper, published in 1944, concerning the ascription of thoughts and feelings of one's own to others.[17] Another experimental exploration of perceptual organization was demonstrated (upon my suggestion) by Michael Finn, in a Ph.D. thesis[18] investigating the concept of reaction formation, showing pictures of a "bad" mother and a "good" mother successively in a tachistoscope. He found that the features of goodness would be strengthened in an attempt to deal, "by reaction formation," with disturbing perceptions of a "bad" mother. Reaction formation is defined as a defense mechanism, operating unconsciously, wherein attitudes and behavior are adopted that are the opposites of impulses the individual harbors either consciously or unconsciously (e.g., excessive moral zeal may be a reaction to strong but repressed asocial impulses). (From Frazier et al., *A Psychiatric Glossary*, 4th ed., American Psychiatric Assn., 1975.)

The Concept of "Splitting"

I have discussed "projection" and "reaction formation" and their experimental verification in order to lead up to the concept of "splitting" as a defense that plays a major role, especially in the work of Kernberg.

Basically, the idea seems to be that in the presence of very inconsistent figures or a limited ability for synthesis, the perception of a "good" figure and a "bad" figure (and their internalization) fails to lead to a good Gestalt formation. It is posited that this synthesis fails to take place because of a fear that the bad figure will destroy the good figure; therefore, an active attempt is made to maintain them separately. Clinically, this means a polarization of seeing one and the same person as good or bad at different times, without ever developing "object constancy," because of this defensive shift. In a social-psychological sense, this process may also be basic, together with projection to the formation of the authoritarian personality, prejudice, and other excessive polarizations of good and bad.

Viewed in a Gestalt theoretical way, splitting and other concepts can be made clearer than they usually are in object-relations theory, and also amenable to experimental demonstration (as with the technique cited for projection and reaction formation). Dreams can probably best be understood as perceptual Gestalten formed by pre-oedipal as well as oedipal perceptions in attempts to master conflicts and resolve problems in various ways and as projections of self and objects. The concepts of Gestalt organization and Gestalt principles can, in fact, best be demonstrated in the formation of dreams and their analysis. It is regrettable that this fact has not been widely recognized by psychoanalysts.

In a very broad overview, I would say then that *object-relations theory is most specifically an addition to an elaboration and refinement of psychoanalysis as a perceptual theory of personality*. More specifically, it extends the structural conceptualization by stressing the concepts and the effects of earlier perceptions.

To the extent to which object-relations theory proposes to explain the acquisition of early perceptual-structural developments and disturbances, it has led to the suggestion of certain technical considerations for the therapeutic structuring or restructuring of these earliest apperceptions, a subject we will also discuss separately. Jacobson, Kernberg, and Kohut share the fact that they are even more difficult to understand than the ordinarily opaque psychoanalytic literature with the exception of Freud himself and Anna Freud, who usually specialized in simplicity. It is best, therefore, at least for a start, to read about their work as described by others.

Kernberg's first two books[19,20] are most lucidly discussed by Segel.[21] In his third book,[22] Kernberg himself has arrived at a more readable and understandable style. Nevertheless, for most readers, derivative sources, panel discussions, etc., are more readily understandable than the original contributions of any of the major authors in the field.

Some Examinations of Object-Relations Theory

Concerning borderline conditions, Segel[21] believes that Kernberg offered an ordering principle in a field beset by a chaos of symptoms as well as theories. He selects Kernberg's formulation of "splitting" as central to his contribution. "Splitting" may be defined as the side-by-side or alternate appearance of opposing ego states or the active process of keeping apart introjections and identifications of opposite quality.[22] Splitting is used as a defense of "good objects" against destruction by "bad objects."

While generally admiring Kernberg's contribution, Segel suggests that the very orderly conceptual progression in Kernberg's theory is more apparent on paper than in actual clinical experience. It seems as if Kernberg has discovered, in the role of splitting, as well as the grandiose self, some valuable factors that, however, occur neither inevitably nor exclusively in narcissistic personalities.

The discussion of the book on object relations comprises much that is mentioned elsewhere in this report. It traces Kernberg's kind of object relationship not only to his predecessors but also to insights he had in the treatment of borderline personalities and extrapolated to a more general theory of early ego development, with splitting playing a role in his general theory. The clarity of this condensed account plus critique does not lend itself to further abstracting here. Read this review. I warmly recommend it for a general orientation in this difficult area.

Applications to Psychoanalysis

Kernberg himself discusses basic aspects of object-relations theory and the applications to psychoanalytic technique in a very informative paper.[23] He clearly says there that he conceives of psychoanalytic object-relations theory as "a special approach or focus within psychoanalysis that examines the metapsychological and clinical issues in terms of the vicissitudes of internalized object relations." He thus clearly disavows any separatist school of thought. He goes on to say that

object relations theory considers the psychic apparatus as originating in the earliest stage of a process of internalization of object relations. This process covers, roughly speaking, the first three years of life — and results in the formation of substructures of the psychic apparatus that will gradually differentiate. The stages of development of internalized object relations — that is, the stages of infantile autism, symbiosis, separation-individuation, and of object constancy — reflect the vicissitudes of these earliest substructures of the psychic apparatus. Discrete units of self-representation, object representation, and an affect disposition linking them are the basic object-relations-derived substructures that gradually evolve into more complex substructures (such as real-self and ideal-self, and real-object and ideal-object representations). Eventually, they will become integrated as intrapsychic structures in the ego, superego and id.

Kernberg then proceeds to differentiate object-relations theory based on Jacobson's, Mahler's, and his own work from that of the British school of psychoanalysis, in that it is integrated with ego psychology in the structural concepts and does not place all development into the first year of life. He also differentiates object-relations theory as outlined by himself from Sullivan's approach—which, in distinction to his own metapsychological approach, was entirely interpersonal. He finally sees psychoanalytic object-relations theory merely as a refinement of the structural viewpoint, which links structure more closely with developmental, genetic, and dynamic aspects of mental functioning and places it between the level of abstraction entailed in metapsychology, on the one hand, and direct clinical observations, on the other.

Moving on to the technical implications of object-relations theory, Kernberg believes that unconscious conflicts are never simply conflicts between impulse and defense but are, rather, conflicts between intrapsychic structures. It is here that a Gestalt psychological formulation would be infinitely clearer than the rather obscure language used and would come closer to attaining operational definitions. For instance, when Kernberg says that the overall consolidation of intrapsychic structures—namely, the ego, superego, and the id—results in integration of internalized object relations, he writes that this "obscures the constituent units within the overall structures, (and) in the course of psychoanalysis, one observes the gradual redissolution of pathogenic superego and ego structures. . . . " It would be clearer to state this obscuring of constituent units as in Gestalt formation, which in turn becomes reconstituted into its parts in the course of psychoanalytic process and transference manifestations.

And when he says, later on, "dissociative mechanisms stabilize such dynamic structures and permit the contradictory aspects of these conflicts to remain—at least partially—in consciousness," the experiments on reaction formation cited earlier here could be a good paradigm. In distinction, with healthier people, he feels, the transitory changes that occur within the transference situation permit the patient to maintain a certain distance and perspective on the transitory distortions of self and object representations without losing the capacity for reality testing.

Maintaining a Balanced Empathy

From these differences in Gestalt formation and integration, Kernberg derives systematic differences between transference and countertransference. He believes that the analyst needs to maintain a balanced empathy towards the patient; trying to understand the patient cognitively requires an empathic attitude that incorporates what the patient cannot tolerate in himself. When the patient's behavior cannot be directly understood in relation to

genetic and structural aspects, Kernberg infers what part of his development—his mental stage—the patient may be bringing into the transference
and recommends "as if" interpretations: that is, saying to the patient, You
behave "as if" you would want me to be mother with a breast and father with
a penis.

It is this special kind of empathy that could lead one theoretically and
practically onto thin ice. It remains to be experimentally demonstrated
that—say, in videotaped material—several object-relations therapists would
arrive at the same interpretation of the transference distortions and similar
empathic formulations. Until this is done, the risk of arbitrariness and
subjective distortion by the analyst appears even greater than in the earlier
traditional classical analytic process.

A detailed discussion of technical consequences of object-relations theory may be found in the proceedings of the meeting of the American Psychoanalytic Association chaired by Ernst Ticho.[24] In summary and oversimpli-
fied, the therapeutic technique is influenced by object-relations theory by
virtue of the fact that it postulates that very early precepts, called variously
"part-self" and "part-object," appear in the transference relationship and
have to be recognized as such. Much of this recognition is accomplished by
empathy on the part of the analyst, and that is where grave doubts arise as to
what might be fact ascertainable by a controlled experimental technique.
For greater believability, it would be necessary that the videotaped material
be blindly submitted to several object-relations theorists and some attempt
made to see if they could independently agree on what was being brought
into the transference, and what intervention should be made.

Projective Identification and Splitting

One of the two concepts most basic to object-relations theory and technique
is projective identification; the other is splitting, discussed elsewhere. Projective identification is an amplification of the original concept of projection, which constituted an ascription of feelings or thoughts of one's own to
the external world for purposes of defense. Projective identification involves
the same process, referred to in object-relations therapy as an externalizing
of self and object images. The projector maintains an empathic relationship
with real objects onto whom these images are projected. The projector also
attempts to control the object—which he now fears, as a result of his projection. This concept has apparently been usefully employed in group therapy,
where it has been observed that one person may actually manipulate relationships in such a way as to make another member as aggressive as his own
needs for projection of his own aggression make necessary. In the ordinary
transference situation, this phenomenon manifests itself as distrust and fear

of the therapist, whom the patient, in turn, tries to control aggressively. For a detailed examination of the concept of projective identification, see also Meissner.[25]

Controversy over the Concept of "Splitting"

Examining one of the basic concepts of object-relations theory in an unusually elegant paper,[26] Pruyser looks at the concept of "splitting" in a grammatical and historical context, asking "What splits in splitting?" He points out that this verb can be used transitively or intransitively, and he examines the use of this word by Janet, by Freud as early as 1891, and by authors from then on—especially in connection with hysteria. By way of Freud's use of the term "splitting" in his 1927 paper on fetishism, Pruyser suggests that in this case one really speaks of disavowal or denial. As a result of asking many searching questions of a theoretical nature, Pruyser concludes that "the verb splitting applied to mental phenomena, and especially the term splitting of the ego, pose more problems than they solve." He, in fact, goes on to examine the use of the term "split" in connection with schizophrenia, again giving a remarkable review of the history of the concept and asking "Who splits what?" In connection with Bleuler's use of splitting of associations, he points out that this means the same as loosening of associations.

Turning next to schizoid character, Pruyser moves to Fairbairn's use of the term "splitting of the ego" in connection with schizoid phenomena. Fairbairn apparently assumes a split between a more superficial part of the ego, representing its higher levels, with a deeper part of the ego, representing its lower levels, apparently having in mind a horizontal split. Pruyser believes that Fairbairn's "splitting" of the ego is analogous to Freud's repression, that Fairbairn (following Melanie Klein) has essentially substituted internal objects or "bad" objects for Bleuler's "complexes," and that nothing really "splits" in Fairbairn's ego because there never was a complete homogeneity between the central ego and the various subsidiary egos. If one follows Fairbairn's description of schizoid states and the power given to the role of splitting as one of the very first mental operations, "splitting is then no more than the beginning of that long-term process of separation between subject and object that is precipitated by birth."

Pruyser also examines the use of the term "splitting" in other object-relations theories, including those of Guntrip, Bion, and Winnicott. He finds Mahler's definition of "splitting" the most acceptable—namely, that what appears to be split are the attitudes and affective responses to the outside world in children who alternately cling and act negativistically. He dwells especially on Kernberg's formulations and is more satisfied with them to the extent that the words are used more in a phenomenological sense, describing behaviors as being disjointed, as contrasting with each other, and as lacking in blending or a commonsensical give-and-take as an aspect of desirable integration.

All in all, Pruyser concludes that the word "splitting" is "both too slippery and too hard. It does not fit what we know about the mental life. . . . Splitting is too spatial and at the same time extremely indefinite. . . . Elevated to a psychological concept, the words 'splitting' and 'split' create more problems than they solve." He contends, "I hope they will be banned from the psychological vocabulary and predict that their banishment will set us free to make new discoveries."

The Technical Consequences of Object-Relations Theory

In a panel on the technical consequences of object-relations theory,[24] the chairman, Ticho, sees the theory as a link between metapsychology and the clinical experimental level of psychoanalysis. He finds the contributions of object-relations theory especially useful in the second analysis of patients who seem to have acquired a good understanding of themselves in the first analysis but can apply these insights—and integrate them—only after an analysis of the pre-oedipal components.

The first paper was contributed by Kramer, who discusses Mahler's symbiosis-separation theory by stressing nonverbal communications, such as scratching and flushing, as related to screen sensations analogous to screen memories. By virtue of "coanesthetic empathy," the analyst can then understand pre-oedipal conflicts. Mahler then goes on to discuss, with the use of case material, the working through of individuation-separation in the transference of adults in psychoanalysis.

Kernberg then discusses, among other concepts, a patient's re-enacting of early self-representation while projecting the object representation onto the analyst. He also stresses that the analyst's understanding is aided by empathy through transitory identification with the patient's own experience (though he takes pains elsewhere to make clear that empathy must be paralleled by interpretation and reconstruction). He enumerates the four specific applications to the psychoanalytic situation: (1) the nature of the conflicts to be interpreted; (2) the varying relationship, genetic history, and early development; (3) the communicative process and its regression in the analytic process; and (4) the question of regression and empathy in the transference.

This is one of Kernberg's most systematic, condensed presentations, and it is highly recommended for a first reading.

Lichtenstein then discusses questions raised by object-relations theory for the theory and practice of psychoanalysis. He believes that object-relations theory points to the importance of feeling states close to the surface in the patient-analyst relationship. When he speaks of having to discover a unifying theme — e.g., one patient's constant search for reaffirmation through instant contact and stimulation — I am reminded of Alfred Adler's concept of a "fictive goal" and a "style of life" deriving from it.

There is no telling what will be rediscovered next.

Some Aspects of Self-Psychology

In a panel on the bipolar self reported by Meyers,[27] Ornstein presented a paper on the bipolar self in the psychoanalytic process. He discusses the development of Kohut's concept[28] in general and of the bipolar self in particular without, however, even once defining the concept. Ornstein addresses himself to the analysis of Mr. Z., the case that opened Kohut's eyes to the importance of the analysis of pre-oedipal material, which was the primary goal of Mr. Z.'s second and presumably much more successful analysis.

(Critics have maintained that the difference between the first and the second analysis of this patient was not so much one of theoretical orientation as one of poor technique in the first analysis.)

Basch then presented a paper on the self-object disorders in which his most important point is probably the technical one that in the management of the self-object transference "no role playing with — or indulgence of — the patient is called for"; this refutes the criticism that Kohut gives up therapeutic neutrality in his treatment by empathizing with the patient.

In a panel on current controversies in psychoanalysis,[28] Gedo states at the outset that Kohut's ideas, when first presented, were greeted with the usual skepticism by the "traditionalists," who insisted that the narcissistic syndromes were variants of the oedipal neuroses and regarded his propositions as the opening wedge for radical revision of psychoanalysis. Kohut continued to proclaim his acceptance of the greater part of the analytic heritage and felt his views were supplements necessitated by the broadening field of applicability of psychoanalytic treatment. Gedo notes that controversies of this type rarely lead to sober scientific evaluation of the reliability of observational data and that Kohut's work is no exception.

Gedo reviews casebooks of Goldberg and Firestein, which dealt with two differing premises. The first, titled *The Psychology of the Self*, includes six patients. Gedo claims that at least half of the illustrative practices in the casebook are flawed as models for the natural unfolding of the analytic transference. Gedo compares this work with cases prepared by Firestein in his study of analyses terminated under the aegis of the Treatment Center of the New York Psychoanalytic Institute. The New York patients seem indistinguishable from Goldberg's in Chicago, except that significant oedipal problems were found in every one of the New York cases.

Contrasting the two groups, Gedo found the New York patients to have had a less favorable outcome. The Oedipus complex in each New York case remained unresolved. Even with the relatively inadequate analyses reported in the Chicago casebook, the patients had more favorable outcomes after certain pregenital issues were emphasized. However, Gedo does not mean to imply that he agrees that analysis conducted in accord with Kohut's recommendations produces better results. He claims that the therapeutically effective procedures were fitted into Kohut's explanatory schema rather arbitrarily. He is particularly skeptical about the concept that repair of a developmental deficit takes place via "transmuting internalization." The effectiveness of several analyses in Chicago was based principally upon correction of a deficit in the capacity to regulate tension, a useful contribution of Kohut's.

Gedo claims that Kohut's entire system of thought departs in a subtle way from the customary intrapsychic framework; he now tends to view psychic life within the dyadic model of object relations. Kohut regards symbiotic needs of childhood as primary; Gedo believes they are only secondary adaptive devices. Kohut looks upon empathy as more than a tool of observation; Gedo believes this differs from Freud's absolute quest for knowledge. He believes that Kohut's new system of values remains unspecified and has to be inferred from the therapeutic choices he advocates. Finally, in contrasting Goldberg and Firestein, Gedo sees some important improvement in tension regulation and in reorganizing behavior in a more coherent manner, but feels that many other issues stemming from the less archaic sector of the personality are neglected by self-psychology.

The Concept of the Bipolar Self

The "bipolar self" is a concept that has become central to the thinking of Kohut and his school. (It has nothing to do with the diagnostic category, bipolar affective disorder.) Kohut devotes an entire chapter with that title to the introduction of the concept in his volume on the restoration of self.[29] Unfortunately, after reading the chapter several times, I am still unable to define the concept. Though Kohut touches on all kinds of interesting matters, including Proust's problems, there is not one sentence that says something like "By the bipolar self, I mean . . . " or "The bipolar self is. . . . "

I mention this point out of annoyance and, in part, to prepare the reader for frustration if he explores this literature. It is bound to be frustrating as well as stimulating, with all kinds of insights offered on the circuitous pathways around the central, undefined concept. At best, one can speak of a definition by innuendo — although there is not enough innuendo for one to be sure what is meant. I should hasten to add that if the latter-day writers on Kohut's concept think that definition is unnecessary because everybody knows what the term means, my experience does not bear that out. Of a dozen well-read psychoanalysts I buttonholed in the course of a number of dinner parties, not one could define "bipolar self" for me even approximately.

Thus, rather than passing on a possibly wrong definition, I recommend perusal of the original.

In the panel on the bipolar self,[27] Wallerstein makes the valuable observation that Kohut's central clinical contribution has been in seeing so many aspects of the psychopathology of pregenital development, not as a regressive defense against the emergence of oedipal transference *alone*, but centrally also as re-creations of deficient childhood constellations. He then goes on to say that

we do not deal with an either/or situation; the patient suffers neither from pregenital difficulties alone or from oedipal ones, but usually from both — at one time from one and at another time from another with defensive regressions and with developmental arrests, with defensive transferences and defensive resistances and with recreations of earlier traumatic and traumatized psychic states. . . .

Thus, Wallerstein very logically insists that Kohut's self-psychology has something valuable to add which can be taken into clinical consideration without justifying a completely new theory of personality or invalidating classical psychoanalytic propositions.

Concluding the panel, Kohut himself commented in a way that was conciliatory with classical analytic viewpoints. He ventured, however, into philosophical differences between the Freudian conception of man as born helpless vis-à-vis reality and the tyranny of the drives and of self-psychology, which "sees man as born strong not weak, because it takes account of the fact that he is born into the psychological matrix of responsive self-objects, just as he is born into the physiological matrix that contains oxygen." This seems to me an unnecessary and useless flight into philosophical fancy. It is similar to an argument over whether a glass of water is half full or half empty. Indeed the infant, born helpless, cannot survive on his own and has to struggle for years to master the environment. On the other hand, there is no question that the infant comes with an anlage of a great many propensities: intelligence, an immune system, as well as the psychological readiness to mature and to grow.

Kohut tends to want to provide in the transference experience whatever the child's earlier environment did not provide. While the point is made that Kohut's empathic approach to the patient must be distinguished from Alexander's "corrective emotional experience," there is a considerable similarity in some of the basic propositions.

The panel concluded with agreement that self-psychology made some important contributions and needs to be integrated into the main body of psychoanalysis. The main disagreement concerned the question of whether the concept of the bipolar self should be seen as superordinate, subsuming the drives as well as narcissism, or whether that is an unnecessary aggrandizing concept. I tend to subscribe to the latter opinion.

Kernberg's Recent Appraisal

Interestingly enough, the most recent and probably the most comprehensive, well-balanced, and evenhanded (but highly critical) evaluation of Kohut's self-psychology comes from none other than Kernberg,[30] his rival in the field of narcissistic personality. In a critique of a volume of papers edited by Goldberg[31] that also includes a contribution by Kohut himself, Kernberg reviews the basic concept that narcissistic personality disorders are caused by an insufficient development of the self. There is a fixation at an early stage. The grandiose self is a fragile structure. Such people develop idealizing and mirroring transferences (which are pathognomonic) and require a technique in which the analyst is empathic and nonthreatening and becomes the vehicle for further maturation of the patient's self and from there proceeds safely to the id-ego-superego structure of classical analysis after the psychic deficit has been made up.

The task of the conference was to attempt to integrate self-psychology with classical psychoanalytic theory, and Kernberg takes sharp issue with the attempts of several of the dozen or so contributors. Above all, Kohut's co-workers, as well as he himself, seem to readily discard observational data (e.g., from the work of Margaret Mahler) and substitute empathic introspection for observation and cognitive insight. Kernberg rightly points out the danger inherent in such purely speculative propositions.

Kohut, he says, made useful observations concerning some narcissistic resistances and overexpanded these possibly useful observations into a whole new theory of personality. I am paraphrasing freely here because this seems a clear parallel to what others have done: Adler, Horney, Sullivan—all contributed a few building blocks to psychoanalytic theory. Carried away by their daring, they attempted to make a whole new house from their few blocks, and their structure became a chimera.

Developmental Theory

Aside from object relations theory and self psychology, developmental theory has come to play a new and somewhat dissident role in basically classical psychoanalysis. The term "developmental" is confusing, as from the earliest days of Freud, a great deal of interest was shown in the development of the child, e.g. in terms of the libidinal zones and aims. "Developmental theory" is meant to refer to data and theory derived from direct child observation.

The work of Escalona, Mahler, and Spitz play a leading role here. One recent extensive discussion of developmental data and theory is offered by Pine[32] who emphasizes the contributions of observation and child rearing to the appreciation of the importance of pre-oedipal development. He discusses the importance of concepts such as self-other differentiation, the development of basic trust, the development of self-esteem, and the role of deficits in distinction to conflict.

Again, the importance of new findings, new theoretical formulations seem exaggerated at the expense of established psychoanalytic propositions. Once again, it is extremely likely that the valuable contributions which developmental data and theory can make to psychoanalysis will be incorporated without the necessity of throwing out the data of genetic theory.

Contemporary Issues

Rangell[33] makes comparisons between the status of psychoanalysis as a process and as a treatment in 1954 and in 1979. He discusses the controversies surrounding several areas: transference versus historical reconstruction, oedipal versus pre-oedipal, and the cognitive-affective duality. He also considers the qualitative factors in the negative therapeutic reaction, the fate of signal anxiety, and the role of the patient in the process of cure.

Rangell begins by pointing out that in 1954 an attempt was made to distinguish psychoanalysis from dynamic psychotherapy, by which it was in danger of being engulfed and rendered invisible. He attempts to view the state of psychoanalysis as a process and treatment in relation to changing historical times.

Discussing transference versus reconstruction, Rangell notes: "It is not a question of transference vs. reconstruction but of transference only vs. transference and the original neurosis. Transference cannot be the sole activity of the analytic clinician. Past and present are continually reciprocal, transference facilitating recall of the past and the past illuminating the current in the transference." Rangell mentions Strachey as the initiator of a trend to put inordinate emphasis on the analysis of transference, an emphasis which obscured all other important and necessary elements of the analytic process. Centrality of transference is not limited to the Kleinian or British object-relations theory school. Transference seems to be one of the central points of controversy in the analytic world, and there is a great deal of debate on the subject. While analysts of diverse persuasions have been quoted as being united on the issue of the centrality of transference, the nature of the concept of transference varies with their theoretical orientations.

Rangell's thesis is that the transference neurosis is the path to the patient's past neurosis. Separate schools have arisen over the importance of transference from oedipal and pre-oedipal years. Rangell compares the work of Kohut and Kernberg. He does not believe that there now exists a different stratum of patients. Some of the original "classic" cases of Freud's he believes would be so-called "borderline" in today's terms. "Because we know more does not mean patients are more disturbed." What was true for Kohut's and Kernberg's patients was true for all patients. Rangell says that Kohut first presented his ideas within existing psychoanalytic theory—the "psychology of the self"—and ended up by replacing structural and metapsychologic theory altogether with his "psychology of the self." With regard to Kernberg, the opposite trend seems to be occurring. He has gradually moved into the mainstream of psychoanalytic theory. His description of self- and object-representation has become closer to the formulations of Jacobson; the theories of Mahler, Hartmann, and Rapaport; and the techniques of Stone, Lowenstein, et al. Kernberg states that there is no borderline patient without oedipal conflicts, albeit distorted by pre-existing ones. Rangell would have us benefit from continuities as much as from separation.

Rangell discusses cognitive-affective duality—or the conflict between knowing and feeling—intellectually formulating an understanding of the case and empathically reverberating to the patient's affective experiences (Fenichel, 1941). The use of empathy as the principal therapeutic tool is reminiscent of Reik's (1933) distrust of theory—the idea that having a blueprint will only constrict the patient. Bion (1970) similarly felt that analysis burdened by knowledge, memory, and understanding conspires against fact and truth.

Rangell believes that both are necessary and that neither is contradictory to or exclusive of the other. Humanist and scientist are combined in the analyst. Empathy, while indispensable, should not be confused with transference. This goes back to the debate over what transference is.

The conflict over the decades has been one between an anti-intellect, antirationality, antiscience wave and the adherence to cognitive understanding firmly rooted in coherent theoretic framework based on objectively observable facts. The duality in psychoanalysis ranged from the Freud-Jung clashes, through Ferenczi-Rank-Reik controversies, to Kleinian-Freudian transference versus reconstruction and the oedipal versus pre-oedipal issues.

During each period of controversy rationality was always cited by those who dubbed themselves the humanists to "dehumanize" the patient—a position that Rangell believes to be unfounded.

Problems of Psychoanalytic Technique

Some current and recurrent problems of psychoanalytic technique are discussed by Blum.[34] Blum contends that psychoanalysis—while not an absolutely rigid, predictable process—is a defined process: a unique form of treatment with rules, methods, and characteristics. The technique evolved in conjunction with psychoanalytic theory and is therefore not immune from the current controversies surrounding that theory. There is obviously a reciprocal relationship between technique and theory. Blum suggests that in exploring psychoanalytic technique, one must ask not only how it is to be done but also why and toward what goals.

The psychoanalytic process has evolved in association with the expansion of psychoanalytic theory and knowledge. The process and technique of psychoanalysis require carefully applied scientific methods.

In this review, Blum notes that discussions of transference and resistance have been going on for generations, and therefore chooses to focus on newer develoments. "More current concerns are differing concepts of the alliance toward analytic work, the inception and fostering of the alliance as if the alliance required special support, the alliance as support of critical ego functions, and the alliance itself as a progressive force. . . . "

As a matter of fact, one might add at this juncture that the development of the concept of the therapeutic alliance as developed with slight variations by several analysts is something of a bridge between the classical, strictly cognitive conception of analysis, closely related to the analyst's "tabula rasa," and the grossly participant observer of the existential "here and now" school, discussed in greater detail elsewhere in this review.

According to the present view of technique held by the object-relations school, analysis of the countertransference is almost as important as analysis of the transference. Countertransference becomes the major vehicle for understanding patients' conflicts, affects, and past object relations. The essential analysis of the transference and the countertransference has become confused.

Blum notes that while empathy is essential, it will not repair developmental deficit or assure the resumption of development. Empathy is complementary to natural-science observation. By itself, empathy is not enough.

Aside from this dealing with the role of empathy assigned by object-relations theory, Blum also addresses himself to the embattled role of the analyst. Enlightenment concerning early development enriches analysis but does not necessarily call for changes in technique. He stresses that many ingredients work synergistically in analysis and that — with regard to transference relationship or the "real" relationship, oedipal or pre-oedipal material, stuctural conflict vis-à-vis structural deficit — no mutual exclusiveness is appropriate. He believes that all of it can be encompassed within the framework of classical psychoanalytic theory.

In a book-review essay, Kanzer[35] provides another very valuable overview of developments in psychoanalytic technique.

In a panel on contemporary problems in psychoanalytic technique reported by Simons,[36] Blum also presented certain views as similarly stated in his paper "Some Current and Recurrent Problems of Psychoanalytic Technique."[34]

The single most interesting observation was made by Stone, who mentions that those treated by Freud reported his naturalness or freedom in his relationship with his patients. This attitude so contrasts with what he calls the "severely austere" and ritualized analytic attitude of some contemporary analysts — which might therefore be more properly called the "neoclassical" analytic attitude, reserving classical for the emphasis on the humane relationship that Freud maintained and Stone considers essential for a genuine psychoanalytic process. Stone suggests that the clearest codification of the "neoclassical" point of view was represented by K. Eissler in 1953, when he suggested that the hypothetical normal ego was susceptible to change by interpretation alone and that any other kind of intervention must be considered a parameter that may be introduced only under highly specified conditions. Stone asserts that "if one was forced to choose, one would do better to choose Freud's early naturalness over the robot-like anonimity of some of Freud's followers." Stone does not believe, however, that such a choice is really necessary.

Stone discusses some of his ideas more extensively in a paper on the value of the "here and now" in psychoanalysis.[37] Valenstein[38] discusses the term "classical" psychoanalysis both historically and conceptually. Beginning with the question, "What is meant by 'classical analysis'?", he notes that before 1936–37 and Anna Freud's *The Ego and the Mechanisms of Defense*, analysis was predominantly "id" analysis, and that it was then considered a "classical" procedure — depending upon transference and an actual understanding of the transference neurosis. Thereafter, the technique came to include the "ego" analysis, which approached the unconscious through analysis of the defenses. From 1937 on, ego analysis became part of "classical Freudian analysis," with interpretation as the main therapeutic agent. This is an important example of growth within the classical model.

The attempt to treat borderline conditions previously considered unanalyzable led to active therapeutic procedures and interventions aside from interpretation. Valenstein traces this trend as beginning with Ferenczi and

Rank and continuing with Kohut's postulation of the independent development of narcissism and Kernberg's ascribing defective ego structures to a failure to integrate split introjects during early development.

Valenstein concludes that psychoanalytic theory in the present "tends toward the external and the real world of object and the analyst as a real person." This coincides with disillusionment with rationality and science. If enlightened understanding was the ideal of the 19th century, then learning through free living and changing through direct encounter and involvement and catharsis have become the current trends. The tilt in psychoanalysis as part of the Zeitgeist is thus now toward affect and experientialism, rather than interpretation and insight. It seems certain that, in time, "self" analysis and object-relations techniques will also be incorporated into the concept of "classical psychoanalysis."

The Status of Meta-Psychology

Freud originally utilized what is commonly known as the topographical theory — namely, that there is a conscious, preconscious, and unconscious mind that interact in certain ways. Later he changed to the so-called structural theory, the tripartite model wherein three structures — primarily the ego, superego, and id and conflicts between each of them, and in turn between *all* of them and reality — constituted the basic variables of psychoanalytic psychology within a topographical framework.

Freud's most ambitious attempt to understand and define psychological phenomena was contained in his meta-psychological theory, which proposed that every psychological event could be understood and analyzed in terms of adaptive, genetic, topographical, economic, dynamic, and functional modes. The metapsychological theory is certainly the most inclusive theory of personality yet developed. But for many it remained a theoretical model very difficult to apply in clinical practice. While Kubie was probably the first to criticize meta-psychology from a theoretical standpoint, a number of clinical psychologists well trained in psychoanalysis have been the major critics of meta-psychology. Holt[39] particularly criticized the economic theory involved in meta-psychology and felt that Freud's conceptualization of the so-called hydraulic model of repression was a product of his period of science (especially physics) and was neither useful nor accurate for contemporary psychoanalysis. George Klein[40] held that meta-psychology was too far removed from clinical observation and too much of an abstraction. But in recent years, Roy Schafer[41] and others have sought to simplify meta-psychology by introducing an "action language."

These various attempts to modify theory have found vigorous opposition. Above all, in my opinion it seems impossible for these psychologists to suggest a useful clinical working hypothesis that would better serve than the tripartite model in particular and meta-psychology in general. For instance, the principle of catharsis in terms of the release of material which has been repressed (as if indeed, primitively speaking, it were kept under hydraulic pressure), is still most useful clinically. Recalling and expressing buried memories is a catharsis which leads to relief—limited as such relief certainly is. Who has not experienced it—in himself and in others and in patients—and how else other than in terms of libido theory and "Freudian units" to explain that anyone in love with *one* person or involved with *one* particular interest doesn't seem to have "any energy left over" for other involvements?

These propositions have been addressed by Meissner[42] in a paper, "Meta-psychology—Who Needs It?" He answers affirmatively: "everybody."

In a lengthy paper on meta-psychology and psychoanalytic theory, Brenner[43] discusses a large number of criticisms of meta-psychology. He rejects a basic idea, introduced by Waelder,[44] that psychoanalytic theory consists of different levels of abstraction, with clinical observation as the most concrete and verifiable and metapsychology as the most abstract and least valuable. A large number of psychoanalysts derive their own thinking from this proposition, and Brenner takes particular exception to it. He points out quite convincingly that the simplest concrete observation in psychoanalysis or any other science involves ideas of the highest order of abstraction. He believes, I think quite rightly, that the correct basis for a hierarchy of theories is the degree to which the theory is supported by relevant data.

Like Brenner, I believe that the various aspects of psychoanalytic theory are interrelated. It is this interrelationship—most of which is, I believe, experimentally verifiable—that makes psychoanalysis a uniquely encompassing psychology of personality. The various attempts to see psychoanalysis divorced from a scientific basis or separate from the natural sciences seem antiquated to me. To posit a duality between social science and natural science seems equally nonsensical as the nature-nurture conflict, since cause and effect play equally important roles in both social and natural science.

Brenner discusses in considerable detail the contributions of some proponents of the idea that psychoanalysis is a science of meaning, which sets it apart from natural science. He quotes particularly from Victor Rosen (1968), who "claimed that the patient's symptoms and dreams differed from a factual statement primarily because they are in different languages. Therefore, nothing causes symptoms—it is just a thought in a different language." It is interesting to note that this 1968 paper antedates the excitement caused in France by Lacan, who would also have it that psychoanalysis is a branch of linguistics. Thus, what is simply one aspect of metapsychological psychoanalysis—namely, its concern with unconscious content as a verbal statement to be translated into secondary process language—is conceived of as

the whole of psychoanalysis. This attempt at reductionism is not unrelated
to Schafer's attempt to substitute metapsychology with actual language, a
proposition vigorously examined and rejected by Rawn.[45]

The interest in language in relation to epistemology probably had its
modern origin in the "Vienna Circle of Philosophy"—also known as logical
positivism—represented by Schlick, Karnap, and Wittgenstein. Logical positivism led to operationalism—especially as developed in America by
Bridgman, who was a major influence on psychology around the middle of
the century—and to the development of a special branch of investigation
flourishing for some years as "science of science" and "semantics," devoted
primarily to linguistic analysis. It is probably from this background that
American psychologists active in psychoanalysis still derive their interest in
noncausal models—especially linguistic formulations as substitutes for the
clinically more useful, operationally demonstratable hypotheses of psychoanalysis, hypotheses which are particularly valuable for being interdependent
and applicable to different levels of consciousness.

Perhaps the best paper on this controversy of the value of meta-psychology is the one recently published by Modell.[46]

If the ego and its relations to the human environment is not seen as a closed system,
it is then possible to conceive of defenses against object relationships without abandoning the psychoanalytic stance. If our metapsychological model is not closed off,
it is then possible to describe events between the self and the object that are not based
on the simplistic theory of inter-personal relationships or a rarified system of "internalized objects."

He quotes Balint. "Balint observed: 'All the events which lead ultimately
to therapeutic changes in the patient's mind are initiated by events happening in a two-person relationship, i.e. happening essentially between people
and not inside only one of them.'"

Modell concludes that the concept of the self or self-psychology still
remains to be integrated with meta-psychology. He sees that not as a reason
for abandoning meta-psychology but only as an occasion for its appropriate
modification.

Dream Interpretation in Current Psychoanalysis

In 1900, Freud spoke of "the interpretation of dreams" as the cornerstone of
his work and considered the dream the royal road to the unconscious. Well
he might have, since dream interpretation permitted him to establish the
continuity between waking life and sleeping life as at other times he could
speak of the continuity between childhood and adulthood and between
normal psychological phenomena and pathological ones. The interest in

dream theory, as well as its clinical aspects, continues to be lively in classical psychoanalysis. It is my impression that ego psychology plays an increasing role in the clinical application of dream interpretation, but I find it difficult to document with references to the literature.

In my own mind I see dreams, to a large extent, as an attempt at problem-solving. I have studied their cognitive aspects, including what perceptions of the past and the present might be involved. Problem-solving aspects can best be seen when the patient has several fragments of dreams or several dreams in one night, and it becomes clear that they represent different forms of solving a problem. For example, in the course of a night's dreaming the same problem may be "solved" by complete submission or by complete aggression, with some stops in between. In some patients the first fragment will primarily show the work of the defenses, and may be almost inpenetrable, whereas the last part may be a frank representation of the problematic affects, with fragments in between showing different stages of that struggle between drive and defense. (I have observed similar phenomena in successive stories told by the same subject in response to one picture of the Thematic Apperception Test and likewise through interpretation of the Rorschach.) A number of analysts have been engaged in sleep research, but application of such research to dream interpretation has had only meager impact.

A lively debate, however, regarding the validity of Freudian dream interpretation has come into focus.[47] Among the antagonists is McCarley. He takes issue with Freud, whom he claims utilized a reflex model of neuronal psychic operation — that is, stimuli outside supplied the energy necessary to excite the neurons and cause them to discharge.

McCarley instead feels that what actually occurs in dreaming is an endogenous cycle of REM and non-REM sleep independent of outside stimuli — which he believes contradicts the hypothesis that dreaming occurs when repressed wishes are stirred up. McCarley believes that if Freud's theory held true, dreams would occur erratically instead of in regular periodic fashion. According to him the activation-synthesis hypothesis, namely periodic firing of neuronal energy, explains the occurrence of dreams. McCarley does not deny that the dream has elements of personal significance or meaning and that we can interpret the dream and provide information about the person recording it. Reiser, after McCarley, spoke of different systems (a neurological one and a psychological one) and postulated that the demonstration of certain physiological processes does not negate the understanding of psychological processes. Despite some better understanding of physiological aspects of dreaming (about which, incidentally, there is still a great deal of controversy), Reiser sees little in what McCarley had to say that seems to invalidate "dreams as reflecting motivational states, cognitive structures and memories."

McCarley's argument seems to be mostly against the wish-fulfillment-disguise theory of causation of dreams, appearing to deny psychological motivation. This seems to me not only entirely unnecessary but also contrary to the current endeavor to finally do away with the mind-body duality (by interaction in terms of system theory)—a theoretical orientation with which McCarley seems to agree.

I have had considerable doubts myself about the fact that all dreams are wish-fulfilling or protectors of sleep, even though undoubtedly some dreams are blatantly wish-fulfilling and some clearly for the protection of sleep—when the dieting person dreams of attending a sumptuous banquet or when a dreamer hears the ringing of Easter bells which keeps him sleeping a little longer while the alarm clock raises havoc. I doubt, however, that it is necessary to assume that *all* dreams are wish-fulfilling. In the broadest sense, they constitute a compromise formation between various drives and reality and the superego and attempt to resolve the conflict in the best possible way for the particular person. I would say that dreams constitute an attempt at optimal conflict resolution and problem-solving by optimal Gestalt formation rather than "wish-fulfillment," which seems a relatively naïve psychological concept.

On the Current Practice of Psychoanalysis

Probably the most specific document of this field is a summary of a 1976 survey on psychoanalytic practice[48] made public in November, 1981. This report delineated changing trends in the practice of psychoanalysis and condensed the principal findings.

The survey reports that in April, 1976, the average active member of the American Psychoanalytic Association was treating about five patients in analysis. He spent slightly more than half of the office treatment time engaged in doing analysis per se. While this meant that the amount of analytic practice had declined about 9% from the number of patients in treatment a decade earlier, by and large the findings were more favorable than one might have expected.

To this I must add, however, that probably a disproportionate percentage of the people in analysis were analytic candidates in treatment with training analysts. The report, in fact, identifies a midcareer crisis in the life of the analyst, particularly among those two-thirds of the profession who are not appointed to be training analysts, complicated by a sharp decline of the analytic case load and a growing reduction in their interest and participation in analysis. This system of two class members contributing to staleness in the analytic community has long been recognized as a critical problem.

Aside from these findings, the survey reported predictably that analysts spent a great deal of time in activities not strictly analytic — from psychotherapy to teaching and administration. The majority of patients were drawn from a narrow slice of the upper stratum of population distribution in terms of income, occupations, and education. The treatment, lasting an average of four to five years, or 850 sessions, was extremely expensive for the individual patient, although the actual amount charged in 1976 varied from only $35 to $40 per hour. This amount was less than the charge for psychotherapy because, obviously, the greater frequency of sessions placed a greater burden on patients. This fact accounted for a much smaller income of psychoanalysts than for most other medical practitioners, including other types of psychiatric practitioners.

Thus, the basic economic problem of analysis persists: the cost for the individual patient is too high, and the income the analyst can derive from the small group of patients he can treat is too small to be consistent with the income of other physicians or other professionals who have undergone a comparable course of education.

Contemporary Psychoanalysis in Europe

Psychoanalysis in Germany was completely destroyed in the Nazi period. It was rebuilt largely thanks to the efforts of Mitscherlich and his associates in Frankfurt and now flourishes widely. In essence, the classical psychoanalytic positions in Germany have a high correlation with those in the United States. In addition to the classical group, there are two or three major nonclassical, nonpsychoanalytic organizations — e.g., Günter Ammons' group, which has developed a self-psychology of its own brand in which the occurrence of "holes" in the self and their repair play a major role.

In Austria, specifically Vienna, a large group of classical psychoanalysts re-emerged with an orientation that can probably be best described as identified with the conservative group in the United States. There are several nonclassical splinter groups.

England, of course, was a staging ground for the development of object-relations theory with the entrance of Melanie Klein followed by various disciples, many with differing views, all of whom stand in distinction to the classical group, which rallied around Anna Freud and her Hampstead Institute.

France is probably the surprise of the decade. In that country, until about ten years ago, psychoanalysis had relatively little popular appeal among educators and philosophers, or any other group outside of psychologists and the psychiatric profession itself. Then, perhaps characteristically, Lacan attained increasing popularity with his linguistically oriented notion of psychoanalysis. As mentioned earlier, he saw psychoanalysis primarily as a science of meaning rather than as a natural science. He developed a technique that one can only characterize as erratic, in that he sometimes felt that five minutes was enough for an analytic session. A review of a selection of Lacan's papers[49] by Anton Kris[50] suggests that Lacan had "a mischievous pleasure in dissent, a fine sense of irony, at times a creative wit—along with an apparently limitless self-confidence." And he adds, "I found it impossible to understand at first reading what Lacan intends. For Lacan psychoanalysis is exclusively the science of human discourse, conscious and unconscious." Kris's view greatly resembles the sentiments expressed in Rossner's earlier quote: "His undisciplined theoretical exposition leads me to doubt that the clinical psychoanalysis of his practice bears resemblance to the clinical psychoanalysis of my own practice," concludes Kris.

From my limited understanding of Lacan and my brief meeting with him a few years ago (he died in 1981), I can only support Kris's impressions. In spite of the popularity of Lacan in France, classical psychoanalysis nevertheless retains its importance in that country—for instance, in the person of Serge Lebovici. Although he is indeed of the classical school, he is not so exclusively classical as to be prevented from playing a major role in French community psychiatry. Together with Widloecher, Lebovici published a survey[51] of the variation in theory and in practice of psychoanalysis in France.

In Scandinavia, in my limited personal acquaintance, a primarily classical and rather conservative strain of psychoanalytic theory and practice exists, although most analysts have a primarily psychotherapeutic practice rather than a psychoanalytic one.

A small analytic interest exists in some of the Iron Curtain countries, such as Czechoslovakia, Yugoslavia, and Hungary—in distinction to the Soviet Union, where psychoanalysis has been officially banned since 1933.

Psychoanalysis Applied

Freud and his immediate associates applied clinical psychoanalytic concepts to many other fields with great enthusiasm and not always with the greatest caution or rigor.

Currently, a great deal more methodological care and sophistication are applied to the attempts at psychoanalytic interpretation of literature, art, anthropology, and other fields. Psychohistory especially flourishes in a more sophisticated form.

Psychoanalysis has also come to terms with its applications to various forms of psychotherapy, including psychoanalytically based brief therapy and group psychotherapy. The cries of heresy are much rarer, and official psychoanalytic journals at times actually publish contributions from these related fields to which psychoanalytic therapy may be applied.

Outstanding in the field of psychoanalytic group theory (as distinct from a dozen other more or less carefully defined forms of group therapy) are the works by Scheidlinger.[52,53] Scheidlinger's volume contains classical papers on psychoanalytic group psychology, some of them early contributions, the second part of those of the object-relations school. The third part deals with ego psychological group theories.

Thus, this volume provides an extensive overview of some ideas in depth of the usefulness of psychoanalytic theory for the understanding of groups and for the practice of group therapy.

More psychoanalysts than ever before are now engaged in group therapy and family therapy, and the combination of individual psychoanalysis or psychoanalytic psychotherapy with group therapy is increasingly accepted by classical psychoanalysts.[54]

Conclusion

The current status of psychoanalysis is characterized by a new synthesis of classical tenets infused with concepts from object relations theory, especially, and from self psychology.

The past decade has been characterized by a vigorous, and, at times, sharp interchange between these schools of thought. The antithesis seems to have been healthily resolved. Classical analysis had found itself limited in understanding and treating character disorders, borderline conditions and narcissistic aspects of other disorders.

The tremendous increase in various narcissistic conditions in the 1960's probably spurred the sudden blossoming of offshoots of object-relationships theory which had been extant for decades in the forms of Melanie Klein's theories and those of her followers.

In the course of vigorous dissension, strictly Kleinian object-relations theory seems to have been relegated to the role of an extreme polarity. More readily acceptable theories of the early role of cognition arose from several more or less independent sources within Kleinian ranks, e.g. Fairbairn, Winnicott, Bion and Guntrip. Edith Jacobson and Margaret Mahler developed their theories from their own observations. Kernberg borrowed from both schools, and in the course of the debate with the classical school managed to integrate his version of object relations theory into the structural concepts of classical analysis: He stresses the importance of early pre-oedipal cognition of the self and of objects and their vicissitudes without excluding the importance of oedipal developments or of conflict theory.

In this modified form, a sizeable number of classical analysts have, in turn, been willing to modify meta-psychology and take advantage of the technical aid pre-oedipal structural hypotheses offer them therapeutically: the susceptibility to treatment of a variety of patients who had been difficult to deal with without that aspect of theory.

For most of these years Kohut's self psychology ran neck and neck with Kernberg's formulations and was similarly embattled. At present, it seems that Kohut and his followers have gone to unsupportable extremes to postulate in a very vague form some concepts of the independent development of narcissism and to formulate a self-psychology that seems to lead back once again to the inadequate concept of a variety of "corrective emotional experiences" and earlier theories of the Sullivanians. In terms of Kohut and his followers, the empathy of the analyst who permits the patient to ascribe all his own grandiosity onto the therapist in the transference situation, in order to deal with the patient's underlying real feeling of helplessness, is not without usefulness. Especially since Kohut's death, his psychology is in danger of becoming more mythology than science in the hands of his followers. Still, some aspects of Kohut's self-psychology, especially the self representations of the self, are important contributions; the dramatic dream of one of his patients who saw himself as a satellite, i.e. only barely related to others are bound to remain valuable influences on analytic practice.

Much remains to be done. The terminologies of object-relations theory and self-psychology are shambles. Definitions seem even less customary and concepts are even less clear than in psychoanalysis generally. Systematic, if not experimental exploration is largely wanting, except in the case of infant observations. Independent evaluation of ongoing analysis, such as that done by Bellak and Smith[13] is desirable to test the validity of the hypotheses of object relations theory.

However, the sum total of the status of classical psychoanalysis, including the scope broadened by object-relations theory and self-psychology, is one of splendid health. With the new armamentarium and new interest, new attention to the field will follow, and psychoanalysis as therapy, as well as theory, seems sounder than it has been for many years. Even in a forbidding economic climate, it will find its place as analysis per se and as derivative in psychoanalytic psychotherapy.

Cognitive science, together with neuroscience, is adding a great deal of understanding of the human mind. Yet, rather than being a substitute or competitor, it is increasingly obvious that the future lies in an understanding of the interaction of the experimental and the biological substratum.

Behavior therapy in its original form, announced as the substitute for psychoanalysis, died of its own. Cognitive behavioral therapy is primarily a diluted form of psychoanalytic dynamics aided by some behavioral techniques — in fact, less and less of the latter. Psychoanalysis, in turn, might benefit from well-conceptualized use of behavioral techniques as adjuncts in some cases.

The same is true for psychopharmacology. Far from being a substitute or a rival, psychotropic drugs are a valuable asset in the psychoanalytic treatment of the more disturbed patients. The psychodynamic role of energizers in the treatment of phobias and obsessions, as well as depressions, may open new vistas to the understanding of drive interaction, and the combination of drug therapy and psychoanalysis or psychoanalytically oriented psychotherapy promise a great deal of hope.

In all, it seems that out of the doldrums, psychoanalysis has risen to new heights. There must be hope that behavioral scientists will help further the methodological and conceptual advance of analysis.

The childhood days of applied psychoanalysis, e.g. in psycho-history and other applied sciences seem to be over as well. Systematic attempts to study literature in psychoanalytic terms seem to have superceded the anecdotal and the whimsical.

Indeed, a surprising spirit seems to pervade psychoanalysis. In the first issue of the Psychoanalytic Quarterly of 1988, Arlow and Brenner suggest a curriculum in psychoanalytic institutes that is less concerned with studying the pioneering but outdated papers of Freud and more with contemporary issues and formulations.[55] Since this comes from the pens of the most stalwart defenders of the "purity" of psychoanalysis and generally most conservative representatives of the field, it suggests a new awakening indeed.

A review by Wallerstein in the first issue of the Journal of the American Psychoanalytic Association of 1988[56] on psychoanalytic science and psychoanalytic research also shows enthusiasms for change, albeit rather minor actual accomplishment thus far and an altogether too great a tendency to rest on a very small wreath of laurels.

To conclude then, a bright picture lies before us with regard to psychoanalysis as a theory, a therapy, a technique.

References

1. Lowenfeld H, Lowenfeld Y: Our permissive society and the superego: Some current thoughts about Freud's cultural concepts. *Psychoanal. Q.* 39:590–608, 1970.

2. Bellak L: Contemporary character as crisis adaptation. *Am. J. Psychother.* 25: 46–55, 1974.

3. Boyer B, Giovacchini PL: *Psychoanalytic Treatment of Characterological and Schizophrenic Disorders*, Science House, New York, 1967.

4. Jacobson E: *Depression: Comparative Studies of Normal, Neurotic and Psychotic Conditions*, International Universities Press, New York, 1971.

5. Mahler M, Pine F, Bergman A: *The Psychological Birth of the Human Infant: Symbiosis and Individuation*, Basic Books, New York, 1975.

6. Jacobson E: *The Self and the Object World*, International Universities Press, New York, 1964.

7. Bellak L, Antell M: (Book review): *Depression: Comparative Studies of Normal, Neurotic and Psychotic Conditions*, by Jacobson. *Contemp. Psychol.* 10(1): 1974.

8. Kohut H: *The Analysis of the Self*, International Universities Press, New York, 1971.

9. Freud S: Fetishism (1927). In Strachey J (ed. and transl.): *The Complete Psychological Works: Standard Edition*, Vol. 21, W. W. Norton, New York, 1976.

10. Hartmann H (1939): *Ego Psychology and the Problem of Adaptation*, International Universities Press, New York, 1958.

11. Reik T: *Der Ueberraschte Psychologe*: Ueber wechselseitige Erhellung und wiederholte Spiegelung. *Almanach der Psychoanalyte*, Band V, 1936, pp. 25-58.

12. Glover E: *The Techniques of Psychoanalysis*, International Universities Press, New York, 1955.

13. Bellak L, Smith MB: An experimental exploration of the psychoanalytic process: Exemplification of a method. *Psychoanal. Q.* 25:385-414, 1956.

14. Spence D (ed.): *The Broad Scope of Psychoanalysis: The Selected Papers of Leopold Bellak*, Grune & Stratton, New York, 1967.

15. Hunt M: *The Universe Within: A New Science Explores the Human Mind*, Simon & Schuster, New York, 1982.

16. Bellak L: *The TAT, CAT and SAT in Clinical Use (Third Edition)*, Grune & Stratton, New York, 1975.

17. Bellak L: The concept of projection: An experimental investigation and study of the concept. *Psychiatry* 7:353-370, 1944.

18. Finn M: An investigation of apperception distortion in the obsessive-compulsive character structure by three methods: Verbal, graphic-emotional, and graphic-geometric. Unpublished Ph.D. thesis, New York University, 1951.

19. Kernberg O: *Borderline Conditions and Pathological Narcissism*, Aronson, New York, 1971.

20. Kernberg O: *Object-Relations Theory and Clinical Psychoanalysis*, Aronson, New York, 1976.

21. Segel N: Book review: *Borderline Conditions and Pathological Narcissism and Object-Relations Theory and Clinical Psychoanalysis*, by Otto Kernberg. *J. Am. Psychoanal. Assoc.* 29:221-236, 1981.

22. Kernberg O: *Internal World and External Reality: Object-Relations Theory Applied*, Aronson, New York, 1980.

23. Kernberg O: Some implications of object relations theory for psychoanalytic technique. *J. Am. Psychoanal. Assoc.* 27 (Suppl.):207-238, 1979.

24. Richards A: "Technical Consequences of Object-Relations Theory," chaired by Ernst Ticho, Ph.D., scientific proceedings. *J. Am. Psychoanal. Assoc.* 26:623-636, 1978.

25. Meissner WW: A note on projective identification. *J. Am. Psychoanal. Assoc.* 28:43-67, 1980.

26. Pruyser P: What splits in "splitting"? A scrutiny of the concept of splitting in psychoanalysis and psychiatry. *Bull. Menninger Clin.* 39:1-46, 1975.

27. Meyers S: Panel report: "The bipolar self." *J. Am. Psychoanal. Assoc.* 29: 143–175, 1980.

28. Gedo J: Reflections of some current controversies in psychoanalysis. *J Am. Psychoanal. Assoc.* 28:363–383, 1980.

29. Kohut H: *The Restoration of the Self*, International Universities Press, New York, 1977.

30. Kernberg O: Book review: *Advances in Self Psychology*, edited by Arnold Goldberg. *Am. J. Psychiatry* 139:374–375, 1982.

31. Goldberg A (ed.): *Advances in Self Psychology*, International Universities Press, New York, 1980.

32. Pine F: *Developmental Theory and Clinical Process*. Yale University Press, New Haven, 1985.

33. Rangell L: Contemporary issues in the theory of therapy. *J. Am. Psychoanal. Assoc.* 27 (Suppl.): 81–112, 1979.

34. Blum H: Some current and recurrent problems of psychoanalytic technique. *J. Am. Psychoanal. Assoc.* 29:47–65, 1981.

35. Kanzer M: Book essay: Developments in psychoanalytic technique. *J. Am. Psychoanal. Assoc.* 27 (Suppl.):327–374, 1979.

36. Simons R: Contemporary Problems of Psychoanalytic Technique (scientific proceedings), chaired by Harold Blum. *J. Am. Psychoanal. Assoc.* 29:643–658, 1981.

37. Stone L: Some thoughts on the "here and now" in psychoanalytic technique and process. *Psychoanal. Q.* 50:709–733, 1981.

38. Valenstein A: The concept of "classical" psychoanalysis. *J. Am. Psychoanal. Assoc.* 27 (Suppl.):113–136, 1979.

39. Holt R: A review of some of Freud's biological assumptions and their influence on this theories. In Greenfield NS, Lewis WC (eds.): *Psychoanalysis and Current Biological Thought*, University of Wisconsin Press, Madison, 1965.

40. Klein G: *Psychoanalytic Theory: An Exploration of Essentials*, International Universities Press, New York, 1976.

41. Schafer R: *A New Language for Psychoanalysis*, Yale University Press, New Haven, 1976.

42. Meissner W: Metapsychology — Who needs it? *J. Am. Psychoanal. Assoc.* 29: 921–938, 1981.

43. Brenner C: Metapsychology and psychoanalytic theory. *Psychoanal. Q.* 49: 189–214, 1980.

44. Waelder R: Psychoanalysis, scientific method, and philosophy. In Guttman SA (ed.): *Psychoanalysis: Observation, Theory, Application*, International Universities Press, New York, 1976.

45. Rawn M: Schafer's "action language": A questionable alternative to metapsychology. *Int. J. Psychoanal.* 60 (Part 4):455–466, 1979.

46. Modell A: Does metapsychology still exist?" *Int. J. Psychoanal.* 62 (Part 4): 391–412, 1981.

47. Dream theory: The debate about revision continues. *Roche Report: Frontiers of Psychiatry* 11(12):4, 5, 11, 1981.

48. Shapiro D (cochairman, Ad Hoc Committee on Psychoanalytic Practice):

Summary of Report of the Survey of Psychoanalytic Practice, 1976. Memorandum of the American Psychoanalytic Association, November 16, 1981.

49. Sheridan A (transl.): *Ecrits: A Selection by Jacques Lacan*, W. W. Norton, New York, 1977.

50. Kris A: Book review: *Ecrits: A Selection by Jacques Lacan*, translated by Alan Sheridan. *J. Am. Psychoanal. Assoc.* 28:223–224, 1980.

51. Lebovici S, Widloecher D (eds.): *Psychoanalysis in France*, International Universities Press, New York, 1980.

52. Scheidlinger S (ed.): *Group Dynamics: Basic Readings*, International Universities Press, New York, 1980.

53. Scheidlinger S (ed.): *Focus on Group Psychotherapy: Clinical Essays*, International Universities Press, New York, 1982.

54. Bellak L: On some limitations of dyadic psychotherapy and the role of group modalities. *Int. J. Group Psychother.* 30:7–23, 1980.

55. Arlow J, Brenner, C: "The future of psychoanalysis." *The Psychoanalytic Quarterly*, Volume LV11, No. 1, 1988, p 1–15.

56. Wallerstein R: "Psychoanalysis, psychoanalytic science, and psychoanalytic research — 1986. *J. Am. Psychoanal. Assoc*, Vol. 36, No. 1, 1988, p 3–31.

6

Transference
Anthony Storr

EDITOR'S NOTE

In this chapter, the author highlights the importance of transference in the relation-ship between patient and therapist, tracing the origin of the concept from the early writings of Freud, who first described the phenomenon, to current thinking, which emphasizes the reality of the doctor-patient relationship while simultaneously reedu-cating the patient as his distortions of the relationship appear in the here-and-now.

Transference is essentially the process by which a patient attributes to his analyst or therapist attitudes and ideas that derive from previous figures in his life, especially from parents and other significant authority figures. It is, in fact, a universal phe-nomenon, occurring in all human relationships and highlighted in the context of helplessness that usually motivates the patient to seek care. In analysis, transference usually manifests itself first as resistance—interrupting the flow of free association. It may be negative, characterized by feelings of hostility or rejection, or positive, such as expectations of powerful assistance or intervention, fulfillment of dependen-cy needs, love, and sexuality. Feelings of love and sexual attraction toward the therapist require careful management: on the one hand, they cannot be arbitrarily dismissed as simply unreal; on the other, they are often quite unreal and require correct interpretation and resolution.

The more obscure the nature of the psychotherapist's own personality, the more transference reactions will emerge. This implies that the more the therapist feels the need for transference issues to be present and negotiable, the more he must conceal his own identity to permit this to occur. In traditional psychoanalysis this technique seems central; in other forms of psychotherapy, the therapist's stance is more varia-ble, and how much of his own personality should enter into the therapeutic situation remains an area of controversy.

All agree, however, that the therapist must not take advantage of the patient's helplessness and that the ultimate goal of treatment is the resolution of transference factors in such a way as to permit the patient to become self-reliant, extending what he has learned in therapy to his relationships with others.

Definition

Transference is the process by which a patient attributes to his analyst attitudes and ideas that derive from previous figures in his life, especially from his parents. It is the way in which a patient relates to his analyst as if he were such a previous figure, and thereby endows him with emotional significance. The term "transference" has also been extended to include the patient's total emotional attitude toward the analyst.

Freud's Discovery and Portrayal of Transference

Freud was the first to describe transference. Although modifications of his point of view have been introduced, his contribution is still so influential that a thorough understanding of it is essential.

The first mention of transference in the psychoanalytic sense occurs in Freud's paper "The Psychotherapy of Hysteria."[1] This is the last section of *Studies on Hysteria*, which Josef Breuer and Sigmund Freud published in 1895 as joint authors. Freud describes a patient in whom a hysterical symptom took origin from a repressed wish that a particular man should kiss her. During the analysis, a similar wish, which horrified the patient, came up in her mind about Freud. Freud refers to the patient as "transferring on to the figure of the physician the distressing ideas which arise from the content of the analysis."

In 1905, Freud published "Fragment of an Analysis of a Case of Hysteria,"[2] in the postscript to which he defines "transference" as

new editions or facsimiles of the impulses and phantasies which are aroused and made conscious during the progress of the analysis; but they have this peculiarity, which is characteristic for their species, that they replace some earlier person by the person of the physician. To put it another way: a whole series of psychological experiences are revived, not as belonging to the past, but as applying to the person of the physician at the present moment.[2]

Freud goes on to say that there is no way of avoiding transference, refers to it as a "creation of the disease" that must be combated, and asserts that it is only after the transference has been resolved that the patient becomes convinced of the "validity of the connections which have been constructed during the analysis." This predominantly negative attitude of Freud's toward transference is somewhat modified by a sentence from the same paper. "Transference, which seems ordained to be the greatest obstacle to psychoanalysis, becomes its most powerful ally, if its presence can be detected each time and explained to the patient."

In 1910, Freud was still exhibiting distaste for transference, in spite of recognizing its importance. In a letter to Pfister, he wrote:

As for the transference, it is altogether a curse. The intractable and fierce impulses in the illness, on account of which I renounced both indirect and hypnotic suggestion, cannot be altogether abolished even through psycho-analysis; they can only be restrained, and what remains expresses itself in the transference. That is often a considerable amount.[3]

In his paper, "The Dynamics of Transference," first published in 1912,[4] Freud points out that the intensity of transference to the doctor, which exceeds "anything that could be justified on sensible or rational grounds," is due to libidinal impulses that are unconscious and date from early childhood. He goes on to make the important observation that when a patient's free associations are halted, it is because associations connected with the analyst have come into his mind. Transference manifests itself first as resistance. Freud suggests that this is because it is difficult to admit "any proscribed wishful impulse if it has to be revealed in front of the very person to whom the impulse relates." But since a number of patients come to trust the analyst to the point at which they can say anything to him, this cannot be the whole explanation.

At this point Freud subdivides transference into "negative" and "positive." It is obviously difficult for the patient to admit hostile feelings toward the analyst; this is why negative transference must be understood and interpreted. However, positive transference also contains unacceptable elements that are difficult to admit. It is easy enough to confess "friendly or affectionate feelings toward the analyst." But such feelings have their roots in infantile erotic impulses, and these are harder to admit. It is in this paper that Freud makes his famous remark: "Originally we knew only sexual objects; and psychoanalysis shows us that people who in our real life are merely admired or respected *may* still be sexual objects for our unconscious."[4]

In "Observations on Transference Love,"[5] Freud discusses the difficult problem of how a male analyst deals with a female patient who has fallen in love with him. He states that neither gratifying the patient's craving nor suppressing it meets the case.

The course which the analyst must pursue is neither of these; it is one for which there is no model in real life. He must take care not to steer away from the transference-love, or to repulse it or to make it distasteful to the patient: but he must just as resolutely withhold any response to it. He must keep firm hold of the transference-love, but treat it as something unreal, as a situation which has to be gone through in the treatment and traced back to its unconscious origins and which must assist in bringing back all that is most deeply hidden in the patient's erotic life into her consciousness and therefore under her control.[5]

Although Freud insists on treating transference-love as "unreal," he does admit that "the state of being in love which makes its appearance in the course of analytic treatment has the character of a 'genuine' love." If it appears abnormal, this is because love in ordinary life is "more similar to abnormal than to normal mental phenomena." However, transference-love differs from normal love in that it is provoked by the analytic situation, is intensified by resistance, and has less regard to reality than love in ordinary life.

In Lecture 27 of "Introductory Lectures on Psycho-Analysis," Freud reiterates his conviction that transference must be treated as unreal:

We overcame the transference by pointing out to the patient that his feelings do not arise from the present situation and do not apply to the person of the doctor, but that they are repeating something that happened to him earlier. In this way we oblige him to transform his repetition into a memory.[6]

In one of his last writings, "An Outline of Psycho-Analysis,"[7] Freud returns to the topic of transference. Discussing the technique of psychoanalysis, he writes:

A number of other things happen, a few of which we might have foreseen but others of which are bound to surprise us. The most remarkable thing is this: The patient is not satisfied with regarding the analyst in the light of reality as a helper and adviser who, moreover, is remunerated for the trouble he takes and who would himself be content with some such role as that of a guide on a difficult mountain climb. On the contrary, the patient sees in him the return, the reincarnation, of some important figure out of his childhood or past, and consequently transfers on to him feelings and reactions which undoubtedly applied to this prototype.[7]

Freud goes on to say that, because the analyst is put in the place of father or mother, he is enabled to modify the patient's superego by a process of "after-education." Freud warns against exploiting this power, which can be misused because its exercise can keep the patient in a state of infantile dependence. In other words, the good parent is one who lets his child go free and does not overload him with maxims as to how he should live his life.

Freud's Attitude to Transference

It seems clear from the extracts quoted above that Freud, although acknowledging the vital importance of transference, deplored its inevitability. It must be remembered that Freud was trained as a scientist, who gave up his research in the laboratories of Brücke to take up medical practice only because he needed more money in order to get married. Freud's early work, reluctantly abandoned, which became known as "The Project" but was originally titled "Psychology for Neurologists," attests to his desire to make psychoanalysis into a science based on anatomy and physiology. Scientists, by definition, must be detached observers, unaffected by the phenomena they are studying and scrupulous in ensuring that their own emotions do not affect the objects of their scrutiny. Freud, I believe, would have preferred his patients to adopt a similar attitude toward him. He would like to have been regarded as a technical expert, as a surgeon or, as he suggested, as a mountain guide: someone who knew the intricacies of the mind and who could guide the patient through the maze of his difficulties but who was not of any more emotional significance to his patient than such a role implied.

Freud's idea of the analyst's role is closely paralleled by the wish of a contemporary professor of psychology who affirms that the practitioner of behavior therapy should be regarded in the same light as a dentist: kind, considerate, but, above all, technically accomplished — not a person likely to play any significant part in his patient's emotional life. Freud's ambivalence toward the phenomena of transference, which is amply illustrated by the extracts from his writings quoted above, bears witness to his reluctance to admit that psychoanalysis is not, and could never have been, a science in the sense in which physics and chemistry are sciences. Paradoxically, it can be argued that it was Freud's detachment and refusal to become personally involved with his patients that both promoted the phenomena of transference and made these phenomena apparent.

The reason for this paradox is that transference is a form of projection, and patients are more likely to project upon a comparative enigma than they are upon a person with whom they are having an ordinary personal relationship. Freud's technique of not revealing himself and of sitting out of sight behind the patient encouraged the latter to have fantasies about him that would not have been so obvious had he been more forthcoming. Nature abhors a vacuum, and we all tend to have fantasies about people we have met but do not yet know at all well. In fact, getting to know someone is as much a matter of correcting false impressions as of gaining new information.

The analyst's comparative anonymity and refusal to answer questions about himself make him function like a Rorschach inkblot. There is enough there to stimulate fantasy but not enough actual information to discourage it. Apprentice therapists often feel that preserving comparative anonymity is artificial and that it would be more human and more helpful to reveal more about themselves to the patient. But if they do so, they deprive themselves of an important source of information about the patient. It is perfectly possible to withhold information about oneself and at the same time convey that one is concerned and anxious to understand and help.

Projection of Parental Figures

Why is it that parental figures are projected upon the analyst? It is actually a natural phenomenon that can be seen in many situations in ordinary life, though highlighted in analysis. Anyone seeking psychotherapy is to some extent bound to regard the analyst as an authority by the very fact of his seeking help from him. He is therefore likely to invest the analyst with the attributes of the most significant authorities from his past, and these are likely to be parents. Less commonly, the analyst may find that he receives the projection of other figures: grandparents, teachers, or other significant authorities. The more distressed the patient, the more he needs an authority to whom he can turn and upon whom he can temporarily rely, until he is well enough to regain his autonomy.

Negative Transference

However well disposed a patient may appear, and however anxious he is for help, his attitude toward the analyst is bound to contain some negative elements. There are two reasons for this. First, if the patient's previous experience is of being criticized, unloved, or ill used by parents, he will bring similar expectations to his analysis. Second, even if his previous experience has been favorable, he is bound somewhat to resent being temporarily reduced to the condition of seeking help and to have some rebellious feelings against the analyst upon whom, for the time being, he is dependent.

It is generally agreed that negative transference, in the sense of expectation of rejection, must be analyzed and interpreted at the earliest opportunity. This is partly because, if it is not, the analysis is likely to be broken off and partly because the correction of the patient's negative assumptions is powerfully therapeutic. Patients who come into analysis are, in many instances, people who do not believe that anyone cares for them, wants them, or understands them. Often such people feel that there is something basically unacceptable about them that precludes intimacy with another person. If the analysis goes well, the patient will gradually come to feel that there is at least one person in the world who accepts him as he is and who values him as a person, and he is likely to generalize this positive experience with the analyst to other people. The analysis of negative transference is thus a corrective emotional experience in which negative assumptions about other people are gradually modified.

The other aspect of negative transference—that is, the resentment of dependency and of being in the mildly humiliating position of having to ask for help—is actually healthy. It may be compared with a child's wish to be free of parental authority and become independent, which inevitably contains elements of rebellion against that authority. Regrettably, there are a few patients who lack much drive toward autonomy and who would like to remain in analysis forever.

Positive Transference

Some degree of positive transference is probably necessary if therapy is to proceed. The patient's attitude may vary from one of reasonable appreciation and gratitude to an irrational adoration in which the analyst is almost equated with the Deity. This is often embarrassing to analysts who are aware of their human limitations, but it should not lead the analyst to try to correct the patient's idealization by self-deprecatory remarks. Although the analyst can neither replace the patient's parents nor entirely make up for what has been missing (or is thought to have been missing) in the patient's early childhood, the patient's experience of the analyst as an idealized parent may have a healing effect that premature interpretation would dispel. The more damaged and insecure the patient, the more he or she may temporarily require an omniscient, all-loving parent who is regarded as "the only one who understands." As the analysis proceeds, such a patient will usually go through the same stages as a child growing up. Just as the child comes to realize that his parents have limitations and failings, so the patient will gradually come to see the analyst as another fallible human being like himself, albeit possessing special skills.

Erotic Transference

As Freud noted, erotic transference is especially likely to be overt when the patient is female and the analyst male; he had, of course, little experience with the alternative situation—a male patient with a female therapist. Since the patient endows the analyst with attributes that are predominantly parental, it follows that when erotic elements coincide, the patient is often trying to make the analyst into a combination of parent and lover. Freud interpreted this as a repetition of the past—which it is, in part. Other writers have emphasized that in very deprived patients the transference may be an expression of a wish to make up for what has been missing in childhood, together with an admixture of sexual feelings that belong to the present. It is important to realize that dependency and sex are ill-matched partners. One of the most common reasons for the failure of a marriage is that one partner has sought a parent in the other rather than a relationship on equal terms.

Freud may have been right in seeing in the Oedipus complex the core of neurosis, but he emphasized the erotic tie to the parent rather than the dependent tie. Many analysts today think of dependency as being the chief obstacle to the attainment of mature relationships, and consider that the wish that a parent or parent-substitute in the shape of the analyst should also be a lover is a way of avoiding the risks of adult responsibility and adult relationships.

The analyst must accept declarations of love with tenderness and understanding, but he must also make it clear not only that there is no hope of the patient's desire being fulfilled but also that such a step would be regressive and would hinder progress toward autonomy. It must be recalled that we all start life with a disappointment in love, since the parent of the opposite sex can never be ours.

The fact that erotic fantasies concerning the analyst are often inescapable elements in the therapy can lead to certain risks, especially in the case of adolescent girls. It is not unknown for such patients to tell their parents and others that the analyst is in love with them or has actually seduced them. Fortunately, the fact that hysterical patients often seem unable to distinguish fact from fantasy has become more generally recognized; but it is a problem that all analysts must be aware of and guard against.

Resolution of Transference

In favorable cases, the analyst may become incorporated, or "introjected," within the patient's psyche as a "good object," just as parents become, or ought to have become, incorporated. In the beginning, every human being is totally dependent; the gradual attainment of independence is encouraged by the loving support of parents. It is those who have not had such support who continue to look for parent substitutes. Relying on oneself is actually relying on something that, in the first instance, was taken into the self from experience with good parents. The same process happens in analysis. The patient, through his experience of the analyst as a reliable figure, begins to form within himself a reliable figure to whom he can turn in case of difficulty. In time, the image of the analyst disappears as a definable entity, just as the image of parents as people to whom the child turns for support fades as the child grows up. The process of becoming autonomous is aided by the positive aspect of negative transference, as one might call it — that is, by the patient's rebellion against the analyst as a restrictive authority, as discussed above.

Failure of Resolution of Transference

In a minority of cases, it is difficult or impossible to resolve a positive transference. Instead of the patient's experience with the analyst being extended toward other people in the external world, the analyst remains for the patient the only person who accepts and understands him. This is likely to happen with very isolated, schizoid patients, who may never have formed close relationships with anyone and who continue to regard the world as predominantly hostile. There are also some patients who are persistently and deeply dependent and who cannot conceive of themselves as ever becoming autonomous. Such cases are best dealt with by a very gradual process of weaning—that is, by extending the interval between appointments from days to weeks to months. Provided such patients know that they have another appointment, however far away, they often manage far better than one might have supposed. The solution may not be ideal, but it is far better than dismissing the patient altogether.

Alternation of Positive and Negative Transference

A few patients swing wildly between two extremes. One day, they may idealize the analyst to the point of making him into a savior; on the very next day, they may treat him as a devil who is an evil persecutor. Such patients demand the highest skill on the part of the analyst. They attest to the acuteness of Melanie Klein's observation that there is what she called a "paranoid-schizoid" position in the child's development in which objects are regarded as wholly good when they are satisfying the child's desires and wholly bad when they are frustrating them. According to Klein, normal development requires that this early paranoid-schizoid position be succeeded by the "depressive position," in which the child begins to realize that the same person who provides food, warmth, and comfort may also, at times, postpone or fail to satisfy immediate needs. Patients who show this violent alternation within the transference are generally maternally deprived to a formidable extent, and have had no chance to develop emotionally beyond this primitive stage. It requires great patience and understanding on the part of the analyst to tolerate what may be quite vicious attacks upon him; if he does so, however, his patience will be rewarded.

Modern Developments

Since Freud's day—and, more particularly, since the emergence of the "object-relations" school of psychoanalysis—there has been a shift of emphasis in understanding and interpreting transference. Freud's tendency was to interpret any emotions the patient might exhibit toward the analyst in the here-and-now. He also thought much more in terms of instinctive drives seeking satisfaction wherever it might be found, rather than in terms of interpersonal relationships. Today many analysts believe that human beings, from the beginning of life, are seeking fruitful personal relationships (which, of course, include instinctual satisfaction) and that neurosis is not so much a matter of inhibited or underdeveloped instinct as of failure to make satisfying human relationships on equal terms. Interpretation of transference, therefore, depends on the analyst's detecting and commenting on the way in which the patient is relating to him in the present: whether he is fearful, compliant, aggressive, competitive, and so on. Such attitudes of course have their history, which needs to be explored; but the emphasis is on understanding in what way the patient's attitude to others is distorted through perceiving in what way his attitude to the analyst is distorted. To do this effectively implies the recognition that there is a real relationship in the here-and-now, and that analysis is not concerned solely with the events of early childhood. The analytical encounter is, after all, unique. In no other situation in life can anyone count on a devoted listener who is prepared to give so much time and skilled attention to the problems of a single individual without asking for any reciprocal emotional return, although requiring professional remuneration. The patient may never have encountered anyone in his life who has paid him such attention or even been prepared to listen to his problems. It is not surprising that the analyst becomes important to him, and recognizing the reality of this is as necessary as recognizing the irrational elements of the transference, which date from childhood.

References

1. Freud S (1895): The psychotherapy of hysteria, *Standard Edition*, Vol. II, pp. 302–303.

2. Freud S (1905): Fragment of an analysis of a case of hysteria, *Standard Edition*, Vol. VII, pp. 116–117.

3. Freud S (1910): Letter to Pfister, quoted in Jones E (1955): *Sigmund Freud*, Vol. II, Hogarth Press, London, p. 497.

4. Freud S (1912): The dynamics of transference, *Standard Edition*, Vol. XII, pp. 99–108.

5. Freud S (1915): Observations on transference-love, *Standard Edition*, Vol. XII, pp. 159–171.

6. Freud S (1917): Transference, Lecture XXVII, "Introductory Lectures on Psycho-Analysis," *Standard Edition*, Vol. XVI, pp. 431–447.

7. Freud S (1940): An outline of psycho-analysis, *Standard Edition*, Vol. XXIII, pp. 174–182.

Further Reading

Alexander F, French TM: The transference phenomenon, chapter 5 in *Psychoanalytic Therapy*, Ronald Press, New York, 1946.

Fairbairn WRD: On the nature and aims of psycho-analytical treatment. *Int. J. Psychoanal.* 39:374–385, 1958.

Greenson RR: Transference, chapter 3 in *The Technique and Practice of Psycho-Analysis*, Vol. I, Hogarth Press, London, pp. 151–356.

Guntrip H: Object-relations theory and psychotherapy, chapter 13 in *Schizoid Phenomena, Object Relations and the Self*, Hogarth Press, London, 1968.

Jung CG: Psychology of the transference. In *Collected Works*, Vol. 16, Routledge & Kegan Paul, London, 1946, pp. 163–321.

Storr A: Transference, chapter 8 in *The Art of Psychotherapy*, Methuen, New York, 1980.

7

Countertransference
Anthony Storr

EDITOR'S NOTE

The concept of countertransference, which originally referred to the unconscious responses within the therapist to his patient that derived from his own personal background and experiences, has been enlarged in usage to include all those reactions that the psychotherapist has toward his patient. The author calls this a form of projection; past experience tells us something about how to deal with people new to us and this can be partly adaptive and helpful, but partly distorting, interfering with the process of understanding and communication. None of us is without bias. We react to how a person speaks, how he or she dresses, to their social and economic status, to certain traits that we do not deem masculine in men or feminine in women. Although the purpose of a therapist's personal psychoanalysis is to reduce the impact of such perceptions so as to free him to work with greater flexibility and latitude, such freedom is never obtained in full.

Compatibility is a central feature of a successful therapeutic relationship, and, the author holds, when it is not there it often leads to early termination of treatment and is frequently the result of "paranoid" projections on one side or the other. He cites several attitudes in particular that can readily interfere with psychotherapy: holding the patient in fear or awe; being unduly afraid of being manipulated by the patient; too strong a need to offer direction and play the authority figure; too great a need to be liked; too great an identification with the patient leading to injudicious self-revelations. Exploitation of patients and sexual relations are not only unethical but represent actions significantly detrimental to progress in therapy.

Countertransference feelings can, of course, be a rich source of information about patients as well, offering clues and directions that can be constructively utilized in the course of therapy. While it is evident that the author's comments focus on long-term psychotherapy and various forms of psychoanalysis, they clearly apply to all forms of psychotherapy as well.

Definition

Just as transference may be defined as the process by which a patient displaces onto his analyst feelings and ideas that derive from previous figures in his life, countertransference may be defined as the process by which the analyst displaces onto his patient feelings and ideas that derive from figures in his life.

In this, the original and limited sense, transference and countertransference are distorting processes that interfere with the progress of analysis.

However, the concept of countertransference has now been extended to include the analyst's response to various items of his patient's behavior and also his total emotional attitude toward his patient.

Historical Background

The first mention of countertransference in Freud's writings occurs in a paper of 1910, "The Future Prospects of Psycho-Analytic Therapy":

> Other innovations in technique relate to the physician himself. We have become aware of the "countertransference," which arises in him as a result of the patient's influence on his unconscious feelings, and we are almost inclined to insist that he shall recognize this counter-transference in himself and overcome it. Now that a considerable number of people are practicing psycho-analysis and exchanging their observations with one another, we have noticed that no psychoanalyst goes further than his own complexes and internal resistances permit; and we constantly require that he shall begin his activity with a self-analysis and continually carry it deeper while he is making his observations on his patients. Anyone who fails to produce results in a self-analysis of this kind may at once give up any idea of being able to treat patients by analysis.[1]

(Freud later insisted that self-analysis should be replaced by training analysis conducted by another person.) There is a later discussion of countertransference in "Observations on Transference-Love."[2] In this paper, Freud confines himself to discussing how analysts should behave toward female patients who fall in love with them and why it is inadmissible for the analyst to proffer love. As the editors of the Standard Edition observe, "it is hard to find any other explicit discussions of the subject in Freud's published works."

Projection

Countertransference, like transference, is a form of projection. It is not confined to the analytic situation. Our perception of any new person is bound to be influenced by our previous experience of other persons. This is automatic and inescapable. Whenever we meet a new person, we try to "place" him or her; this "placing" activity is biologically adaptive in origin. Primitive man, encountering a total stranger, needed to know whether he was friend or foe and wanted all the clues he could get in order to know how to approach and address the unknown person. Although we may try to be as objective as possible, we cannot avoid making assumptions and guesses about strangers. Much of the process of getting to know another person is correcting our guesses and assumptions—that is, withdrawing our projections.

The mechanism of projection is both a help and a hindrance. We need our previous experience in order to know how to assess and approach new persons, but our experience is necessarily limited and may lead us to make unjustified assumptions about others. We are also bound to harbor certain prejudices derived from our own upbringing and social milieu, and we may be quite unconscious of such prejudices until they have led us into error.

Prejudices

The way a patient talks—his accent, turn of phrase, or speech rhythms— may lead an analyst to make unjustified assumptions based on his previous experience of people who speak similarly. For example, a Southern accent might lead an analyst to assume a whole set of attitudes and opinions that the patient does not actually profess.

The same is true of the way people dress. Although style of dress may express aspects of personality, it may also be an attempt at compensation for deficiencies. Beginners sometimes assume that women who dress fashionably and take a great deal of trouble with makeup and grooming are sexually active, but they soon learn that girls who look like models are often frigid.

Analysts often assume that "good mothers" behave in certain specified ways that usually turn out to be derived from their own childhood experience. Acceptable parental behavior varies widely from class to class even within the same culture, and family life is so completely different in other cultures that some analysts refuse to take on such patients for treatment. For example, it is obvious that the oedipal situation is not the same for a child brought up in an extended family in which the father has more than one wife as it is for a child raised in the nuclear family conventionally found in middle-class Western culture.

Some prejudices are more emotionally loaded and spring from deeper roots within the analyst's own psychopathology. Male analysts often find it difficult to cope with female patients who are assertive and dominant. Women analysts are sometimes intolerant of men who are dependent and passive. Such emotional reactions on the part of analysts call for self-examination and perhaps further personal analysis.

Certain types of sexual behavior on the part of patients are liable to evoke irrational responses from analysts. This is particularly true of pedophiles, who are also likely to evoke hatred and violence from fellow prisoners when they are confined in penitentiaries. Some analysts (Wilhelm Reich being one example) are intolerant of homosexuals. Although no one can be entirely free of prejudice, such emotional reactions as part of countertransference can interfere with the progress of analysis. It is not uncommonly true that what we most dislike in other people is something we have not accepted in ourselves; such reactions should, therefore, disappear or be very much modified in the course of training analysis. Yet no one, however thoroughly analysed, can boast that he is entirely free of prejudice, and most analysts recognize that they cannot be successful with every type of patient.

Like and Dislike

Psychiatrists in training often inquire whether it is necessary for them to like their patients if they are to help them. Although, at the beginning of psychotherapy, the analyst may find that he is somewhat "put off" by certain aspects of his patient's behavior or manner, he will usually find that such things become unimportant as therapy progresses. Although it is inevitable that analysts have preferences among their patients it is hardly possible to get to know anyone as intimately as happens during analysis without coming to like them. Real incompatibility between patient and analyst almost always results in treatment's being broken off before intimate knowledge of the patient has been achieved. Such incompatibility is generally due to paranoid projection on one side or the other. In fact, one of the rewarding aspects of practicing psychotherapy is that the therapist finds that he comes to appreciate a wider range of different people than he did before he took up his profession.

Emotional Attitudes Toward Patients
That May Hinder Progress

Fear and Awe: Analysts may find themselves asked to treat patients who are much older than themselves or are more intelligent, more gifted, or in superior social positions. Such patients may inspire fear or awe. It is helpful to the analyst to recall that high intelligence and emotional maturity do not necessarily go together and that even the most impressive persons not only started life as helpless babies but also have the same emotional needs as the rest of mankind.

Fear of Being Manipulated: Analysts often approach patients suspiciously, because they have been taught that patients are likely to be manipulative. In their overanxiety not to be caught out and made to feel foolish, they tend to make negative interpretations of the patient's behavior when such is not justified. Comparatively few patients are either dishonest or deliberately manipulative. Those who are have learned in childhood that this was the only way that they could get what they needed from their parents, and analysis provides a setting in which they have the opportunity of learning that such maneuvers are unnecessary. They will do this only if the analyst's attitude is one of trust. It is far better that analysts should occasionally be deceived or manipulated than that they should display significant mistrust of the patient.

Authority and Advice: Conventional medical training encourages physicians to become authorities who give their patients advice and instructions. Analysts, on the other hand, need to be *relatively* passive. The object of analysis is to help the patient understand himself better so that he can become more autonomous and more competent in making choices and decisions. This will not be achieved if the analyst acts as an authority who tells him what to do. As Jung once said, "Good advice is often a doubtful remedy but generally not dangerous since it has so little effect." Doctors who are learning to become analysts find it difficult to abandon their traditional authoritarian role and often feel ill at ease if they are not handing out prescriptions or instructions. It is a considerable advance when such doctors learn that the capacity to listen patiently is itself therapeutic.

The Analyst's Need to Be Liked: Some analysts are so anxious to be loved that they dare not make interpretations that might upset the patient. It is important not to make interpretations that are hurtful before rapport has been established; but parts of any analysis are bound to be painful and disturbing to the patient, since we all deceive ourselves into thinking that we are better than we are. When positive transference has been established, most patients will tolerate "home truths" without too much distress; it is antitherapeutic to encourage self-deception by failing to draw attention to the patient's less creditable motives.

Identification with the Patient: A certain degree of identification with the patient is necessary for the establishment of rapport and for the analyst to be able to understand the patient. However, identification that goes beyond this may hold up progress, because the analyst will then lack an objective base from which he can make interpretations. I once saw a woman who had been in treatment for some time with a female therapist. It turned out that the latter had identified herself so closely with the patient that no progress had been made. As the patient reported of her former therapist, "We just sat and chatted about how dreadful men were."

Identification Leading to Self-Revelation: Inexperienced analysts who recognize their own problems in what patients tell them sometimes fall into the trap of saying: "I know what you must be feeling; I've been through it myself." This is especially true of sympathetic analysts, who feel that it is pretentious to adopt the traditional analytic attitude of not revealing oneself and who do not wish to set themselves up as being superior. There are good reasons why such self-revelation is inadvisable. First, if the patient comes to know the analyst as a person in the way that he knows his friends, he will no longer produce the fantasies about the analyst that are so valuable to the analyst in understanding how his patient has developed and what his attitudes to unknown people are. In other words, self-revelation on the part of the analyst can interfere with the development of transference. No analyst can — or should — be an entirely "blank screen." He is bound to reveal a good deal about himself by his attitude toward the patient, his way of speaking, and so on. But deliberate self-revelation of the kind proffered by sympathetic friends deprives the analyst of a valuable source of information and is apt to convert the relationship into one of friendly exchange rather than analysis.

It will also be difficult, if self-revelation has begun, to prevent it from going further. It is important that the patient remain in ignorance of the analyst's private life so far as this is possible. If, for example, a male homosexual patient knows that the analyst is married, he may assume that there are areas of his own experience the analyst cannot understand. If a female patient knows that the analyst is married, it may inhibit her from producing fantasies about marrying him herself; this kind of inhibition may prevent the analyst from discovering a great deal more about the patient's wishes and fears in regard to the opposite sex.

Analysts must accept that, while they are practicing their profession, they are agents of their patients and fulfilling a professional obligation. Revealing their own problems injudiciously strips them of their professional function and makes things more difficult for the patient, not less. Self-revelation on the part of the analyst is often self-indulgence — a wish to be understood and accepted by the patient. Patients, of course, realize that it is not by accident that the analyst came to adopt his profession; but while they are in treatment, what they want and need is an analyst whom they can trust and upon whom they can rely — not someone whom they perceive as wrestling with unsolved problems of his own.

Exploitation of the Patient: The analyst who talks about himself is often exploiting the patient by demanding the latter's interest and attention. There are other, grosser forms of exploitation. Patients who have strongly positive transference feelings toward the analyst may long to perform services for him, load him with presents, or give him stock-market advice if they are in a position to do so. In my opinion and experience it is wrong to take advantage of the patient's dependency and gratitude. One analyst had taken into treatment an occupational therapist who worked in his clinic. She masochistically stayed on late to help him, acted as an unpaid secretary, and devoted herself in every way to his interests. No doubt she enjoyed her self-sacrifice, but the analyst's acceptance of it made it quite impossible for her to solve her own problem: her wish to remain a child and to serve a protective father.

Presents: It is generally agreed that it is usually detrimental for analysts to accept presents during the course of treatment. Although presents may express a genuine gratitude, they may also be bribes, designed to obtain reciprocal special favors from the analyst. Occasionally, if patients offer creative work (for example, books they have written), it may be hurtful to refuse and better to accept such gifts, provided they are not of any great commercial worth. It is also permissible to accept modest gifts when analysis is terminated. The giving of such tokens may have the positive effect of making the patient feel on more equal terms — that he, too, has something to give.

Prolongation of Analysis: Some analyses go on for many years without achieving much in the way of therapeutic benefit. If the patient is rich, he may not mind paying the analyst's fees for many years; it is obvious that such an arrangement may suit an analyst who is short of money or else grasping. Some analysts, usually unwittingly rather than deliberately, encourage the dependency of patients and fail to interpret this aspect of the patient's behavior, ensuring that the patient goes on obtaining gratification for his dependent needs rather than becoming self reliant.

Obsessional Analysts: No analysis is ever perfect, but some analysts are sufficiently obsessional to want their analyses to be so and therefore encourage their patients to pursue analysis long after maximum therapeutic benefit has been achieved. Patients who collaborate in this kind of analysis are usually themselves obsessionals. One analyst was convinced that, at some early stage of his childhood, his patient had been the subject of a homosexual assault, the memory of which he had entirely repressed. The analyst was sure that if only his patient could recall this incident, his neurotic problems would be solved. They therefore pursued this will-o'-the-wisp for many years. Obsessional patients are often "good" patients, who keep their appointments, pay their bills promptly, and appear to be extremely cooperative. Since they are often anxious to pursue analysis so no stone of their psychopathology is left unturned, it is easy for the analyst to lose objectivity, acquiesce in their indefinite attendance, and fail to see that they are actually failing to make progress.

Sexual Exploitation: Since Masters and Johnson have taken it upon themselves to provide sexual partners for some of their patients,[3] the idea that analysts sometimes become sexually involved with their patients is no longer as shocking as it used to be. However, there are powerful reasons why analysts should not have sexual relations with their patients. First, if the analyst is medically qualified, he is running the risks consequent upon infringement of medical code of ethics. Second, however much the analyst may deceive himself into thinking that sexual experience with him might be good for his patient, the reverse is almost always the case. One psychiatrist could not bear the distress of his female patients, and would put his arms round them to comfort them. This soon led to sexual involvements. The psychiatrist thought that he was helping his patients by offering them love and did not realize that he was using the therapeutic situation as a way of gaining sexual gratification for himself without the risk of being rejected. He was a diffident man who, besides being frightened of being rejected by women in ordinary life, was reluctant to assume the responsibilities that generally follow upon sexual involvement between peers.

From the patient's point of view, sexual involvement with the analyst is generally harmful because it raises hopes of a continuing relationship that are usually doomed to disappointment. It is also often a repetition or acting-out of a situation that is at the heart of the patient's problem. Many patients entering analysis do so because they cannot free themselves from oedipal ties and thus cannot form adequate sexual or other relationships with their peers. The analyst, because of the transference projections upon him, is bound to be in a parental role to some extent. Combining a sexual role with that of a parent compounds the patient's problem and makes it much more difficult for her to form attachments to persons who are not in a "special" relationship with her. In other words, sexual intercourse between analyst and patient is incestuous in spirit if not in fact and effectively prevents the patient from resolving the transference and getting on with life. Both analysts and patients sometimes want to make analysis into a substitute for life, which it can never be.

Emotional Attitudes Toward Patients That Promote Progress

Research has established that analysts need to be capable of genuine concern and warmth toward their patients. The stereotype of the remote, olympian analyst who is quite unaffected by anything his patient says to him is not only false but outmoded. Warm acceptance facilitates personality change.

Analysts can learn to use their own countertransference feelings as useful information. Irritation with a patient, sexual feelings toward a patient, special hopes or interest, may all be revealing not only the analyst's psychopathology (which he ought, of course, to be aware of) but also of the patient's. For the analyst's emotional response is a response to something the patient is doing or feeling—something of which the patient may be quite unconscious. Good analysts become adept at using their own countertransference emotions as thermometers reflecting the patient's state. Patients who are latent psychotics often arouse very uneasy responses in their analysts, and these may be treated as warning signs that the patient is more disturbed than has hitherto been apparent.

What is the "correct" attitude toward the patient in analysis? There is obviously no one correct attitude that can be adopted as a professional stance by every analyst. Indeed, adopting an attitude can be a pretense that is soon seen through by the patient. There is, in fact, no substitute for genuine concern; but it is a concern that differs from that we show to friends in trouble. With friends, we are merely involved in support and sympathy. With patients, analysts are also concerned with the possibility of personality change and with pointing out how the patient has become embroiled in a particular form of trouble and how he may be contributing to it himself. Of course, not all misfortunes are of the patient's own making, but the analyst must always be alert to that possibility and may make interpretations demonstrating that the patient's way of dealing with calamity may not be the only one or even appropriate.

C. G. Jung wrote:

If the doctor wants to guide another, or even accompany him a step of the way, he must *feel* with that person's psyche. He never feels it when he passes judgment. Whether he puts his judgments into words, or keeps them to himself, makes not the slightest difference. To take the opposite position, and to agree with the patient offhand, is also of no use, but estranges him as much as condemnation. Feeling comes only through unprejudiced objectivity. This sounds almost like a scientific precept, and it could be confused with a purely intellectual, abstract attitude of mind. But what I mean is something quite different. It is a human quality—a kind of deep respect for the facts, for the man who suffers from them, and for the riddle of such a man's life.[4]

Although this passage of Jung's conveys to most people what the attitude of the analyst should be, it is clear that Jung's "unprejudiced objectivity" is underpinned with a respect for the individual human being that is not wholly unprejudiced or entirely objective. What he is postulating is something very similar to Carl Rogers' "unconditional positive regard." Both Jung and Rogers believe that the analyst should be on the patient's side, however much he may dislike some of the things the patient does or says. It is well known that analysts tend to overvalue their patients, just as parents overvalue their children. It is almost inevitable that analysts have some degree of irrational prejudice in favor of those whom they come to know so intimately. This seems to be a part of countertransference that not only is inevitable but also may be a therapeutic factor of considerable importance. What is more important in life than believing that, whatever one's character or problems, there is at least one person who is unequivocally on one's side?

References

1. Freud S: *Standard Edition of the Complete Psychological Works*, Vol. 11, ed. 2, Strachey J (transl.-ed.), Hogarth Press, London, 1953, pp. 144–145.

2. Freud S: *Standard Edition of the Complete Psychological Works*, Vol. 12, ed. 2, Strachey J (transl.-ed.), Hogarth Press, London, 1953, pp. 159–171.

3. Masters WH, Johnson VE: *Human Sexual Inadequacy*, Little, Brown & Company, Boston, 1970.

4. Jung CG: *Collected Works*, Vol. 11, Routledge and Kegan Paul, London, 1932, pp. 338–339.

Further Reading

Winnicott DW: Hate in the countertransference. In *Collected Papers*, Tavistock, London, 1958.

Heimann P: On countertransference. *Int. J. Psychoanal.* 31, 1950.

Little M: Countertransference and the patient's response to it. *Int. J. Psychoanal.* 32, 1951.

Reich A: On countertransference. *Int. J. Psychoanal.* 32, 1951.

Gitelson M: The emotional position of the analyst in the psycho-analytic situation. *Int. J. Psychoanal.* 33, 1952.

Money-Kyrle RE: Normal countertransference and some of its deviations. *Int. J. Psychoanal.* 37, 1956.

Racker H: Transference and countertransference. The International Psycho-Analytical Library No. 73, Hogarth Press and Institute of Psycho-Analysis, London, 1968.

Storr A: Objectivity and intimate knowledge. Ch. 7 in *The Art of Psychotherapy*. Methuen, New York, 1980.

8

Listening Processes in Psychotherapy

Fraser N. Watts

EDITOR'S NOTE

Listening constitutes a central activity in all psychotherapy, yet it may often be skewed or faulty and thus impede correct evaluation of a patient and progress in treatment. Here the author explores some current psychological investigations into the nature of listening, pointing out how these may prove valuable to the psychotherapist.

He asks, for example, why it is sometimes so difficult to grasp the meaning of what a particular patient may be saying. Perhaps the patient has little previous experience in articulating emotional experiences, or he may lack the concepts necessary to grasp their significance. For a variety of reasons, such as embarrassment, his motivation to communicate may be ambivalent. A distinction is made between manifest content and latent content. He cautions that manifest content may not be as easily attended to as most people would assume; the influence of what the psychotherapist expects to hear can readily cloud the objectivity of his listening. Paying too much attention to one aspect of communication—latent as opposed to manifest, for example—sets the stage for missing important cues and often for inferring the presence of attitudes or feelings that are not really there.

Knowing the signs of critical moments in therapy is essential. A change of voice quality, altered movement and posture, moments of unintelligibility, and novel metaphors are a few such clues.

To the question of whether the therapist should engage in active or passive listening, the obvious answer—too often ignored in practice—is that it depends on the patient and on the phase of therapy taking place.

Introduction

How psychotherapists listen to their patients has attracted surprisingly little attention in the extensive literature on psychotherapy. Theodor Reik's *Listening with the Third Ear*[1] is still a classic, yet the time may now be ripe to progress with this important topic. Major recent advances in cognitive psychology that are concerned with general processes involved in understanding language and acquiring knowledge[2] provide the framework for a formulation of the listening skills of the psychotherapist. A number of authors[3-5] have recently approached psychotherapeutic listening from this point of view. The cognitive processes involved in psychotherapeutic listening are very complex, and it must be admitted that there has been very little direct investigation of these processes.

Patients' Language

Before considering how psychotherapists should listen to patients, it will be helpful to note the properties of patients' speech. Like most impromptu spoken language, it will frequently be unclear or ambiguous, but for several reasons there may be particular difficulties in understanding patients in psychotherapy.

First, patients will try, at least sometimes, to express things that are at the boundaries of their conscious awareness and of which they have little previous experience articulating.

Second, some patients will systematically lack the concepts necessary to grasp the significance of important aspects of their experience. Psychosomatic patients, for example, have been said to have poorly developed emotional concepts.

Third, the patients' motivations to communicate may be ambivalent. Important material may be embarrassing to disclose, and the patients' attitudes to disclosure may fluctuate depending on the state of their relationships with the therapist.

Last, the material that eventually needs to be presented (the linking of current relationships and concerns, an autobiography from infancy onwards, and the therapeutic relationship) is extremely complex. Information hinted at can only be properly understood in the light of other material. Sometimes this other necessary material will not have been presented at all. At other times the therapist will need to relate a single statement of the patient to a great deal of scattered material that was previously revealed in order to make sense of the statement. This point is underscored in a masterly study of therapeutic disclosure,[6] in which one of the principal methods discussed was how a single remark of the patient needed to be expanded to include extensive material from many other statements if its implicit meaning was to be fully explicated.

All this emphasizes the difficulty of comprehending the psychotherapeutic patient. The main factor to set against this is that the patient normally has a basic need and wish to be understood. Partly because of this, and partly through involuntary processes, important material is likely to be repeated. Patients usually give their therapists more than one chance to grasp an important point.

Manifest and Latent Content

The primary question concerning how therapists should listen is to what extent should a therapist accept at face value what the patient says. Psychotherapists have often made a distinction between the manifest content of what the patient says (i.e., its ostensible, surface meaning) and its latent content (i.e., the unconscious themes that can be discerned beneath the surface meaning). How should therapists divide their attention between manifest and latent content?

Manifest Content: The first point to make is that attending accurately to manifest content is not nearly as easy as many assume. Shapiro,[7] in an important paper on assessment interviewing, has provided an excellent exposition of the problems. The most substantial body of relevant empirical information comes from studies of listening deficiencies in opinion survey interviews. It confirms that the expectations of interviewers determine what they think they have heard. Particularly interesting are some of the factors that affect interviewers' errors in recording responses accurately. Ambiguous statements present particular problems, and are likely to be either omitted or distorted in the interviewers' accounts of what was said. Another finding, which will surprise no psychotherapist, is that behavior stressful to the interviewers results in their making more listening errors. However, it may also be salutary for psychotherapists to know that errors are high among interviewers who are oriented toward creating a good interpersonal relationship rather than to addressing the task in hand.

We do not really know how far such findings of inaccuracies in nonclinical interviews are paralleled by similar deficiencies in psychotherapists. How much the progress of psychotherapy is impeded if a therapist misunderstands what the patient has said is an open question. However, the provisional conclusion must be that errors in listening to surface content are easy to make and are probably quite common.

Reading Between the Lines: It is not sufficient in psychotherapy just to attend to the manifest content of what patients say. This follows from the assumption that material that is central to the patient's problem and has particular anxiety attached to it is unlikely to be produced easily. So, if the therapist is not to miss issues that are really important to a particular patient he will need to learn to "read between the lines" of what is actually said.

Spence[8] has provided some very elegant evidence that illustrates one way in which the patients' underlying concerns may be revealed under camouflage. In studying the words used by patients suspected of cancer, he found that the word "death" was commonly heard among patients whose diagnosis of cancer was subsequently confirmed. Many uses of the word occurred in contexts that had no obvious connection with illness (e.g., "I was tickled to death"), and such usages would have been missed by a therapist attending only to manifest content. Spence coined the term "lexical leakage" to describe this phenomenon. We do not know how common it is, but it is only one of many ways in which unconscious concerns emerge in camouflaged ways in patients' speech.

Risks in Listening Strategies: Before looking in further detail at other ways in which latent material can manifest itself, and the strategies psychotherapists can use in listening for it, we must consider the different kinds of risks associated with attending to manifest and latent content. Exclusive attention to manifest content may result in the therapist's missing important material. On the other hand, an overeager search for latent content carries with it the opposite risk: the therapist may think he has identified important unconscious themes that are not actually present.[9] The possibility of such an error occurring, and the difficulty of checking for it, seem to have been seriously underestimated by psychotherapists.

For example, a therapist may pick up a range of cues that could indicate hostility. Sometimes the cues he has discerned will really represent hostility, other times they won't. It is rather like listening to a poor quality radio and trying to distinguish between real signals and background noise. This analogy with signal detection, which has been extensively used in psychology, will help us here. Two very different factors can result in a listener picking up genuine signals of hostility more often. One is a real improvement in his acuity, i.e., in his capacity to distinguish between genuine hostility and misleading "noise" that does not indicate hostility. The other possible factor is simply that the listener has lowered his criterion for what he accepts as a signal of hostility. He may simply have decided to accept almost anything as a signal of hostility. This would result in his picking up more correct signals of hostility, but at the cost of more "false alarms" too — cases in which he thinks he has detected hostility, but is actually mistaken.

There is some disturbing, albeit inconclusive, evidence[9] that as psychotherapists improve their ability to detect signals of hidden themes such as hostility, the improvement might be done partly by lowering their criterion for what they accept as a signal rather than by improving their ability to distinguish true signals from background noise. This problem arises because people, psychiatrists included, tend to base confidence in their judgment on the number of times they are right and take little notice of the number of times they are wrong. In the example of hostility, therapists' confidence may be inflated by the increasing number of times they correctly recognize hostility, but may not be correspondingly deflated by the number of mistakes they make.

Listening for Latent Content: Most psychotherapists develop rules, which are often only implicit, to help them listen for important concerns of patients that may be only latent in what they say. Such rules fall into two main groups. Some simply alert the therapist to moments in therapy when important material may be close to the surface. Others can be used as a more direct guide to the patients' assumptions and preoccupations. The next two sections contain an illustrative list of such implicit rules, largely drawn from papers by Peterfreund,[4] Rice,[10] and Watts.[5] It should be noted, however, that in many cases we have no scientific evidence to indicate whether or not these are good rules for psychotherapists to use.

Important Moments in Therapy

Several cues can alert therapists to the fact that the patient may be touching on something of particular importance. They are not infallible, but they indicate moments when the therapist should listen with unusual care.

Voice Quality: The tone of voice that patients use is one of the best indicators of how emotionally involved they are at any particular point in a therapy session. Rice and Wagstaff[11] have reported important research findings on voice quality as an indication of productive periods in a psychotherapy session. Rice[11] describes the kind of "focused" voice involved thus: There is a kind of voice quality that seems to indicate an inner focus on something that is being seen or felt freshly. Sometimes in the midst of a long client discussion expressed in a highly externalizing voice quality one hears just a small blip of focused voice. The voice slows, softens without losing energy, pauses, and loses the "premonitored" quality of the externalizing voice. This should be an indicator to the therapist that this part might be heard and responded to.

Movement and Posture: Related aspects of posture and movement can help alert the therapist to important material, including shifts in body posture, sudden changes in direction of gaze, and signs of increased physical tension.

Moments of Unintelligibility: The therapist should be alert for times when the patient says something that the therapist does not understand. This may be a cue that the patient is struggling to articulate something of emotional significance that is difficult to grasp consciously. A related cue is when the patient's affect is not appropriate to what he says.

Sequence: Just as the therapist should attend carefully to things he does not understand, so he should note carefully abrupt changes of topic in which no logical connection exists.

Slips of the Tongue: Freud's classic monograph on the psychopathology of everyday life[12] drew attention to the significance of slips of the tongue. They help to alert the therapist to topics that may be emotionally important. Peterfreund[4] gives an example of a patient who had had a vasectomy speaking first of being "still sterile," then correcting it to "again sterile," when he actually meant "now sterile."

Novel Metaphors: Important moments in therapy are associated with the patient's use of novel or unusual metaphors. Pollio et al.[13] have provided convincing evidence that moments of insight are associated with the use of novel metaphors, though trite or "frozen" metaphors are hardly ever used at such moments. Rice[10] has drawn attention, for example, to the unusual use of sensory words such as a patient speaking of a "stretched" smile on the face.

Assumptions and Preoccupations

Some of these listening rules also help therapists grasp important themes in patients' material. The sequence in which topics are raised can be an important clue to their significance. Slips of the tongue may reveal unconscious thoughts. Novel metaphors, besides alerting the patient to important moments in therapy, can reveal idiosyncratic concepts that may be important in understanding the patients' experience and psychopathology. There are other aspects of the patients' language that reveal such concepts.

Conjunctions of Adjectives: The conjunctions that link the adjectives used in describing an important person are often revealing. Listen, for example, to whether a patient talks about people being "strong and loving" or "gentle and loving" and you can see what assumption he makes about how these qualities are related. Kelly[14] has argued powerfully for the importance of such "personal constructs" in explaining personal development.

Evaluative Terms: Evaluations — favorable or unfavorable — expressed by a patient often reveal important assumptions and personal needs also. Expressions of criticism are often richer in content than are expressions of approval.

Frequency of Topics: Topics that the patient uses frequently are likely to be important too. Therapists, therefore, listen carefully to the frequency with which a topic comes up, as well as what is said about it. For example, if a patient frequently raises the topic of hostility but denies that it is a problem, the therapist would begin to suspect otherwise.

Frequency of Words: In addition to topics, the therapist will attend to what words are used with unusual frequency. The previously described research on lexical leakage by Spence[3] makes the point that important concerns can manifest themselves in frequent use of a word such as "death."

Listening for Particular Content Categories: The areas of content that are particularly important probably vary from one kind of presenting problem to another, and from one stage of therapy to another. The therapist may, therefore, adopt a strategy of attending very closely to material of a certain kind. Hedges[15] has recently published a survey of four therapeutic approaches in terms of the listening focus on which they are based. The listening perspectives she considers correspond roughly to the psychotic, borderline, narcissistic, and neurotic categories of patients. The experienced therapist develops an ability to focus on material that is believed to be relevant to a particular kind of psychological problem.

Active vs. Passive Listening Strategies

What is perhaps the most fundamental issue about listening in psychotherapy has been left until last: Should the therapist be active in listening out selectively for certain kinds of material and relate it to his emerging formulation of the patient or should he simply maintain what Freud called "evenly-suspended" or "free-floating" attention.

Working Models: Peterfreund[4] has provided a statement of the active approach to psychotherapeutic listening, centered around the concept of a "working model." Working models encapsulate information that has been acquired about a particular topic, shape our perceptions by sensitizing us to some events rather than others and giving form and structure to our perceptions, and guide our responses, making possible prediction, action, and other adaptive functions. Working models are continually updated as new information becomes available. Such a concept is an accepted feature of contemporary cognitive psychology,[2] though it goes under a variety of names ("schema" being one of the most common) and is defined in a variety of ways. However, there is general agreement that an important aspect of the comprehension of linguistic material is its relationship to internal cognitive structures such as "working models."

With this in mind, Peterfreund proposes that the analyst develop a series of working models to underpin his professional work, one of these being the model of the individual patient (though this would be based in part on more general models of the development of psychopathology, etc.). Once a model of a patient has begun to develop, it can be used to structure the listening process. One simple use is to distinguish old material that has already been incorporated into the model from new material that may require a revision of the model. Information will also be categorized according to its relevance to the model, and irrelevant information ignored. In general, material that is consistent with internal models is better remembered than incongruent information, though there may be exceptions to this rule.[5] This is worrisome because it may result in the therapist's clinging to a prematurely formulated model of the patient's pathology when an open-minded and unselective evaluation of the material available would lead to its being rejected or radically modified. Finally, material tends to be distorted so that it agrees better with the model. This is probably what accounts for many of the mistakes that were noted in the discussion of listening to manifest content. All these consequences of working models, or schemata, for the perception and comprehension of linguistic material have been well established as general principles.[2] So far there has been no satisfactory empirical investigation of whether they apply to listening processes in psychotherapy, though it seems reasonable to assume that they do.

"Evenly-Suspended" Attention: It is an interesting fact that Freud anticipated many of these issues, even though they had not yet been demonstrated by modern scientific methods, and he discussed their consequences for psychotherapy. In the series of lectures known as "Recommendations to Physicians Practising Psychoanalysis,"[16] he said:

For as soon as anyone deliberately concentrates his attention to a certain degree, he begins to select from the material before him . . . and in making this selection he will be following his expectations or inclinations. . . . In making the selection, if he follows his expectations he is in danger of never finding anything but what he already knows; and if he follows his inclinations he will certainly falsify what he may perceive.

Equally interesting is Freud's solution to this problem, which is that the therapist should adopt a style of "evenly-suspended" or "free-floating" attention, which "consists simply in not directing one's notice to anything in particular and maintaining the same 'evenly suspended attention' (as I have called it) in the face of all that one hears."[16] He adds that " . . . this rule of giving equal notice to everything is the necessary counterpart to the demand made on the patient that he should communicate everything that occurs to him without criticism or selection."

This concept of evenly-suspended attention has been discussed at length by Reik.[1] The contemporary psychoanalytic theorist, Bion,[17] has developed a similar concept of attention "without memory or desire."

It can be seen that there might be a number of advantages in this strategy. One that Freud does not explicitly mention is that it might be of help in reducing the impossible cognitive burden that would fall on a therapist who tried, in an open-minded way, to consider all possible formulations of the material available to him and the implications of everything the patient said. Attempts to do this consciously and rationally would simply break down, because the amount of information processing required would quickly exceed capacity. Freud's concept of evenly-suspended attention probably involves processing much material "preconsciously" rather than consciously, thus bypassing the point (i.e., consciousness) at which constraints on processing capacity are most severe.

However, it is questionable whether adopting this kind of rather passive, unselective processing strategy in fact reduces selections and distortions due to "expectations" and "inclinations." While it might do so, it is also possible that evenly-suspended attention would increase the amount of distortion of material that took place. It may do nothing to prevent distortion to accord with the therapist's working model of the patient but instead could simply reduce the level of conscious vigilance against such distortion.

Finally, it is doubtful whether it is realistic for a psychotherapist to follow Freud's advice, or indeed whether Freud himself did so. Evenly-suspended attention would make it very difficult for the therapist to develop a coherent formulation of the patient's psychopathology or even to remember the material, because memory is largely dependent on contact between incoming material and mental "working models." Later in the same lecture to physicians, Freud acknowledges the difficulty a psychotherapist encounters when recalling at will a patient's material. However, he argues that the material that arises serves to aid recall of related material revealed previously, a process now known as "cued" recall.

Two Stages: Freud's declared strategy of evenly-suspended attention does not carry conviction if taken to extremes or used as a sole listening strategy, though most would agree that it has a place alongside a more active approach to listening. The relative importance of the two concepts may depend in part on the stage of therapy, and many would accept the suggestion (made, for example, by Langs[18]) that psychotherapeutic listening goes through two phases. In the first phase, evenly-suspended attention has its place, and the psychotherapist needs to be unguarded in his receptiveness to primary processes and to make full use of his unconscious sensitivities. However, this approach needs to be superseded by a second phase that, while retaining a degree of unguardedness, relies fundamentally on cognitive efforts at organization and formulation.

References

1. Reik T: *Listening with the Third Ear*, Farrar Straus, New York, 1948.

2. Bransford JD: *Human Cognition: Learning, Understanding and Remembering*, Wadsworth, Belmont, Calif., 1979.

3. Spence DP, Lugo M: The role of verbal cues in clinical listening. In Holt RR, Peterfruend E (Eds.): *Psychoanalysis and Contemporary Science*, Volume I, Macmillan, London, 1972.

4. Peterfreund E: How does the analyst listen? On models and strategies in the psychoanalytic process. In Spence DP (Ed.): *Psychoanalysis and Contemporary Science*, Volume IV, International Universities Press, New York, 1975.

5. Watts FN: Strategies of clinical listening. *Br. J. Med. Psychol.* 56:113–123, 1983.

6. Labov W, Fanschel D: *Therapeutic Discourse: Psychotherapy as Conversation*, Academic Press, New York, 1977.

7. Shapiro MB: Assessment interviewing in clinical psychology. *Br. J. Soc. Clin. Psychol.* 18:211–218, 1979.

8. Spence DP: Lawfulness in lexical choice—a natural experiment. *J. Am. Psychoanal. Assoc.* 28:115–132, 1980.

9. Watts FN: Clinical judgment and clinical training. *Br. J. Med. Psychol.* 53:95–108, 1980.

10. Rice LN: A client-centered approach to the supervision of psychotherapy. In Hess AK (Ed.): *Psychotherapy Supervision: Theory, Research and Practice*, John Wiley & Sons, New York, 1980.

11. Rice LN, Wagstaff AK: Client voice quality and expressive style as indices of productive psychotherapy. *J. Consult. Clin. Psychol.* 31:557–563, 1967.

12. Freud S: The psychopathology of everyday life. In Strachey J (Trans.): *Standard Edition*, Volume VI, Hogarth, London, 1958.

13. Pollio HR, Barlow JM, Fine HJ, Pollio MR: *Psychology and the Poetics of Growth*, Erlbaum, Hillsdale, N.J., 1977.

14. Kelly GA: *The Psychology of Personal Constructs*, Norton, New York, 1955.

15. Hedges LE: *Listening Perspectives in Psychotherapy*, Jason Aronson, New York, 1983.

16. Freud S: Recommendations to physicians practising psychoanalysis. In Strachey J (Trans.): *Standard Edition*, Volume XII, Hogarth, London, 1958.

17. Bion WR: *Attention and Interpretation*, Tavistock, London, 1970.

18. Langs R: *The Listening Process*, Jason Aronson, New York, 1968.

9

The Rorschach
Part I: Psychoanalytic Theoretical Implications
Michael Joseph Miller

EDITOR'S NOTE

The Rorschach test is one of the most commonly used and valuable diagnostic adjuncts available to us, not only to determine the nature of a patient's psychopathology, but to secure important data regarding personality structure and pertinent psychodynamic issues as well. In this chapter, and the one following, the author reviews the history of the development of the Rorschach, pointing out the central role the projection mechanism plays in the test's execution.

The Rorschach test consists of ten ink blots of which five are achromatic and five have color. The examination consists of two phases — the performance proper and the inquiry. During the first stage, the examiner, without comment or question, hands the blots to the patient one at a time and in no preordained order; the patient is given the opportunity to produce his own spontaneous responses. During the inquiry stage, the examiner refers to each response and asks the patient to explain, if he can, how he arrived at his impressions.

The Rorschach is especially sensitive to the patient's fantasy life. It is also a highly effective way to ascertain his ability to deal with the phenomenon of regression. Freud defined regression as a shift of attention from the outer to the inner world, from words to pictorial representations, from the reality principle to the pleasure principle, from ego activity to ego passivity, from the adult to the infantile. Regression is essentially a return to an earlier, more primitive, archaic mode of personality functioning. It is a universal experience; under stress, many people temporarily revert from secondary process operations to primary process ones, as the more logical thinking mechanisms give way to more unrealistic, personalized, egocentric, and emotionally charged ones. Regression in the service of the ego, as defined by Kris, has a definite beginning and end, is completely reversible, and is a function of successful adaptation to stress or change. The ability to regress and return from episodes of regression are an inherent part of the creative process; this is also a *sine qua non* for the patient who can successfully undergo traditional psychoanalysis. Extreme and fixed states of regression are seen in many schizophrenic patients.

How an individual deals with regressive differences, as shown during Rorschach examination, can tell us a great deal about a patient's psychopathological state and overall personality integration.

Historical Background

In 1911, a promising young Swiss medical student, Hermann Rorschach (1884–1922), began experimenting with inkblots in the examination of mental patients. After completing his psychiatric residency and after some ten years of inkblot experimentation, Dr. Rorschach published his findings in his book *Psychodiagnostik*.[1] This gifted psychiatrist, prematurely dead at the age of 38, introduced, in this one short monograph, a projective technique that became the inspiration of an entire discipline of clinical practitioners engaged in the study of personality and psychopathology. His contribution was most provocative, the result of a deeply probing mind.

In the words of his colleague, friend, and editor, Dr. W. Morgenthaler, Rorschach possessed the characteristics so necessary and valuable to a psychiatrist:

Flexibility of character, rapid adaptability, fine acumen, and a sense for the practical were combined in Hermann Rorschach with a talent for introspection and synthesis. . . . In addition to this rare nature, which tempered personal emotional experience with practical knowledge, he possessed sound traits of character, . . . an unerring tendency to search for the truth, a strict critical faculty which he did not hesitate to apply to himself, and a warmth of feeling, and kindness [Epilogue, *Psychodiagnostics*].[1]

Armed with these personal attributes and a serious dedication of purpose to the study of personality through perception of inkblots, Rorschach ushered in the world of projective techniques. However, neither the inkblot technique itself nor the idea behind the technique was completely original with him. As Z. Piotrowski[2] notes: "Interest in the possible meaning of vague, indefinite and ambiguous visual phenomena is as old as humanity."

In antiquity, Greek artists developed a practice of throwing a sponge, soaked in different colors, at a canvas or wall in order to create spontaneously derived imagery. During the Renaissance, Leonardo da Vinci (1452–1519) drew attention to the link between such accidentally created graphic forms and subjective imagination. In his use of paint blots, he reported that "various experiences can be seen in such a blot, provided one wants to find them in it — human heads, various animals, bottles, cliffs, seas, clouds or forests and other things. . . . "[3] Leonardo went on to use paint-blot responses in his evaluation of aspiring pupils. "All that is good or inferior in you, will appear in the corresponding parts of your figures."[2]

During the 19th and early 20th centuries, a number of thinkers and psychologists began to use inkblots. In 1857, Justinus Kerner (1786–1862) used inkblots to stimulate the mind. In 1895, Alfred Binet (1857–1911) suggested use of inkblots as a method of studying individual differences in personality. In 1898, George V. Dearborn recognized that inkblot responses could reveal complex traits of personal functioning. At about the same time, Sharp and Kirkpatrick of Harvard University published their results of children's reactions to inkblots.

Although these psychologists recognized the usefulness of inkblots, they were not fully cognizant of the implicit idea behind the technique—that is, the idea of projection. The anticipation of the "projective hypothesis" came from a completely different source. It is to German philosophy—in particular the work of Friedrich Nietzsche (1844–1900)—that the origins of projection can be traced. Nietzsche, in his writings on "perspectivism" (*The Will to Power*),[4] drew attention to the extent to which our interpretations of the world are unlimited, symptomatic, need-determined, and (to put it in one word) projective:

No limit to the ways in which the world can be interpreted; every interpretation a symptom. . . .

It cannot be doubted that all sense perceptions are permeated with value judgments.

Ultimately, man finds in things nothing but what he himself has imported into them.

It is our needs that interpret the world; our drives and their For and Against. We have learned that sense impressions naively supposed to be conditioned by the outer world are, on the contrary, conditioned by the inner world.

. . . Sense perceptions [are] projected "outside." . . .

Neitzche's contribution to our understanding of projection cannot be overestimated. Yet he was not alone. Not long after he had put down these thoughts on paper, another contributor was to come along to provide a further elucidation and elaboration on this most important of psychological phenomena. Beginning in the 1890s, Sigmund Freud was already making reference to projection as a form of defense. By 1911, the very year in which Rorschach was initiating his inkblot experimentation, Freud presented this concept of projection as a defense in a specific case, the Schreber case. In the same case study, he also drew attention to the notion of projection as a natural human phenomenon to be found in a variety of normal circumstances:

The most striking characteristic of symptom-information in paranoia is the process which deserves the name of projection. An internal perception is suppressed, and, instead, its content, after undergoing a certain degree of distortion, enters consciousness in the form of an external perception. In delusions of persecution the distortion consists in a transformation of affect; what should have been felt internally as love is perceived externally as hate. We should feel tempted to regard this remarkable process as the most important element in paranoia and as being absolutely pathognomonic for it, if we were not opportunely reminded of two things. For, in the first place, projection does not play the same part in all forms of paranoia; and, in the second place, it makes its appearance not only in paranoia but under other psychological conditions as well, and in fact it has a regular share assigned to it in our attitude towards the external world. For when we refer the causes of certain sensations to the external world, instead of looking for them (as we do in the case of the others) inside ourselves, this normal proceeding also deserves to be called projection[5] [p. 66, S.E.].

These twin ideas of projection have stood the test of time. Although clinical practitioners have sometimes confused one with the other, and although a full theoretical elaboration of the relationship between the two has yet to be developed, both notions of projection have proved themselves to be pregnant with clinical possibility.

Projection as a defense has contributed much to our understanding of psychopathology, in general, and paranoidal pathology, in particular. And projection conceived as a mode of human behavior has provided us with the theoretical underpinning of projective techniques, in general, and the Rorschach, in particular. Although neither Nietzsche nor Freud nor, for that matter, Rorschach introduced the term "projective technique" into the literature, the phrase itself is considerably indebted to their work. Actually, it was not introduced until 1939, when Lawrence Frank published his paper "Projective Methods for the Study of Personality." Yet the term, though late in coming, clearly rests upon the concept of projection. This idea of projection was there before Rorschach, although the method was not. And those who had previously used inkblots had the method but not the idea. It remained for Hermann Rorschach to explicitly couple the method to the idea, the inkblot to projection. In one simple stroke, he gave us a tool to systematically study personality projections—the Rorschach inkblot test.

The Rorschach Inkblot Test Procedure

The Rorschach test procedure consists of a set of ten inkblots (five achromatic and five in which color is combined in part or all of the blot). The ten nearly symmetrical inkblot designs are individually printed and centered on a piece of white cardboard about 7 by 9½ inches. Although there is no standard formulation for introducing the cards, the usual procedure is to invite the patient to tell you what he sees. For example,

People see all sorts of things in these inkblot pictures; now tell me what you see, what it might be for you, what it makes you think of. There are no right or wrong answers. Take as long or as short a time as you please. You can see as many or as few things as you want. It's up to you.[6]

The examination consists of two phases: the performance proper and the inquiry. In the performance proper, the examiner, without comment or question, hands the blots to the patient, one at a time, and the patient is given every opportunity to produce his responses as spontaneously as possible. Upon completion of all ten inkblots, the examiner returns to all of the patient's responses, beginning with the first card, in order to conduct an inquiry to determine how the patient arrived at his spontaneous responses.

Implicit in this Rorschach invitation of perceptual spontaneity is the assumption of perceptual selectivity on the basis of personality. Presented with ambiguous, indeterminate stimuli of varying forms, colors, and shades, the patient is encouraged to freely select visual images according to his own personality predilections and preferences. There are no directions to see anything in particular. There are no specific expectations. Rationality is not encouraged; nor is logic; nor is conscious effort. This relaxation of logical thinking is designed to get at the patient's spontaneous play of associations. The focus on an external task is an attempt to deflect the patient's awareness away from self. Ignorant of personality traits elicited, he is more likely to reveal such traits. Such a relaxation of selfconsciousness permits a free flow of visual imagery.

The Rorschach, in its activation of imagination, is particularly sensitive to the patient's fantasy life. Such fantasies, wishes, visual images, imaginative play of ideas, free associations, etc., are the very "stuff" of Rorschach protocols. They, too, are the concern of psychoanalytic theory. Both Rorschach technique and psychoanalytic theory assume that these perceptual manifestations of the inner life are guided by—and, therefore, revelatory of—personality. Both technique and theory are one in their sensitivity to such personality phenomena. Although the technique is simple, the theory is demanding. A psychoanalytic appreciation of the Rorschach requires careful study of a few select concepts. These psychoanalytic concepts, although small in number, have very large implications for both theory and applicability of the Rorschach.

Psychoanalytic Theory

Perhaps it is no accident that in the very year Rorschach was initiating inkblot experimentation (1911), Freud was publishing his psychoanalytic understanding of projection. Rorschach was well acquainted with psychoanalytic theory. Such central concepts as regression and the primary process had already been introduced by Freud to the psychiatric world. Although Rorschach might not have been cognizant of the full implications of such psychoanalytic concepts for his work and although Rorschach rejected the use of his technique as a tool for probing unconscious content, he was well aware of a certain kinship to psychoanalytic theory. He did make explicit reference to psychoanalysis in his publications.

This relationship between Rorschach methodology and Freudian theory has become closer over the years. In addition to projection, Freud's concepts of regression and the primary process, with Kris's elaboration of regression in the service of the ego, are central contributions to a psychoanalytic understanding of the Rorschach.

Regression

The psychoanalytic concept of regression was first introduced by Freud (1900) in his *Interpretation of Dreams*,[7] in which he distinguished three forms:

1. Reversal of sequence impulse, motor discharge to the sequence impulse, hallucination.
2. Formal regression, in which the psychic apparatus functions on a more primitive level.
3. Regression in remembered time to earlier stages of development.

Freud used these conceptions of regression to describe the general shift of attention from the outer to the inner world, from words to pictorial representation, from the reality principle to the pleasure principle, from ego activity to ego passivity, from the adult to the infantile, and from concern with the present to concern with the past. Although the initial application of the concept of regression was to the dream process, it was later extended to various forms of psychopathology and to childhood development. Psychic shifts — whether from words to images (as in dreams), from reality relations to autism (as in schizophrenia), or from a socialized level of development to a more primitive level (as in the response to frustration) — are all considered regressive. Essentially, regression is a return, in some measure, to an earlier, more primitive, more archaic mode of personality functioning. As Gill and Brenman[8] put it:

A regressive process is one in which the balance of forces shifts so that freer and more primitive impulses come to expression, while the control system likewise becomes more primitive and relatively less stringent and determining of the course of psychic life vis-à-vis the impulses [p. 106].

Although, originally, such regressive shifts were specifically discussed in reference to the processes of the dream, the psychopathological state, and childhood play, they have been recognized as relatively universal phenomena. Schafer[9] has referred to their general applicability to psychic states, ranging from daydreaming to purposeful visualizing, to wit and humor, to artistic creativity and the audience's response to it, to productive fantasy and imaginative processes, to problem solving, to hypnosis, to free association, to the psychotherapeutic process, to the capacity for orgasmic experience, to ego-building identifications, to motherliness, to empathy, to intimacy and love, and, finally, to the Rorschach. In this context, the Rorschach has been considered an invitation to regress in thinking.

Although the thought process is not necessarily indigenous to such regression, it is the process most commonly referred to and most frequently elaborated on in the psychoanalytic discussions of regression, particularly as they relate to the Rorschach. Such regressive thinking is psychoanalytically conceptualized as a process returning to a primary, developmentally earlier psychic mode of thinking. This process, the primary process, has proved to be one of the cornerstones of the psychoanalytic interpretation of the Rorschach.

The Primary Process

So important is the concept of the primary process within psychoanalytic theory that Ernest Jones regarded it as one of the most fundamental of Freud's contributions. He even went so far as to suggest that it was one of his greatest insights, if not *the greatest*.[10] Whether one is in agreement with such an extreme statement or not, the central historical and theoretical position of the primary-process concept within psychoanalysis can be readily conceded. Among the earliest concepts propounded by Freud, the primary-process concept was introduced in 1895, in the unpublished paper "Project for a Scientific Psychology," in which he wrote:

A primary neuronic system, having thus acquired a quantity, employs it only in order to get rid of it through the connecting path leading to the muscular mechanism, and thus keeps itself free from stimulus. This process of discharge is the primary function of the neuronic systems[10] [p. 262].

Building on this early sketch, Freud later, in Chapter VII of *The Interpretation of Dreams* (1900), more fully explicated the conceptual foundations and actual workings of both primary- and secondary-process functioning.

Since Freud, more often than not, relied on economic conceptualizations, his early theoretical statements on the primary and secondary process were usually in economic terms. For example, the primary process, defined in "The Unconscious" (1915), was "mobility of cathexis," whereas the secondary process was the binding of cathexes. This means that the primary process seeks immediate discharge of energy and immediate gratification operating according to the pleasure principles, whereas the secondary process is able to inhibit energy discharge and to delay instinctual gratification operating according to the reality principle. Again, in "The Unconscious," Freud characterized the workings of the primary process in the following economic terms:

By the process of displacement one idea may surrender to another its whole quota of cathexis; by the process of condensation it may appropriate the whole cathexis of several other ideas. I proposed to regard these two processes as distinguishing marks of the so-called "primary psychical process"[10] [p. 264].

The primary process was termed "primary" by Freud, not because it came first chronologically. Developmentally more primitive, more archaic, and more infantile than secondary processing, primary processing is, in its organizing principles, less differentiated, less abstract, less realistic. Its cognitive forms are concrete, its modes of ideation are often visual, its configurational properties are illogical; its organizing principles are "unrealistic," its cognitive activity is fluid and its modes of reasoning are autistic. The "primary processor" does not follow the ordinary rules of logic; he is not bound to realistic limitations of time and space; he may resort to magic, both in image and word; he frequently transforms reality into his own personalized, subjective world. This element of subjectivity is a central criterion of the primary process. The primary processor's organization of experiences is self-centered, personalized, and egocentric. His approach is a self-referential one. He may experience a loss of emotional distance, a loss of self-boundary, a sense of bodily participation, and a confusion of fantasy and reality. He is relatively autistic in functioning and his percepts are fluid, his concepts undiscriminating, his affects loosely controlled, and, finally, his images archaic.

All these workings of the primary process have been subjected to considerable Rorschach study. One direction of study has been the schematic attempt to pinpoint the specific cognitive manifestations of the primary process. The purpose of such an attempt has been to provide a further delineation and elucidation of its workings. Stimulated by Freud's original description (1900) of the three major primary-process mechanisms of condensation, displacement, and symbolization, others have attempted to extend this work. For example, Fliess[8] has suggested that the chief characteristics of the primary process, in addition to the three noted by Freud, are picturization, allusion, representation of the whole through a part, concretization, and representation through opposites. Robert Holt[11-13] has been in the process of developing an elaborate classification scheme serving to identify such Rorschach primary-process manifestations as image fusion, composition, clang association, fragmentation, impressionism, image symbolism, color symbolism, autistic logic, autistic elaboration, perseveration, transformation of percept, self-reference, contradictions, etc.

Such cognitive features, although frequently characteristic of, for example, schizophrenic thinking, are not exclusively so and, in point of fact, may be readily apparent in any of the many regressive states referred to above. The whole point here is that such primary-process manifestations are expressed in a variety of activities, ranging from the creative to the pathological. Holt has been attempting to operationalize the "vital distinction between primary process that serves the ego's adaptive purposes in humorous, scientific and artistic creativity, and primary process that invades the ego to its detriment as a result of decompensated defenses and cognitive controls"[12] (p. 314). Although both expressions of the primary process are conceptualized as regressions, the former is considered to be in the service of the ego.

Regression in the Service of the Ego

Although Freud never made explicit reference to "regression in the service of the ego," he did allude to such a process in his discussion of the workings of the primary process. For example, in relating two such varied activities as joking and dreaming, he implied different purposes achieved by the same primary process. In 1905, he wrote: "The interesting processes of condensation . . . which we have recognized as the core of the technique of verbal jokes, points towards the formation of dreams."[10] Moreover, he went on to suggest that the primary process can be an active, constructive process in the search for pleasure.

The fact that such condensations are sources for a yield of pleasure is far from incompatible with the hypothesis that conditions for their production are easily found in the unconscious. We can, on the contrary, see a reason for the plunge into the unconscious in the circumstance that the pleasure-yielding condensations of which jokes are in need arise there easily. . . . The thought which, with the intention of constructing a joke, plunges into the unconscious is merely seeking there for the ancient dwelling-place of its former play with words . . . [10] [p. 284].

Ernest Kris, stimulated by this discussion of a "jokemaking" regression of the primary process, initiated his own investigation into the regressive process in creativity (1936). Kris observed that such regression

. . . occurs not only when the ego is weak—in sleep, in falling asleep, in fantasy, in intoxication, and in the psychoses—but also during many types of creative processes. This suggested to me years ago that the ego may use the primary process and not only be overwhelmed by it. This idea was rooted in Freud's explanation of wit (1905), according to which a preconscious thought "is entrusted for a moment to unconscious elaboration" and seemed to account for a variety of creative or other inventive processes[14] [p. 312].

   This state of regressive creativity, in which "the ego enrolls the primary process in its service and makes use of it for its purpose," was in 1936 conceptualized by Kris as a "regression in the service of the ego."[14] Although Kris coined the conceptual phrase, he was not alone in his discussion of the phenomenon. In 1939, Hartmann[15] spoke of "regressive adaptation," whereby adaptation may be achieved by way of regression. He wrote: "Even in the productive scientific thinking the detour over irrational elements, the use of visual imagery in general and of symbolic elements, far from being a handicap, may actually be helpful." And "adapted and normal behavior of adult persons is actually achieved by way of regression. . . . We also know that the healthy ego, for certain purposes, has to be able to abandon itself to the id (sleep, intercourse)" [pp. 59–60].
   This promotion of adaptation by way of regression was further described by Schafer (1967), who defined "regression in the service of the ego" as a "partial, temporary, controlled lowering of the level of psychic functioning to promote adaptation"[9] [p. 80]. Such a process is "regressive" in that the more primitive, infantile modes of thought, conceptualized as the primary process, are allowed freer play than is common in everyday waking life; such a process, moreover, is "in the service of the ego" in that the primary process is utilized for adaptive purposes. These regressions are circumscribed; they are small-scale, temporary, and under control. Although similar in certain important respects to maladaptive regressions, they, too, are to be differentiated from such regressions. Their important similarity is the increased intrusion of the primary process. For example, in both adaptive and maladaptive regressive states, images wander freely without being bound by rules and properties of the accepted, conventional, familiar, everyday world. Yet such free-wandering imagery is not necessarily adaptive; nor, for that matter, is it necessarily maladaptive. Regression, in and of itself, is not necessarily either healthy or pathological: it may serve either interest. The important task is to differentiate the two. As Gill and Brenman[8] note: "That there is a difference between the regression involved in making a joke and that in a florid psychosis seems perfectly clear, but how are we to define this difference systematically?" [p. 161]. They proceeded to make the attempt by describing "ideal models" of the two regressions. To quote their summary:

A regression in the service of ego is (1) more likely to occur as the ego grows more adaptive and less likely to occur as the ego grows less adaptive; (2) marked by a definite beginning and end; (3) reversible, with a sudden and total reinstatement of the usual organization of the psyche; (4) terminable under certain emergency conditions by the person unaided; (5) one which occurs only when the person judges the circumstances to be safe; (6) one which is voluntarily sought by the individual and is—relative to a regression proper—active rather than passive [pp. 105–106].

In regression proper the ego is helplessly inundated. In regression in the service of the ego, it initiates, lends itself to and uses regressive mental activity for its own purposes [p. 105].

These regressive differences can be discernible on the Rorschach. In its invitation toward regression, the Rorschach is ideally suited to draw forth primary-process ideation. How the individual deals with this invitation to regress may well be the cutting edge in differentiating between the psychopathological and the nonpsychopathological. Or, differently put, this regressive differential may well contribute to the diagnostic differential. Here is where psychoanalytic theory of the Rorschach can contribute to psychiatric practice in the clinic.

Summary

Psychoanalytic theory draws attention to the importance of such phenomena as projection, regression, and the primary process. Such psychoanalytic ideas have been directly related to Rorschach methodology. The "projective hypothesis" has served as a central theoretical underpinning to such projective techniques as the Rorschach. The Rorschach, in its ambiguity, has been conceptualized as a technique designed to promote both projection and regression. The primary process, in particular, is likely to reveal itself and its operations in response to the Rorschach invitation to regress. Individual variations in the adaptation of such regressive processes do have their clinical implications. A clinical awareness of and differentation between such "regressive styles" may contribute to the clinician's twofold tasks of diagnosis and prognosis.

The clinical implications of this psychoanalytically inspired Rorschach methodology suggest the task that stands before us. Hermann Rorschach himself had some important things to say about the clinical application of his test and its psychoanalytic possibilities. The clinical contributions of both Dr. Rorschach and his test will be addressed in Part II of this lesson.

References

1. Rorschach H: *Psychodiagnostics*. Hanns Huber, Berne, Switzerland, 1942.
2. Piotrowski Z: A. *Perceptanalysis*. Ex Libris, Philadelphia, 1974.
3. Rabin AI: Projective methods: An historical introduction. In Rabin AI (Ed.): *Projective Techniques in Personality Assessment*, Springer Publishing Co., New York, 1968.
4. Nietzsche F: *The Will to Power*. Vintage Books, New York, 1968.
5. Freud S (1911): Psychoanalytic notes on an autobiographical account of a case of paranoia (dementia paranoides). S. E., 12.
6. Klopfer B, Davidson HH: *The Rorschach Technique: An Introductory Manual*, Harcourt, Brace and World, New York, 1962.
7. Freud S (1900): *The Interpretation of Dreams*, Science Editions, Wiley, New York, 1961.
8. Gill MM, and Brenman M: *Hypnosis and Related States*, Science Editions, Wiley, New York, 1959.
9. Schafer R: *Psychoanalytic Interpretations on Rorschach Testing*, Grune and Stratton, New York, 1954.
10. Gill MM: The primary process. In Holt RR (Ed.): Motives and thought. Psychoanalytic essays in memory of David Rapaport. *Psych. Issues Monogr*. 18/19, I.U.P., New York, 1967, pp. 260–298.
11. Holt RR: Gauging primary and secondary processes in Rorschach responses. *J. Proj. Techa1. 20:14–15, 1956.*
12. *Holt RR: Cognitive controls and primary processes. J. Psychiatr. Res.* 4:105–112, 1960.
13. Holt RR (1967): The development of the primary process: A structural view. In Holt, pp. 344:383.
14. Kris E: *Psychoanalytic Explorations in Art*. I.U.P., New York, 1952.
15. Hartmann H (1950): Selected problems in psychoanalytic theory. In *Essays on Ego Psychology*. I.U.P., New York, 1964.

Additional Reading

Ellenberger H: The life and work of Hermann Rorschach (1884–1922). *Bull. Menninger Clin*. 17:173–219, 1954.

Miller MJ: Regression in the service of the experiential process. Unpublished doctoral dissertation, New School for Social Research, New York, 1971.

10

The Rorschach

Part II: Assessing Regression as an Aid to Diagnosis and Treatment

Michael Joseph Miller

EDITOR'S NOTE

In this chapter the author continues to explore the basis of the Rorschach test, its value and limitations. Hermann Rorschach himself admitted to diagnostic limitations: "Incorrect diagnoses . . . are made . . . due to the fact clinical symptoms of primary importance may appear unimportant in the test results . . . the test indicating that secondary clinical symptoms (are) of great importance."

In normal people, the Rorschach test makes possible a profile of personality; in patients, it makes possible the diagnosis of illness. It also provides an intelligence appraisal relatively free of previous knowledge, memory, practice, and degree of education. The test also allows the evaluator to draw conclusions about many of the patient's affective relationships.

The value of the Rorschach test lies not so much in the specific content of the responses as in the formal qualities; it is not so much what is seen as how it is seen. It has proved particularly valuable to assessing ego strength, detecting, for example, the presence of more disorganized and disorganizing elements in patients who may appear, on the surface, to be reasonably well put together. Patients who may be good candidates for intensive psychotherapy may be distinguished from those who may not. The prospects for psychotherapy can be evaluated by evaluating the patient's general personality style — his ability to tolerate regression, his cognitive abilities and styles, his basic defense mechanisms, and the presence or absence of subtle ego impairments.

The test should normally be accompanied by other psychological tests; a battery of tests offers a more comprehensive, reliable profile of any patient. A unique feature of the Rorschach, however, is the fact it can be readministered over a period of time to assess progress without intrinsic learning prejudice. For example, in one study, it was found that psychoneurotic patients with the greatest improvement showed an increase in primary-process activity in the Rorschach, whereas those who improved the least showed a reduction in primary-process thinking on subsequent testing. In another study, it was found that schizophrenic patients who improved by means of chlorpromazine demonstrated a significant improvement in defense effectiveness, but no change in the intensity of primary-process activity.

Rorschach on the Rorschach

Hermann Rorschach was both artist and physician. As a young man, he had found himself in a dilemma as to career direction. His decision was to go to medical school but, at the same time, to preserve his interest in art. Once deciding upon medical school, he quickly recognized that psychiatry was to be his specialty. Even as a medical student, he took a special interest in the examination of mental patients. Such work must have activated both artistic and scientific impulses that stirred within him.

Rorschach's own Rorschach would have been very suggestive as to what goes into such an interesting personality blend of artist and doctor. As an artist, he was attracted to the inner world of fantasy. His wife recalls his being visibly moved on their reading of Leonardo da Vinci's imaginative use of paint blots in the exploration of prospective artists' fantasy lives. The inkblot, as a tool of such fantasy exploration, held its fascination for him very early in his training. Yet, trained as a physician, he also was a scientific man. He approached his own creation with a great deal of caution. He was circumspect in his writings about its clinical application. Proceeding with care, Rorschach was not one to oversell the Rorschach. Nor would he have been one to engage in the polemics surrounding the Rorschach after his death.

Yet polemics there were, and they became unusually heated. Sides were drawn up. Those in defense of the Rorschach initially oversold it. Exaggerating its power, they presented the Rorschach as if it, by itself, could encompass the entire personality. An aura of mystery and magic began to surround the Rorschach. It wasn't long, however, before it became apparent that there was no magic here. As Robert Holt reflects in his foreword to *Diagnostic Psychological Testing*:[1]

Elated by the success and acceptance that came to them in the 1940's, clinical psychologists became overconfident and began claiming far too much. They thus set themselves up for a hard fall; the evidence pretty quickly began coming in that they had no magical wands in their grasp [p. 26].

The pendulum soon swung the other way. Testing, in general, and the Rorschach, in particular, were cast under a cloud of suspicion by the scientific community. Those opposed to such testing tended to dismiss the entire Rorschach endeavor out of hand. It was unscientific. They suggested that the only explanation for the Rorschach's continued existence was the failure of its adherents to read the research findings. And the studies, pro and con, accumulated rapidly. Publications defending and attacking the clinical usefulness of the Rorschach continue to this very day. The volume of Rorschach literature has reached well over 5000 publications.

Hermann Rorschach himself would have taken a step back from these polemics. He would have been able to recognize both limitations and contributions of the technique. He did as much even before debate began. For example, in his *Psychodiagnostics*[2] he, in no uncertain terms, alerted the reader to its limitations:

The inadequacy of the test in estimating the quantitative importance of findings can be so great that it cannot be said whether a symptom is manifest or latent [p. 121].

Incorrect diagnoses were and still are made. This is due to the fact that clinical symptoms of primary importance may appear unimportant in the test results, and that the test indicates secondary clinical symptoms as of great importance, so that, while the individual symptoms may be correctly described, the putting together of these to form a diagnosis may be at fault [p. 120]. The test cannot be considered as a means of delving into the unconscious. At best, it is far inferior to the other more profound psychological methods such as dream interpretation and association experiments [p. 123].

Yet, all the while cautioning the reader as to his test's limitations, Rorschach recognized its promise (in *Psychodiagnostics*[2] 1921):

The test has proved to be of diagnostic value. In normals it makes possible differential diagnosis of personality; in patients, the diagnosis of the illness. Furthermore, it presents an intelligence test almost completely independent of previous knowledge, memory, practice, and degree of education. It is possible by means of the test to draw conclusions concerning many affective relationships. The test has the advantage of almost unlimited applicability making possible without further data comparison of the results in the most heterogeneous subjects [p. 183].

After a further period of development it should be possible in almost every case to come to a definite conclusion as to whether the subject is normal, neurotic, schizophrenic or has organic brain disease. Even now it is possible to arrive at a clearly differentiated diagnosis in most patients, and at a specific personality diagnosis in neurotics and normals [p. 120].

Rorschach went on to draw particular attention to the test's psychoanalytic possibilities. In his posthumously published paper, "The Application of the Form Interpretation Test,"[2] he brought the Rorschach into direct relationship with psychoanalysis. His paper represents the first report of a "blind analysis" of the Rorschach protocol of a patient who was under psychoanalytic treatment. The consistency of findings between Dr. Rorschach, the examiner, and Dr. Oberholzer, the psychoanalyst, convinced both men of the test's clinical validity, in general, and of its psychoanalytic promise, in particular.

Rorschach and Psychoanalysis

At exactly what point in time and place Rorschach came into contact with psychoanalysis is unknown. Dr. Henri Ellenberger, in his beautiful, poignant essay, "The Life and Work of Hermann Rorschach (1884–1922)," speculates that Rorschach probably came into contact with the first psychoanalytic group in Zurich (composed of such participants as Bleuler, Jung, Maeder, Binswanger, and Pfister) sometime between 1909 and 1913.[3] Between 1912 and 1914, he was known to have published a number of short papers, notes, and book reviews for one of the very first psychoanalytic periodicals, *Zentralblatt für Psychoanalyse*. Although Rorschach himself was never analyzed (it was not a requirement at that time), he did psychoanalytically treat patients at the asylum of Munsterlangen in 1912–13. He later became quite active in the Swiss Psychoanalytic Society. His final manuscript, "The Application of the Form Interpretation Test," wherein he establishes a deeper relationship between the Rorschach and psychoanalysis, was to be presented to the Swiss Psychoanalytic Society. The presentation was never made, owing to his sudden death (of perotinitis) at the age of 38.

Yet his work lived on. It could be said that Rorschach actually anticipated developments in psychoanalytic theory. His sensitivity to the world of the inkblot seemed to have attuned him to psychoanalytic concerns that would assume centrality in later developments.

Early on, Rorschach himself realized that the value of the Rorschach test lies not so much in the content of the response as in its formal qualities. The very first paragraph in Chapter II of his *Psychodiagnostics*[2] begins:

In scoring the answers given by subject, the content is considered last. It is more important to study the function of perception and apperception. The experiment depends primarily on the pattern [p. 19].

And in closing his book, he re-enforces the point:

The problems of the experiment deal primarily with the formal principles (pattern) of the perceptive process. The actual content of the interpretations comes into consideration only secondarily [p. 181].

It is not so much what is seen as how it is seen. It is not the percept but the perceptual process. It is not the content of the experience, but the form of the experience. "We do not know what he experiences, but, rather, how he experiences"[2] [p. 86]. Psychoanalytically, Rorschach was quite sophisticated in cautioning us against a simplistic depth interpretation of the unconscious meaning of the content. "The test cannot be used to probe into the content of the subconscious"[2] [p. 123]. In his emphasis on formal, organized principles of the perceptual process, he anticipated later psychoanalytic developments in ego psychology.

The underlying assumption for both Rorschach and ego psychoanalytic theory is that personality is revealed through its formal, organizing principles. For Rorschach, the relationship between formal variables determined the personality type. For example, his *erlebnistype* ("experience type") was determined by the relationship between two formal variables (movement and color) elicited in response to the test. It was the pattern between these different variables that was essential in analyzing the protocol. Perceptual types, apperceptual types, *erlebnistypes* were all found to be a function of the ways and means by which the subject organized his responses.

Compatible with Rorschach's focus on this pattern of variables is the contemporary psychoanalytic focus on ego organization. Interest in characteristic ego defenses, "regression in the service of the ego," cognitive styles, and primary-process ideation has in common a concern with the ego's ways and means by which experiences are organized. It is assumed that a study of ego processes will reveal personality and psychopathology. Individual variations in ego defensive styles, in regressive styles, in cognitive styles, and in primary-process styles have been hypothesized to be related to personality characteristics and psychopathological entities. Simply put, we reveal ourselves through our thinking and our perceiving. How we come to know, to see, and to think about the world reflects our psyches. Different psyches "cognize" the world differently. And if this is so, a concentrated study of individual variations in such cognitive processes will enable us to differentiate between different psychological makeups and different psychopathologies.

Psychoanalytically put, Rorschach's study of regression and of the primary process is intended to contribute to such difficult clinical tasks as differential diagnosis and psychotherapeutic prognosis. As an invitation to regress, the Rorschach can provide us with a valuable tool with which to approach difficult clinical questions of patient regression. And this very issue of patient regression — its clinical assessment and its therapeutic promotion — is at the heart of the clinical endeavor.

Regression: Clinical Issues

The clinician is frequently confronted with difficult questions of regression in regard to the diagnosis and prognosis of a variety of different patients. For example, how susceptible is this patient to psychotic regression? What is the tolerance level of this patient for regression? Beneath the apparent neurotic symptoms, may not a latent schizophrenic regressive process be occurring? Will the psychotherapeutic invitation to regress promote an adaptive or maladaptive regressive response in a particular patient? Is psychiatric hospitalization inducing pathological regression in this case? Given a particular patient's readiness to "regress in the service of the ego," should not a more intensive psychoanalytic treatment be undertaken? More ominously, may not the psychotherapeutic regression be contributing to apparent patient deterioration?

We do know that some patients in psychotherapy improve and others deteriorate. We know that some patients are "analyzable" while others are not. We know that patients enter psychotherapy with different abilities to regress. We do know that some patients have a ready accessibility to their primary-process ideation and others do not. These observations on—and difficult questions about—psychotherapeutic treatability present the clinician with a multiplicity of issues in regard to diagnosis, prognosis, and treatment.

The psychoanalytic perspective on these clinical issues suggests that regression—its clinical assessment and its therapeutic promotion—should be considered in patient evaluation. The psychoanalytic utilization of the Rorschach suggests that this inkblot invitation to regress offers just the right opportunity to assess patient regression.

The Rorschach: Clinical Contributions

When one approaches the difficult questions inspired by the issue of patient regression, the clinical advantages of psychological testing, in general, and the Rorschach, in particular, are considerable. Such testing enables the clinician to more carefully examine the patient's ego processes (e.g., defenses, controls, cognitive abilities, cognitive styles) in microstructural detail. The patient's application of his abilities under regressive and nonregressive conditions can be better compared. Subtle ego impairments can be more readily discerned under regressive conditions. For example, the Rorschach's invitation to regress may well uncover ego regressions that are not apparent in structured testing (e.g., intelligence tests) or standardized interviewing (e.g., mental-status examinations). This also draws attention to the necessity of a battery of tests in the evaluation of the patient. (For a further discussion of the need for a battery of tests, as well as the referral process, see the section on referring a patient, p. 145.) No single test or interview can, by itself, make a definitive statement about the patient. But the Rorschach, used in the context of such a test battery, can teach us about the internal workings of the personality. R. R. Holt[1] suggests that

. . . diagnostic tests are the best way of learning about the microstructure of personality, the patterning of defenses, and the interpenetration of motives and thought and affects. Just as the physician must know both gross anatomy and fine histology, any serious student of personality . . . should be trained in both approaches to his subject matter [p. 38].

Another important advantage of such testing is the provision of a relative control for subjectivity. The test stimuli are standard. All patients so tested are administered the same set of stimuli. The possibility of a completely independent opinion through "blind analysis" presents itself. Furthermore, through serial testing, the opportunity for therapeutic evaluation presents itself. For example, a Rorschach given at the time of initial evaluation can be readministered at a later time (e.g., termination of treatment) to assess patient progress. This measure of objectivity introduces the possibility of operationalizing the criteria by which patients are evaluated. The Rorschach lends itself to such operationalization; it provides that measure of objectivity. A scoring system is readily available. One for regression is readily applicable; it has, in fact, already been introduced.

For the past 30 years, R. R. Holt has been studying regression with the Rorschach.[4-7] Over the course of that time, he has developed a *Primary Process Manual* to score such regressive material. The Rorschach has allowed Holt to operationalize the "vital distinction between primary process that serves the ego's adaptive purpose in humorous, scientific and artistic creativity, and primary process that invades the ego to its detriment as a result of decompensated defenses and cognitive controls"[5] [p. 14]. More specifically, the manual is intended to detect the presence, the intensity, the control, and the adaptability of primary-process material. If present, primary-process ideation may reveal itself through either its content or its formal features. "Content" refers to ideational drive representations with libidinal or aggressive aims. "Formal characteristics" refer to the cognitive organization of the material, including such mechanisms as condensation, displacement and symbolization, which Freud (1900) delineated in his original discussion of primary-process thinking.

If either content or formal features of the primary process are present, the intensity of such manifestations is scored. This intensity score is a measure of the degree to which, theoretically, the flagrancy and primitivity of the primary-process material requires defenses — defense demand (DD). At the same time, accompanying every primary-process intrusion are the controls and defenses that reflect the individual's control over his primary process. This control score is a measure of the degree to which the individual effectively defends himself—defense effectiveness (DE). As applied to Rorschach responses, the DE score is a function of (1) perceptual accuracy of the response, (2) control and defenses accompanying the response, (3) affect accompanying the response, and (4) the rater's clinical judgment. Taking this DE score, which serves as an independent measure of primary-process control, and joining to it the DD score, which serves as an independent measure of primary-process intensity, we have a conjoint measure of adaptive regression. This is a relatively unitary measure, which takes into consideration both the control and the intensity of primary-process ideation.

The Rorschach, so operationalized, allows for the refined analysis of individual variations in regression that is so difficult to come by in clinical observation alone. The technique permits both researcher and clinician to put their "regressive hypotheses" to the test. Do, in fact, individual differences in regression correlate with external behavior? A number of research studies utilizing Holt's *Primary Process Manual* suggest that this is the case. Some of these studies do have direct relevance for the clinical practitioner.

Rabkin[8] attempted to relate changes in primary-process thinking to psychotherapeutic change. Applying Holt's manual to before, after, and follow-up Rorschach protocols of psychotherapeutic patients, she attempted to relate major primary-process summary scores to overall level of adjustment and changes in it (as measured by the Menninger Foundation's Health-Sickness-Rating Scale). When Rabkin considered "the quality and quantity of primary-process material conjointly," her findings were most suggestive. For example, she found that "an increase in pripro [primary process] accompanied by effective controls was observable in patients showing greatest improvement of an overall nature, while patients who improved least had less primary-process thinking than they did initially and what there was of it was more poorly controlled than it had been initially" [p. 125]. This finding led Rabkin to encourage the use of the primary-process manual in psychotherapeutic research if only "as an auxiliary tool in research regarding psychotherapeutic change" [p. 121].

Ackman, in her study investigating the effects of hypnotic induction on primary-process thinking, found that more archaic pathological regression, with less adaptive defense patterns may be facilitated by hypnosis while more creative regression may be simultaneously diminished.[9] In another study of hypnotic effects, West and colleagues found that hypnosis resulted in a regressive movement toward a more primitive adjustment, with a lessening of defenses and with shifts toward primary process reasoning.[9]

Kahn,[10] in his study of 43 murderers (males admitted to hospital with pleas of insanity), delineated the factor of primitive, undefended primary process and that of aggressive drive expression demanding considerable defense. In 1964, he found perceptual accuracy to be a useful measure of disorganization. It was one of the few measures that differentiated "legally sane" from "legally insane" murderers.

Lavoie (1964), in comparing mothers of schizophrenic children and those of normal and neurotic children, found the latter to be more balanced in the use of their primary process while the former manifested either an excessive use of primary process ("regressed") or an excessive use of secondary process ("rigid").[9]

Saretsky,[8] in his study of the effects of chlorpromazine on primary-process thinking, found a significant improvement in defense effectiveness for VA schizophrenic patients in the experimental drug group, while the placebo control group showed no significant change. At the same time, neither group showed a significant change in intensity of primary process (DD). Rabkin, summarizing Saretsky, states that

"although psychotic thinking is largely unaffected by chlorpromazine, there is a pronounced favorable change in the patients' attitude toward such ideation and their manner of handling it. Chlorpromazine does not remove signs of psychosis in the structure or content of thinking, but enables the patient to defend and justify it more effectively" [p. 56].

Miller,[9] in his attempt to relate individual differences in regression to psychotherapeutic receptivity, found that subjects who demonstrated a greater accessibility to their primary-process ideation were more likely to prove experientially receptive to psychotherapy. However, an inverse relationship was found between control of the primary process and receptivity to the experiential process. This finding suggested the interpretation of a "resistance to regression." Miller hypothesized that resistance to regressive pulls from within contributes to the avoidance of experiential challenges from without. The overall implications drawn from his findings were that "just as therapies differ in their effectiveness, so do individuals differ in their response. Therapies may be for good or bad. Individuals may succeed or fail" (p. 112).

In conclusion, these Rorschach studies on regression are most suggestive for the clinician, whether he be diagnostician or therapist, or both. In the Rorschach, we have a valuable tool that can tease out individual variations in regression, thereby providing important data to the clinician faced with the difficult tasks of differential diagnosis and therapeutic prognosis. The psychoanalytic awareness of styles in regression, coupled with a clinical testing instrument capable of measuring such regressive styles, arms the clinician with both theory and method in his assessment of a patient's diagnosis and prognosis.

Referring a Patient for Rorschach Testing

It must be born in mind that the Rorschach, by itself, cannot do the total clinical job. One does not simply order a Rorschach. The Rorschach is always used in the context of a battery of tests. The other tests comprising this battery usually consist of the Bender-Gestalt, Projective Drawings, the Thematic Apperception Test, an I.Q. test (for example, the Wechsler), the M.M.P.I. etc. The mix of such tests selected by the examining psychologist will depend, in large part, upon the reason for referral. Referral by problem rather than by test is recommended.

The most frequent types of psychological testing referrals made fall into the following five categories:

1. Intelligence (e.g., This patient appears to be intellectually limited. Please assess for possible mental retardation. Or, this patient has been diagnosed as mentally retarded, but appears to be well able to comprehend his environment. Please evaluate for intellectual capacity.)

2. Neurological Dysfunction (e.g., This patient presents problems in gait and coordination. Please evaluate for difficulties in perception and motoric control, suggestive of brain damage.)

3. Psychopathology (e.g., Please test so as to contribute to differential diagnosis between borderline personality disorder and borderline schizophrenia.)

4. Psychodynamics (e.g., This patient who is presenting pedophiliac behavior is in need of testing to assess sexual conflicts, level of psychosexual maturity and dynamics related to his family with particular attention directed towards mother-son pathology.)

5. Psychotherapeutic Treatment (e.g., Is this a good candidate for psychoanalytic uncovering or is such depth probing treatment contraindicated?)

The ideal referral is clear, lucid, and specific. Rather than an "I want to know more about this patient" type of referral, the referring psychiatrist is encouraged to strive for specificity. Presented with a clear reason for referral, the examining psychologist can then select an appropriate battery of testing tools. The psychologist is more likely to be responsive to the referral request when he knows what the psychiatrist wants. Miscommunication between psychiatrist and psychologist often develops because they are not on the same frequency; it is the responsibility of both to give serious thought to the real reason for this particular referral.

The more knowledgeable the referring psychiatrist is about psychological tests in general, and the Rorschach, in particular, the better able he will be to ask intelligent questions in psychological testing follow-up. The psychiatrist will receive from the psychologist his best considered appraisal and judgment based on an over-all assessment of a battery of testing results. The psychiatrist is very dependent on the competency and quality of that particular psychologist. The interpretation of the tests, themselves, are really no better than the skill and experience of the psychologist himself. Therefore, if the psychiatrist wants more specific information, he has to know the right questions to ask. For example, if the psychiatrist needs to know more about the patient's intellectual capacity, he will want to know not only the I.Q. score, but the scatter in the sub-tests as well as the fantasy resources elicited on the projectives. If the psychiatrist needs to know more about the patient's "psychoanalyzability," he will want to know about the patient's regression on the Rorschach. If, in the process, he learns that the patient's Rorschach has numerous perceptual distortions (F−), arbitrary inanimate movements that are distorted (M−), personalized self-references of a paranoidal nature, and an abundance of morbid color responses, he will certainly think twice before suggesting psychoanalytic treatment. Many patients who have deteriorated in psychoanalytically-oriented treatment could well have been deterred from such treatment by a judicious test evaluation of their regression. Testing can be invaluable when a well-informed psychiatrist knows which questions to ask and a responsible psychologist knows which testing tools to administer.

References

1. Holt RR: Editor's foreword. In Rapaport D, Gill MM, Schofer R (Eds.): *Diagnostic Psychological Testing*, International Universities Press, New York, 1968.

2. Rorschach H: *Psychodiagnostics*, Hanns Huber, Berne, Switzerland, 1942.

3. Ellenberger H: The life and work of Hermann Rorschach (1884–1922). *Bull. Menninger Clin.* 17:173–219, 1954.

4. Holt RR: Gauging primary and secondary processes in Rorschach responses. *J. Proj. Tech.* 20:14–25, 1956.

5. Holt RR: Cognitive controls and primary processes. *J. Psychiatr. Res.*, 4:105–112, 1960.

6. Holt RR: Recent developments in psychoanalytic ego psychology and their implications for diagnostic testing. *J. Proj. Tech.* 24:254–266, 1960.

7. Holt RR: Diagnostic testing: Present situation and future prospects. *J. Nerv. Ment. Dis.* 144:444–465, 1967.

8. Rabkin J: Psychoanalytic assessment of change in organization of thought after psychotherapy. Unpublished doctoral dissertation, New York University, New York, 1967.

9. Miller MJ: Regression in the service of the experiential process. Unpublished doctoral dissertation. New School for Social Research, New York, 1971.

10. Kahn MH: Correlates of Rorschach reality adherence in the assessment of murderers who plead insanity. *J. Proj. Tech. Pers. Assess.* 31(4):44–47, 1967.

11

Contraindications for Intensive, Dynamically-Oriented, Insight Psychotherapy: A Sequential Approach

Sidney Crown

EDITOR'S NOTE

What kinds of patients are not suited for intensive, dynamically oriented psychotherapy? It is important for every clinician to consider this question in each consultation. To begin with, psychotherapy is not always a good thing. According to Hadley and Strupp, about 3 to 6% of patients actually lost ground and never regained it in the course of therapy. Not infrequently, changes in personality and behavior induced by therapy cause complications in the patient's living conditions—divorce for example, or conflict with employers who had been happier with the patient's previous pattern of adjustment. Patients may or may not have the inner and environmental resources to cope successfully with such complications.

Sources of unwanted effects arising from psychotherapy may be found in the patient or in the therapist. A history of poor functioning in society, fragile personality integration, substance dependency, excessive self-punishment, crude expression of emotion via the somatic systems (alexithymia) rigidity, and obsessive-compulsive defenses are among predictors of such negative effects. In therapists, excessive involvement in or commitment to a particular therapeutic technique, narrow training, emotional attachment to particular patients, or a tendency to keep patients in treatment too long are a few more obvious sources.

Iatrogenic negative effects of psychotherapy can be caused by a variety of mistakes, ranging from faulty technique, undue intrusiveness into patients' privacy, premature or inappropriate interpretations, invalidation of the patient's rights and his sense of integrity, and unresolved transference, including undue dependency on the therapist.

When regular therapy is over, patients should feel free to return if and when new life stresses or the need to learn more should occur, and to be able to do so without declaring themselves "sick" or being necessarily required to engage in another period of prolonged therapy.

Introduction

This chapter concerns the background to the issue of contraindications for intensive, dynamically-oriented, insight psychotherapy. These contraindications may be located in the patient, in his or her socio-cultural background, in the therapist, in the therapist's faulty technique, or in the patient-therapist interaction.

The main contribution of the material, however, is to arrange the material in a sequence of possible or likely contraindications that may be detected from time to time of referral of the patient preceding the first meeting through to any potential complications of the post-therapy period. This approach is designed to sharpen the therapist's clinical perceptions.

Background to the Contraindications Issue

Psychotherapists, in their privacy, have perhaps always been aware that not everyone is helped by their therapy. Some patients can get worse.

Freud was certainly aware of the general issue. He was never uncritically enthusiastic about the therapeutic potential of psychoanalysis. He was aware, for example, that paranoid patients seemed unable to benefit, that phobic patients at some stage had to tackle directly their feared situation, that excessively self-centered patients could not establish a viable emotional relationship with the therapist, and that some patients could become addicted to never-ending therapy.

In one of his many epigrams, Freud formulated simple positive criteria for the selection of patients. "Not too old, not too ill." If all else is forgotten, these are still useful guidelines in the avoidance of patients who may be contraindicated for psychotherapy.

What Is An "Unwanted" Effect of Psychotherapy

An unwanted, or negative, effect of psychotherapy is an effect that is relatively permanent and can plausibly be attributed to treatment. Thus, the transient worsening of symptoms in a patient facing up to personal problems for the first time is excluded because the patient should emerge from this crisis a more insightful and coping person.

The formal recognition of the unwanted effect problem is the seminal paper of Hadley and Strupp.[1] These researchers obtained replies from 70 experienced psychotherapists representing the major approaches to psychotherapy: dynamic, behavioral, and humanist-existential. The psychotherapists estimated that three to six percent of patients developed negative effects. These effects might include the worsening of symptoms, developing new symptoms, developing objectionable personality qualities such as sexual promiscuity, "acting-out" so as to endanger self or others, making ill-advised job decisions, breaking up established relationships, and dropping out of treatment. The definitive discussion of these findings is that of Strupp et al.[2]

The definition of a negative effect may differ according to who assesses it: patient, therapist, a third-person, or society in general. Greater self-fulfillment of a patient in a relationship may be exciting for the patient and may be applauded by his or her therapist, but it may disturb the dominance-submission balance of a marriage and lead to elective separation. An employer may view negatively the increased assertiveness in an employee because he or she becomes emboldened rather than compliant as before. Conventional society may view in distinctly negative terms the homosexual doctor or lawyer who "comes out" following psychotherapy.

Sources of Unwanted Effects

Sources in the Patient: Most authorities, and most research data, target the patient as the major source of unwanted effects. Frequently manifested is poor functioning in society, which is related to ego function and/or reality sense, as shown by previous inadequacy in work, relationships, and sexual adjustment. Other unwanted attributes are evidence of fragile personality integration, especially psychotic or borderline functioning; disabling neurotic traits such as suspicion, jealousy, or general paranoid attitudes; tendency to substance dependency; excessive self-punishment shown in an inability to succeed and to enjoy oneself without guilt; pessimistic or depressive life philosophy; inability to tolerate anxiety or external stress; and evidence of crude expression of emotion through somatic systems such as headache, "indigestion," "palpitations," and other such symptoms. These patients are called "alexithymic" — literally, no words for emotions. Rigid personality qualities are contraindications such as extreme religiosity or defensive control of emotion by excessive obsessionality or intellectualization.

Sources in the Therapist: It is hoped that during training, psychotherapists are given the opportunity to recognize, face up to, and hopefully work through their own difficulties. Nevertheless, the psychotherapist should be aware of remaining problem areas within himself, because recognition of these may help him or her to avoid crisis of psychotherapy. They include excessive involvement in any particular therapy technique, intolerance of other techniques, narrow reading and narrow training, emotional attachment to a particular patient or retaining patients in treatment too long, and dislike of certain types of personalities such as the aggressive or the dependent.

A number of these therapist attributes are manageable through prudent avoidance. For example, don't take on patients for therapy that past experience has shown is unconstructive for you. Other difficulties may be dealt with by discussion with a colleague analogous to the way musicians of considerable seniority attend "master" classes.

Sources in the Patient-therapist Interaction: The question here is of goodness or poorness of therapist-patient "fit." Some authorities use the concept of initial concordance, or later convergence between the values and attitudes of the patient and those of the therapist. Of course, "fit" is not a fixed, immutable concept determined at the outset of therapy.

Sources in the Cultural Interface (Ecology) of Psychotherapy: In the U.S. for a long period of time, and in the UK more recently, experts have recognized that cultural or ecological contraindications for psychotherapy must be anticipated. This is particularly true in the verbally based psychotherapies, and less so with those that are behaviorally based. There are unpredictabilities and risks with ethnic subgroups, because communication may not exist even as a concept, let alone as a desirable goal, with many ethnic subcultures. The possibility of a "joint" interview in cases of sexual dysfunction remains remote if, as with many groups outside Western industrial society, women tend to be devalued. In another example, a single-parent mother experiences the ambivalence of society and its impact on her son who becomes "difficult" with her. She complains bitterly, "After all I've done for him. . . . " Intensive psychotherapy in this situation risks leading a previously reasonably functioning person to become preoccupied with guilt and sadness and less able to cope. It may therefore be contraindicated.

The Induction Process

The induction process starts with patient referral, continues with patient assessment, and ends with the establishment of the psychotherapeutic contract. The majority of contraindications for psychotherapy should be detected during this sequence.

Prior Attitudes; Patient Referral: The referral process is strewn with possible traps such as, "I'd be very grateful if you'd see a colleague for me . . . ," or, beguilingly, "You helped a friend of mine. . . . " The local general practitioner may write, "I've been seeing this patient but think now he needs a specialist's treatment. . . . " There are many modes of introduction, and they are not selected at random by the individual who is referring the patient. Look for the "hidden agenda."

A dispassionate appraisal is essential. The professional colleague may be coming only because he feels the need to comply. The GP's patient may be an appropriate referral, or the doctor may have misjudged the difficulty and is passing the problem on. The friend of the friend may be far more ill than the patient you originally treated successfully.

Early countertransference feelings may be generated by the peculiarities of expectancy, curiosity, or antagonism. Beware of feelings of self-importance at being asked or antagonism to the as-yet unseen patient because one feels pressured or because of the supposed diagnosis. Beware of feelings of dejection because the surname suggests an ethnic or religious subgroup you have previously worked with unsuccessfully. This patient may be different.

Preliminary Encounter: By the time you meet the patient in your waiting room, a background of expectation, hope, or doubt has formed in the patient that combines with and relates to similar anticipations in the therapist. A complex encounter occurs, therefore, even in the first few minutes. Non-verbal communication in the form of dress, manner, bodily postures, facial expression, and gesture, as well as the communication through the paralinguistic channel, are far more important. They are more primitive and harder to disguise than verbal communication, which is concerned with the transmission of information.

Don't bury your head in your notes or you will miss much that is important in the early, largely intuitive, assessment of the patient. Watch for the wary manner of the potentially paranoid patient, the exceptionally friendly and open attitude of the professional or paraprofessional colleague who is role-playing a "suitable" patient, and the possible discordance between the verbal and nonverbal communication of the potentially severely disturbed patient. Note grimacing or listening, evidence of the personal muddle characteristic of the severe identity problem, bravado or self-centeredness, or excessive compliance suggesting a dependency problem or complex attitude to establishment figures. Evidence of depression may be revealed before the patient speaks by the way he or she sits, stands, or walks. A couple may touch each other at stressful times in the interview. A patient may adopt unusual or "way out" styles of dress, hair style, or make-up, or, conversely, show meticulous conventionality. Careful observation at this stage may allow a preliminary assessment of the possible suitability of psychotherapy.

Flexibility and tolerance also enter here so that a patient can feel encouraged if he or she wishes to reveal an interest in, say, extrasensory perception, spiritualism, or astrology without sensing that they may be judged a "nut" and refused treatment. Interpersonal judgment is a two-way process: both patient and therapist may be seeking attributes in the other such as formality or informality, male or female, older or younger, religious or agnostic.

Doctor-patient Relationship: Transference and Countertransference: The doctor-patient relationship is the most important of the so-called nonspecific factors in psychotherapy and is highly relevant to psychotherapy outcome. As noted in the previous section, it begins prior to the actual meeting between the patient and doctor. As therapy proceeds, this relationship becomes more articulated and complex.

Part of the doctor-patient relationship is associated with "ordinary" human attitudes of people to one another. Used in psychotherapy, where one person is seen to be trying to help another, the feelings remain basically positive so that a working alliance is maintained despite session-to-session fluctuations that occur as conflicts and problems are presented, are better understood, and are worked through in therapy.

Unconscious forces, however, become increasingly relevant so that the "transference" becomes an important part of therapy. Transference is the process by which the patient's feelings about important figures in the past and present are projected onto the doctor. In countertransference, the doctor's feelings are projected onto the patient. Doctor and patient are both implicated. The two differ in that the patient's feelings for the doctor are unconscious and therefore unguarded and usable in therapy, while the doctor's should be conscious as a result of training and personal therapy or sensitivity training. The therapist should be able to manage his or her own feelings without allowing them to interfere with his management of the patient.

Countertransference feelings may, in fact, often provide clues as to what the patient intends to "do" to others outside the consulting room. For example, the therapist's feeling that the patient "manipulates" him suggests that manipulating others is an important psychological need or conflict in the patient. Most experienced psychotherapists probably use their intuition in this area as one clue to the patient's conflicts.

From the point of view of contraindications for psychotherapy, a patient who cannot establish a therapeutic alliance with the therapist and who cannot, fairly early on, project feelings for others onto the therapist may prove difficult to help in therapy. Malan, an experienced British psychotherapist, considers the early appearance of parent transference to be a significant prognostic factor for successful psychotherapy.[3]

Assessing the Patient

We now focus on the information needed to assess a patient for psychotherapy and to look for contraindications.

Diagnostic Assessment: Formal DSM-III diagnosis is important because it sharpens the psychotherapist's perception to possible contraindications. This may include severe disturbance in mental function, as in paranoid, schizophrenic, or affective psychoses; severe personality disorders such as paranoid, sociopathic, or substance-dependent; or excessive self-centeredness, profound psychoneurotic disturbance as seen in multiple-system (Briquet) hysteria, or obsessive-compulsive neurosis.

Psychodynamic Assessment: Psychodynamic assessment should not just include the traditional areas of psychosexual development, defense and coping structure, superego, and object relationships. It should also include more general dynamic factors such as psychological-mindedness, motivation, inner- versus outer-directedness, value systems, and personality assets.

Psychosexual Development: Symptoms and personality qualities that relate to the earliest phases of psychosexual development appear to be contraindicated for psychotherapy, and they include the psychoses, severe borderline personality disorders, severe manifestations of eating disorders, and the substance dependencies. Some of the most experienced psychotherapists[4] limit psychotherapy to patients whose problems and conflicts relate to later phases of development, especially the oedipal.

Defenses: Two aspects of defense may appear. The first is a general inadequacy of the coping mechanisms. This can be seen in psychotic breaks with reality or by the converse, an absolutely rigid control and fixity. The second is the balance of defenses, including the excessive use of such defenses as denial, intellectualization, or projection. Both symptoms and the patient's ordinary functioning in the world should be examined for evidence in his or her defense structure of their effectiveness.

Superego: The superego should lead to the patient's establishing guidelines for action and appropriate guilt when these guidelines are transgressed. Potential therapists should be on watch either for an apparently ineffective superego with lack of impulse control and an inability to anticipate the consequences of actions, as well as the converse, the punitive superego structure that leads to the activation of guilt in inappropriate situations.

Object Relations: An examination should be undertaken for evidence of established relations with both the same and opposite sex or a need for such relationships which seems to have been blocked. The block can arise either from unconscious inhibitions, which might be resolved with therapy, or from a lack of social skills. In the latter case, social skills training may be usefully added to a dynamic psychotherapy approach.

Areas of Adequate Coping: Positive areas of achievement should be noted in work, social, and sexual adaptation, as well as any successful areas of functioning such as complex interest and hobbies. Positive achievement is something noted too seldom by psychotherapists, yet it is an important part of the overall assessment. Few patients have no established areas of strength or areas of potential strength that may be fostered through psychotherapy.

Motivation for Therapy: This is often treated as a fixed attribute that is present or absent in a potential psychotherapy patient. In fact, motivation is more often a dynamic factor whose potential becomes realized (or inhibited) through the course of the assessment interviews or during ongoing therapy.

Insight and Psychological-mindedness: A patient needs the ability to see problems in psychological, or at least psychosomatic terms rather than to conceptualize them in physical or somato-psychic terms. The alexithymic patient not only lacks the ability to see problems in psychological rather than physical terms but also shows less ability to fantasize or to dream. Psychotherapy is contraindicated for these people.[5]

Inner- Versus Outer-Directedness: Directedness is increasingly being taken into consideration by psychotherapists. It reveals the patient's ability to establish the locus for his problem and the solution in himself as opposed to "out there," to others, or to fate.[6] It also relates to positive self-determination or self-actualization, both important general goals of psychotherapy. Here may be a crucial psychotherapeutic paradox: the only people you can help are those capable of helping themselves.

Trials of Interpretation and Therapy: Also related to the evaluation of the difficult-to-assess patient is a response to a trial interpretation, such as parent-therapist transference interpretation. A negative response with a total inability to gain insight would suggest a contraindication to psychotherapy. If still uncertain, the therapist may offer the patient several sessions as a trial of psychotherapy. Contraindications to therapy that have been missed may emerge at this time.

The Therapeutic Contract

The idea of a "contract" between patient and therapist seems to have two roots. The first is a recognition of the importance of a behavioral component ("homework") in all psychotherapies. The second is the increasing democratization of the client-therapist relationship. Patients have a right to full information about therapy if they are to enter into it. The contract may involve practical arrangements such as time, place, frequency, and payment, as well as the more technical aspects such as the reasons for suggesting a particular psychotherapy or combination of therapies and a discussion of alternatives.

The therapeutic contract should be flexible, and this flexibility is relevant when anticipating possible contraindications for psychotherapy. Because it may not be possible to firmly establish a patient's suitability for psychotherapy early in treatment, any uncertainty can be made explicit to the patient and discussed. If the patient proves unsuitable, modifications can be made to therapy without loss of face or confidence on the part of the patient. Flexibility is also relevant when a decision cannot be made with certainty about the relevance of a joint interview approach to a marital problem or whether a behavioral component should be introduced into psychotherapeutic discussion of a psychosexual problem.

The principle mistake made is with the therapists or patients trying to crystallize the therapeutic contract too early or making the contract too unyielding and inflexible.

Ongoing Psychotherapy: Iatrogenic "Contraindications"

Iatrogenic contraindications are those caused by the therapist particularly through faulty technique. The problems caused by this may falsely appear to come from the patient and he or she may therefore appear "unsuitable" for psychotherapy.

A number of errors have been identified. In group therapy, intrusiveness and excessive control of patients is potentially damaging.[7] The misuse of interpretation is another major fault. An interpretation is a psychological hypothesis suggested to the patient to explain or understand aspects of his or her experience or behavior and interpretations usually postulate unconscious conflicts. Major faults include an interpretation that is made too early in therapy or one placed too "deep" in terms of supposed unconscious processes.

A third fault is invalidation of the patient. This is elaborated in an interesting paper by Meares et al.[8] Examples are poor therapist time-keeping coupled with rigid standards for the patient, denigrating the patient, invalidating the patient's experience, and confusing the patient with conflicting messages.

A further error concerns unresolved transference. Buckley et al.[9] investigated therapists' experience in their own therapy and compared a group of those who reported negative effects of their psychotherapy with those who did not. Unresolved transference was an important component that left excessive transference "residues" and led to unsolved dependency problems.

Termination of Therapy

Again, problems at the termination stage may be iatrogenic, especially when termination is too abrupt. Stopping therapy may be broached by the patient. Provided the request seems to emerge appropriately from the progress achieved, the suggestion must be taken seriously. Alternatively, the therapist may consider that goals have been reached or are unlikely to be reached. Only one rule really applies: Do not terminate suddenly. At least one further session is needed to avoid any unnecessary emotional upset that may lead to the development of further symptoms through a feeling of being "dumped" prematurely. When this happens, the patient may think that he or she has been unsuitable all along. In fact, the fault lies in the therapist's technique of terminating therapy.

Post-therapy: May I Return?

The answer must surely be "Yes." However, immediate return is usually contraindicated and suggests therapy or its termination has been mismanaged. A discussion of returning should be initiated by the patient; if not, by the therapist prior to the termination phase. If psychotherapy is a learning process then — as with other learning processes — the client will use what he or she has learned to continue learning. In this respect, the post-treatment period is extremely important. Patients should be encouraged to experience this stage without capitulating to the understandable desire to return for more psychotherapy when a new, unanticipated stress occurs. If, after a reasonable period, problems still seem to emerge, further psychotherapy may be indicated. *May* is used here because care would need to be exercised in deciding whether more psychotherapy is appropriate or some other modality of psychological treatment is called for. Even at this late stage, the patient may be apparently unsuitable for psychotherapy.

Perhaps most important is that the therapist should remain aware of the power of countertransference feelings. A patient who is attractive in personality or background or in the ability to make good therapeutic progress may be hard to let go. The doctor-patient communication, especially through the nonverbal channels, must be monitored carefully so that potentially independent patients are encouraged to be so, including being independent of their therapists!

References

1. Hadley SW, Strupp HH: Contemporary views of negative effects in psychotherapy. *Arch. Gen. Psychiatry* 33:1291–1302, 1976.

2. Strupp HH, Hadley SW, Gomes SB: *Psychotherapy for Better or Worse. The Problem of Negative Effects*, Jason Aronson, New York, 1978.

3. Malan D: *The frontier of brief psychotherapy: An example of the convergence of research and clinical practice*, Plenum Publishing Corp., New York, 1976.

4. Sifneos PE: *Short-term dynamic psychotherapy: Evaluation and technique*, Plenum, London, 1979.

5. Nemiah JC, Freyberger H, Sifneos PE: Alexithymia: A view of the psychosomatic process. In Hill OW (Ed.): *Modern Trends in Psychosomatic Medicine*, Butterworths, London, 430–439, 1976.

6. Craig AR, Franklin JA, Andres G: A scale to measure locus of control behavior. *Br. J. Med. Psychol.* 57:173–180, 1984.

7. Lieberman MA, Yalom ID, Miles MG: *Encounter groups: First facts*, Basic Books, New York, 1973.

8. Meares RA, Hobson RF: The persecutory therapist. *Br. J. Med. Psychol.* 50:349–359, 1977.

9. Buckley P, Karasu TB, Charles E: Psychotherapists view their personal therapy. *Psychotherapy: Theory, Research and Practice* 18:299–305, 1981.

12

Synchronicity Awareness in Psychotherapy

Carolin S. Keutzer

EDITOR'S NOTE

Sir Alec Guiness, in his autobiography *Blessings in Disguise*, recounts a line from Hamlet, Act V, as a theme throughout his life: "Readiness is all." Reading his story, one sees how much what seems like coincidence may have contributed to the emergence of his personal and professional success, unexpected events for which, although he may not have felt ready, he nonetheless was.

Not infrequently we encounter such phenomena in patients; for example, a young woman who comes to therapy following a series of ill-chosen, disastrous love relationships, works through conflicts that have contributed to her self-defeating behavior and, now free of their influences, finds herself relating with different kinds of men.

Is this strictly coincidence or is there more to it? Carl Jung evolved a theory which he called synchronicity—the simultaneous occurrence of two meaningfully but not causally connected events, "equal in rank to causality as a principle of explanation." It is *meaning* that differentiates such synchronicity from ordinary synchronous happenings.

Jung delineated three different types of synchronicity. First, there may be a coincidence between mental content and an outer event; for example, you may be thinking about a friend just as that person calls you on the phone. Secondly, you may have a dream or vision that coincides with an event taking place at the same moment some distance away. Thirdly, you may have a premonition or vision about something that may happen in the future, and indeed, the event does take place.

There may be a relationship between overall mental health and an awareness of meaningful coincidence, since it may help us feel connected rather than isolated and estranged, and part of a dynamic, interrelated universe. While synchronicity can be fruitfully employed in psychotherapy, its analysis should be approached with the usual caveats, being careful in focusing on it in patients suffering with psychotic, paranoid, and narcissistic conditions. Nor should its analysis overshadow due attention to other issues and everyday reality.

Introduction

Anomalous and elusive phenomena are frequently encountered in the course of psychotherapy. Of special interest are those experiences of patients which go beyond the individual person—the so-called "transpersonal experiences." The term "transpersonal" refers to an expansion or extension of consciousness beyond the usual ego boundaries and beyond the limitations of time and space.[1] Reports from an increasing number of therapists[2] suggest that transpersonal experiences can be potentially valuable for human development and can be useful in facilitating disidentification from superficial roles and distorted self-images. When transpersonal experiences are affirmed, validated, and integrated as meaningful aspects of one's self (rather than being repressed, denied, or avoided), they tend to bring up fundamental questions concerning the nature of reality and one's true identity. The "synchronistic" event is an important experience within the general category of transpersonal phenomena and is an event which can be used as a therapeutic tool.

Definition

C. G. Jung's famous treatise, "Synchronicity: An Acausal Connecting Principle,"[3] written in collaboration with noted physicist, Wolfgang Pauli, hinges on the concept of synchronicity, which he defined as " . . . the simultaneous occurrence of two meaningfully but not causally connected events" or alternatively as "a coincidence in time of two or more causally unrelated events which have the same or similar meaning . . . equal in rank to causality as a principle of explanation. . . . "

Since antiquity, there have been many who spoke in terms of "influences," "sympathies," and "correspondences" to explain events that seemed to be unaffected by the laws of causality. Things could hang together, if not by mechanical causes, then by hidden affinities in an invisible order. The doctrine of the "sympathy of all things" can be traced back to Hippocrates: "There is one common flow, one common breathing, all things are in sympathy." Thus, the Jungian concept of synchronicity is a modern derivation of the archetypical belief in the fundamental unity of all things transcending mechanical causality.[4]

The "Physics Connection"

Although many eminent scientists have been intrigued by Jung's concept of synchronicity, it was not until quite recent times that science could consider such an unconventional phenomenon—an event outside of a space-time, cause-and-effect sequence. Now, it seems, quantum mechanics has demonstrated some synchronicities of its own, most notably the apparent underlying connectedness shown by the "distant correlation" experiments based on Bell's theorem.[4] Without going into the mathematics of Bell's deductions or the empirical verification of Bell's theorem, we can get a flavor of the importance of these findings by a statement from Bernard D'Espagnat of the University of Paris. Summing up the subatomic experiments and their implications, D'Espagnat[5] concludes that, "The violation of separability seems to imply that in some sense all these objects constitute an indivisible whole."

Accepting nonlocality means embracing the temporal paradoxes of an instantaneously connected world in which nothing can really be separated from anything else. These events are no more plausible to our common sense view of reality than are the synchronicities of the psyche described by Jung. Yet each of these events is a clue intimating the possibility that we, and everything in the universe, might be invisibly linked rather than unrelated and separate. And we are reminded that Jung[6] advised us, in what is turning out to be a hauntingly accurate prophecy, that, "Sooner or later nuclear physics and the psychology of the unconscious will draw closer together as both of them, independently of one another and from opposite directions, push forward into transcendental territory, the one with the concept of the atom, the other with that of the archetype." Jung continues to discuss this analogy between physics and psychology:

Psyche cannot be totally different from matter, for how otherwise could matter produce psyche? Psyche and matter exist in one and the same world, and each partakes of the other, otherwise any reciprocal action would be impossible. If research could only advance far enough, therefore, we would arrive at an ultimate agreement between physical and psychological concepts. Our present attempts may be bold, but I believe they are on the right lines. Mathematics, for instance, has more than once proved that its purely logical constructions which transcend all experience subsequently coincided with the behaviour of things. This, like the event I call synchronistic, points to a profound harmony between all forms of existence.[6]

Nature of a Synchronistic Event

Most of us can appreciate the nature of a synchronistic event by recalling a personal experience of an uncanny coincidence accompanied by a spontaneous emotional response of awe, wonder, or warmth and the certitude that something meaningful or significant has just occurred. In Jungian theory, each of us has a "collective unconscious" as well as a personal unconscious. The collective unconscious is a storehouse of latent memories and experiences that transcend personal experience. "Archetypes," the primary components of the collective unconscious, are inherited predispositions which express ancient systems of reactions and attitudes. These transpersonal images are the residue of human evolutionary development and can be activated under the proper conditions. According to Jung, when the "archetypal" level of the "collective unconscious" is touched in a situation, there is emotional intensity as well as a tendency for symbolic expression. At these times dream images of great intensity and symbolic meaning may arise, and synchronistic events are most likely to occur.

"Meaning" differentiates synchronicity from ordinary coincidences or "synchronous" events—events that occur at the same moment. Clocks are synchronized, people sit down at a concert at about the same time, and runners begin a race at the same moment. Yet no one would see anything significant about these concurrences. Synchronicity requires a human participant, for it is a subjective experience, one in which the person gives meaning to the coincidence. Similarly, because the meaningful "coincidence" occurs within a subjective time frame (and therefore outside space-time) the aspects of the synchronistic event need not occur simultaneously.

Importance of Meaning

Since the quality of personal meaning has a central focus in Jung's system of psychotherapy, all events during therapy are examined for the real as well as the potential meanings they may have for the client. Toward this end, Jung used the principle of synchronicity as a nodal point to bring meaning to many phenomena which were inexplicable within a traditional causal or Newtonian paradigm, and he believed that the assimilation into consciousness of synchronistic phenomena was an important aspect of individuation. In speaking of the journey toward individuation, Jung wrote, "It always seemed to me as if the real milestones were certain symbolic events characterized by a strong emotional tone. . . ."[7] Indeed, according to Frey-Wehrlin, "Jung himself and a number of his followers have stated that in many instances a synchronistic factor has played the decisive part in the cure."[8]

Synchronistic events could be particularly powerful in promoting the existential concept of "Augenblick"—a German word that means, literally, the "blinking of the eye," but which is usually translated as "the pregnant moment." It is the moment when a person suddenly grasps the meaning of an important symbolic event. The pregnancy consists of the fact that it is never an intellectual act alone; the grasping of the new meaning always presents the possibility and necessity of some personal decision, some shift in gestalt, some new orientation of the person toward the world and the future. This is experienced by most people as the moment of most heightened awareness (referred to in psychological literature as the "aha" experience).

Types of Synchronicity

Jung[3] delineated three different types of synchronicity. In the first category, there is a coincidence between mental content (perhaps a thought or a feeling) and an outer event. Thinking about a friend just as that friend calls you on the telephone could be an example of this first type. In the second category, a person has a dream or vision which coincides with an event that is taking place at a distance. An historical event in this category is Swedenborg's vision of the great fire in Stockholm in which he described what he "saw" to others around him. Days later, the news arrived of the actual event. Swedenborg had been accurate in every detail with the reports of the catastrophe which had occurred hundreds of miles away. In the third group of synchronistic events, a person has a prophetic image (as a dream, vision, premonition, or intuition) about something that, as it later turns out, does happen. Dreaming of the death of a loved one is frequently reported as an example of this class of synchronistic events.

Methods of Analysis

One of the clearest writings on the therapeutic applications of synchronicity can be found in the book, *The Tao of Psychology: Synchronicity and the Self*, by the psychiatrist and Jungian analyst, Jean Bolen.[9] She believes that unraveling the symbolic meanings of synchronistic events, like monitoring our dreams, adds an extra dimension that can enrich our inner lives, add another facet to our awareness, and call into personal use the creative urges of the collective unconscious.

According to Bolen, synchronistic events can be analyzed in the same way as are dreams. Specifically the twin Jungian techniques of "amplification" and "active imagination" are employed. Amplification requires asking the patient to go into the details of the event and then to produce associations to the key elements. Consulting ancient writings, mythology, fairy tales, religious texts, etymological dictionaries, or just personal hunches and intuitions, the analyst may enrich the meaningfulness of the synchronicity analysis by suggesting possible relationships between the central theme and related symbols, myths, and legends. This method is sometimes called "mutual amplification" because, in contradistinction to free association, it involves a conscious collaboration between the therapist and patient.

This collaboration with focused attention is thought to activate further symbols from the unconscious and thus bring greater and greater clarity of meaning of the key element of the synchronistic event itself. Although the contributions by the analyst do not necessarily have a suggestive effect on the patient — the patient generally being quick to reject any association that does not "click"—Brookes warns that there are times when it seems prudent to keep such contributions to a minimum:

. . . if regressive elements are dominant in a particular phase of therapy and especially if predominantly hysterical or borderline elements are present, the therapist may choose to minimize his or her own contribution to amplification, in view of the possibility of suggestive or ego-disintegrative effects.[10]

In active imagination, the patient starts with an image of a person, place, animal, object, or symbol associated with an emotional synchronistic event. Then, in a relaxed mental state, the patient "sees" or imagines what images will next appear. The process is akin to watching a motion picture except that the screen is in the mind. The next frame of the motion picture is thought to provide some clue, sign, or signal about some important unconscious activity which seeks expression. The procedure can be continued until the patient recognizes some meaningful thought.

Examples

The above two methods of analysis seem most suited to synchronistic events that involve dreams of some nature (Jung's synchronistic types two and three), or that involve series of coincidences in which the meaning remains obscure until further probing and analysis is done. The meaning of synchronistic events in the type one category—a coincidence between mental content and an outer event—seems often to be adduced more directly. Patients frequently report a synchronistic event of obvious personal significance and can readily answer the question, "What does that mean?" or "What was the message to you?" A brief example follows.

My patient, a 28-year-old graduate student who was "stuck" in the process of completing her dissertation, received a book in the mail one day. It was not the title she had ordered but was one that had immediate pertinence to a thorny problem in her dissertation. She took this "mistake" as a sign she should get on with her work and was greatly energized for the task at hand.

This incident recalls to mind the ancient Chinese adage, "When the pupil is ready, the teacher will come." While the above example can be seen to fulfill a compensatory function for the individual (an active intrusion into a general attitude of passivity on the part of the procrastinating student), another example (reconstructed from a personal conversation with the patient) demonstrates the revelatory function of the synchronistic event.

An unmarried female in her mid-thirties was approaching with great ambivalence the last therapy session she was to have before her therapist went on his month-long vacation. Being in the throes of the positive transference, she was, of course, eager to see him; appositively, she was understandably reluctant to bid him goodbye for the month. For the first time in many years, as she attempted to keep her appointment, her car manifested mechanical difficulties. The engine started immediately but then sputtered down and died. This sequence was repeated a number of times until finally she was able to get the car going — to arrive at her therapy session ten minutes late. In the midst of apologizing for her tardiness by describing what had transpired, she, and then her therapist, began laughing. It was obvious to both of them that the recalcitrant car had been mirroring her "stop-start" feelings toward the impending session.

The Therapeutic Context

The beliefs, values, and intentions of the therapist set the parameters of the process and influence the probability of a salubrious outcome in transpersonal therapy. What can take place in therapy is inevitably limited by the personal fears and beliefs of the therapist, just as it is limited by the degree of readiness of the patient to explore certain realms of experience. Thus, the most effective therapist would probably be the one who had an expanded sense of the self (beyond a purely personal identification) and who viewed therapy as the natural unfolding or awakening of the transpersonal self. Since the content of therapy must always reflect the full spectrum of the patient's experience (including the egoic and sometimes the pre-egoic as well as the trans-egoic level of functioning), the adept therapist must be flexible, fluid, and unattached to specific methods or techniques.

Analogously, it is imperative that synchronicity analysis not be undertaken without regard to the context of the relationship. The relationship between patient and therapist is considered to be the crucible in which transformations in *both* parties takes place, much as is suggested by the Jungian metaphor of the alchemical transmutation. Jung saw psychotherapy as a unique and unreproducible dialect between two psyches, in which the actions or interventions of the therapist at any moment arise out of the unique history of the two parties to that moment.[11] Thus synchronicity analysis — as almost any psychotherapeutic strategy — should arise out of and be secondary to the therapeutic relationship.

Advantages

Bolen sees a clear connection between improved mental health and a growing awareness of meaningful coincidence. The idea of synchronicity strongly suggests that our lives are inherently meaningful and that we are therefore responsible to discover and live that meaning:

If we personally realize that synchronicity is at work in our lives, we feel connected, rather than isolated and estranged from others; we feel ourselves part of a divine, dynamic, interrelated universe. Synchronistic events offer us perceptions that may be useful in our psychological and spiritual growth and may reveal to us, through intuitive knowledge, that our lives have meaning.[9]

In addition to providing further meaning to life, expanding awareness, providing a feeling of connectedness with all things, and helping one to get one's bearings, synchronicity can provide yet another tool to help bring about individual change in therapy. If the person can recognize that a problem (perhaps an unconscious conflict) can be reflected in the external environment (that is, accepting the possibility that the world experienced is a type of mirror of the psyche), then the person can take responsibility for changing. As Richard Bach so cogently expressed it in *Illusions*:

Every person,
all the events of your life
are there because you have
drawn them there.
    What you choose
    to do with them is
    up to you.[12]

Actually, whether or not an event is truly governed by the laws of synchronicity is often irrelevant in terms of the therapeutic efficacy of the event. As long as the occurrence is experienced as personally meaningful and it asserts something novel into the patient's consciousness which forces a new perspective, an inviting opportunity, or the felt necessity for change, the progression of therapy can be enhanced.

Limitations and Hazards

The analysis of synchronistic events, as with virtually every other technique in psychotherapy, is not without its caveats, hazards, and limitations. In certain cases, the development of a larger conscious awareness and perspective does not come about; instead, the ego identifies directly with impersonal psychic material. In such instances "ego-inflation" occurs. The possibility of psychosis or paranoia arises when a primitive ego structure copes with its fear of annihilation by identifying directly with archetypal material in a grandiose way. As Brookes[10] warns:

From a Jungian viewpoint—perhaps from any viewpoint—transpersonal events in psychotherapy are a two-edged sword: they provide great potential for further growth and evolution of consciousness, but they strongly tempt susceptible persons to succumb to ego-enhancement, manipulation of others through power, and even paranoid and other psychotic states. For these reasons, a careful assessment of the client's ego-functions during every stage of therapy is essential.

Jung himself constantly warned that the activation of the unconscious always carried with it the possibility of the ego being overwhelmed by transpersonal material.[11]

Another risk of emphasizing synchronicity in therapy is that the patient might become fascinated with the transpersonal aspects of his or her life to the exclusion of everyday reality. It can be very exhilarating to have archetypal experiences that are validated by one's therapist and the temptation is sometimes strong for the patient to become preoccupied with observing, analyzing, and responding to cues which seem to be coming from the collective unconscious. Such a preoccupation can frequently be seen as a defensive maneuver of the ego—a strategy to avoid becoming aware of an unwillingness to assume responsibility for daily living.

Fordham[13] describes further the psychopathological use of synchronicity as he discusses one of his patients whose archetypal conflict with his father was resolved by a synchronistic event (involving boats and racing):

For months afterwards he looked for and found "significant coincidences;" two people, one after the other, looked at him in the same way in the street, or two people wearing the same type of hat, all these and many others seemed meaningful. There arose, indeed a sort of system of coincidences as an echo to the real synchronicity. Jung has pointed out that the occurrence of coincidence does not in itself constitute synchronicity—it is meaningfulness which is important: without this meaningfulness synchronicity cannot be said to have occurred. This case amplifies the proposition and makes it clear that not all coincidences which seem to be meaningful are necessarily synchronistic. There is a psychopathological use of coincidence—it is when a significance belonging to another source is displaced.

Indeed, it would be a sure sign of psychopathology and a hazard to both the mental and physical health of an individual if he or she became so preoccupied with meaningful coincidences that lawful consequences (within the traditional cause-and-effect sequence) were completely disregarded. It must be kept in mind that a central concept in Jungian psychotherapy is *balance*. A competent therapist, therefore, will be vigilant for the possibility of any imbalance in the patient's life—an imbalance between the inner world and the outer world, between regression and progression, and between the investment of psychic energy in the conscious and in the unconscious.

Related Techniques

A number of related and theoretically compatible therapeutic techniques can be used in conjunction with synchronicity analysis. Boorstein[2] discusses logotherapy, the metaphor as experience, gestalt therapy, transcendental meditation, dream analysis, mindfulness meditation, biofeedback training, and perceptual affective therapy as modes of transpersonal therapy. Keutzer[14] explores the rationale for using meditation, "analysis of the personal drama," Sufi tales, and metaphors in therapy (along with synchronicity analysis). Analysis of the personal drama, for example, is a technique by which the patient is helped to disidentify from the restrictions of the purely personal concerns—to gain detachment from the ego and from ensnaring roles and activities; Sufi tales and metaphors are used to provide greater awareness and a broader perspective by bypassing the rational processes and related defense mechanisms.

Conclusion

C. G. Jung was probably the first Western psychotherapist to recognize the importance of transpersonal psychic events in his psychotherapeutic work and his emergent general psychology. In so doing, he greatly enlarged the spectrum of meanings and interpretations that could be attributed to physical events and psychological experiences of his patients. Although the acknowledgement and utilization of synchronistic phenomena are thoroughly embedded in the tradition of human experiences, only recently have these phenomena been explicitly made part of the therapist's armamentarium. While recognizing the limitations and contraindications of their application, we still have much to gain from refining the technique and making judicious use of synchronicity analysis.

References

1. Sundberg N, Keutzer C: Transpersonal psychology. In Corsini R (Ed.): *Wiley Encyclopedia of Psychology*, John Wiley & Sons, New York, 1984.
2. Boorstein S (Ed.): *Transpersonal Psychotherapies*, Science and Behavior Books, Palo Alto, Calif., 1980.
3. Jung CG: Synchronicity: An acausal connecting principle. In Read H, Fortham M, Adler G (Eds.): *Collected Works*, Volume 8, Pantheon, New York, 1952.

4. Keutzer C: The power of meaning: From quantum mechanics to synchronicity. *J Humanistic Psychol* 24:80–94, 1984.

5. D'Espagnat B: The quantum theory and reality. *Scientific Amer* 158 (November), 1979.

6. Jung CG: Anion. In Read H, Fortham M, Adler G (Eds.): *Collected Works*, Volume 9 (Part 2), Pantheon, New York, 1951.

7. Jung CG: *C. G. Jung Letters*, Volume 1, Routledge & Kegan Paul, London, 1973.

8. Frey-Wehrlin CT: Reflections on C. G. Jung's concept of synchronicity. *J Anal Psychol* 21(1):37–49, 1976.

9. Bolen J: *The Tao of Psychology: Synchronicity and the Self*, Harper & Row, New York, 1979.

10. Brooks C: A Jungian view of transpersonal events in psychotherapy. In Boorstein S (Ed.): *Transpersonal Psychotherapies*, Science and Behavior Books, Palo Alto, Calif., 1980.

11. Jung CG: The practice of psychotherapy. In Read H, Fortham M, Adler G (Eds.): *Collected Works*, Volume 16, Pantheon, New York, 1954.

12. Bach R: *Illusions: The Adventures of a Reluctant Messiah*, Delacorte Press/ Eleanor Friede, New York, 1977.

13. Fordham M: *New Developments in Analytical Psychology*, Routledge & Kegan Paul, London, 1957.

14. Keutzer C: Transpersonal psychotherapy: Reflections on the genre. *Professional Psychology: Research and Practice* 15:868–883, 1984.

13

Man as Process: Existential Aspects of Psychotherapy
Hans W. Cohn

EDITOR'S NOTE

Even if not consciously acknowledged, all clinicians employ existential concepts in their approach to psychotherapy. After all, therapy assumes the possibility of change, and the existentialistic vision centers on the issue of becoming, of movement from a particular, presumably unhealthy form of adaptation to a more integrated and effective one.

Existential concepts stress that all time—past, present, future—is equally relevant to the patient; therefore undue emphasis on one to the exclusion of the others does a disservice to patients. In fact, they go so far as to see disturbances in the balance of these three temporal modes as an aspect of all emotional afflictions; the depressed person, for example, seems locked into the past, while obsessional practices are designed to ward off some future danger, and anxious people are dominated by what might happen.

The separation of subject from object—a basic tenant of traditional scientific investigation—is really not tenable in psychotherapy. In carrying out therapy, we can never eliminate ourselves, our views, or our feelings from the total therapeutic situation. Nor is it realistic to pretend we can evaluate and set goals for patients without due consideration of the interpersonal systems within which they exist.

Existential concepts encourage therapists to give credence to things as they are and not always seek hidden, often unsubstantiated, motives and influences. The question "how a patient experiences what he is experiencing" becomes as important as the question "why." They also give us additional ways to view such fundamental issues as man's finiteness, his fear of death, guilt, and his need to make choices about himself, about who he is, and what he shall become.

The Relevance of Philosophy

Freud had great reservation about philosophy and its "Handbooks to Life."[1] He insisted that, " . . . analysis is not, like philosophies, a system starting out from a few sharply defined basic concepts, seeking to grasp the whole universe."[2] Philosophy has, indeed, little to offer to psychotherapy if it presents itself as a rigid "system" trying to encompass the multitude of phenomena by reducing them to a few "basic concepts."

Another matter is the philosophical orientation all of us inevitably bring to whatever we undertake. Every psychotherapist brings, consciously or unconsciously, a certain view of man to the pursuit of therapy; a view of man's position in the world and to other men — in that sense we are all philosophers.

Existentialism, as I see it, is not a school of philosophy but a philosophical orientation, a way of viewing man's position in the world. Most of the thinkers who have been called existentialists have rejected the label, and it is of the very essence of existential thought not to be a "school," rather to be unsystematic. In this way, it falls outside Freud's description of a philosophy.

What existential thinkers share is their approach to certain experiences, such as the experience of the other person, of time, of death. To the extent to which these experiences concern us as therapists, a consideration of the existential approach to them can be of help and interest.

Is There a School of Existential Therapy?

Just as there is no school of existential philosophy, I do not think that there is a school of existential therapy. Though Medard Boss, a friend of the existential philosopher Martin Heidegger, distinguishes "Daseinsanalysis" ("Dasein," literally "being there," is the term Heidegger uses for human existence) from psychoanalysis, in his actual practice he is a psychoanalyst.[3] On the other hand, Salvatori Maddi's article "Existential Psychotherapy" proposes "strategies" that are clearly cognitive.[4] A great many psychotherapists resemble each other in their existential orientation while adopting very different techniques — there are, for example, group therapists and family therapists each of which may call themselves "existential."

The Meaning of Existence

In order to elucidate some of the existential ideas, we need to inquire into the meaning of the word "existence." As most existential philosophers, particularly Heidegger, believe in the etymological examination of words, this inquiry into the meaning of "existence" constitutes an existential practice in itself.

"Existence" has its roots in the Latin verb ex-sistere which means literally "to stand out," and then "to emerge, to proceed."[5] It carries a sense of movement, of "becoming," of "being" as a continuous process.[6] This meaning is very different from everyday usage where we talk of "mere existence." Insofar as all psychotherapy assumes the possibility of change, existence as "becoming," as a process, seems to be implied in most therapeutic endeavors, unless they rely on a mechanistic concept of man where therapy would simply be a rearrangement of parts.

Existential Time

Becoming, process, change, imply an element of time. This is not our everyday linear clocktime, a useful mechanical device of measurement, but which is of limited use when applied to the dynamics of experience. At any particular moment — in the present — I still carry the past within me and live towards a future. For example, when I fall in love, my relationship with people close to me in the past as well as my wishes and expectations will enter the process. Time is three faceted, and a dimension of existence.[7]

Time and Psychotherapy

The exploration of the past was, from the very beginning, the task of psychoanalysis, and the phenomenon of transference — the projection of an important figure from the past onto the therapist — showed the survival of the past into the present. If the relationship between patient and therapist is reduced to the relationship of the patient with the past figure, the "present" aspect of the situation is neglected, and the existential concept of time is violated. The existential view would be that past and present are always there together. It is, in fact, difficult to see how therapy could affect a past that is truly "past."

If one mode of time can be seen as more important than the others, it is that of the future, though it has perhaps not received sufficient attention from the psychotherapists. Heidegger saw man as always "ahead" of himself/herself, and the very concept of "becoming" points towards the future. All therapy wishes to bring about change, that which is "not yet," and our hopes and expectations affect our memories, our dreams, our experiences.

An important aspect of our future is our death. Its inevitability is implicitly present in all our experiences. The fact that our existence is limited in time is part of the reality of psychotherapy. More will have to be said about this at a later point.

Time and Emotional Disturbance

Disturbance in the balance of the three temporal modes (past, present, and future) is an aspect of all emotional afflictions. Minkowski describes a schizophrenic who is unable to make a connection between one day and the next: his present lacks both the past and the future.[6] Depressed persons have bound themselves to the past. Obsessional practices are meant to ward off the future. Anxious people are dominated by what might happen.

Macquarrie points out that an overconcern with possibilities can lead to wish-fantasies and what he calls "irresponsible idealism." A denial of possibilities, on the other hand, makes people submissive to authority and the status quo.[8] It is, as if they had dropped the "ex" from ex-sistere.

The most important denial of the future manifests itself in the denial of death. Yalom has explored the emotional pathology rooted in this denial with great thoroughness.[9]

Being-In-The-World

Heidegger has shown that one of the most important characteristics of human existence is that it is temporal — "in time." He also says that it is always "being-in-the-world"[7] What does he mean by that? Two things need to be noted in this expression — the special use of the word "in," and the hyphens. The use of "in" here is not meant spatially, as when I say "I'm sitting in my car." I can get out of my car, I can dispose of my car: but I cannot get out of the world, I cannot dispose of it, I am always "in" it. The "in" here indicates a state of mutual interrelatedness, as the warp and weft of a carpet. The world and I cannot be seen except in relation to each other. The use of the hyphens underlines this meaning.

But Heidegger does not leave it there. He goes one step further and stresses that we are always in the world with others. "By 'Others' we do not mean everyone else but me — those over against whom the 'I' stands out. They are rather those among whom one is too."[7] Heidegger, in this rather cryptic saying, emphasizes again the mutual relation between me and others: they are not just independent entities who are also there, I am "among" them, connected with them.

A patient's relation to "the others," his/her parents as a child, his/her wife or husband later on, his/her therapist here and now is, of course, of crucial concern to psychotherapy. Heidegger's way of describing our being in the world with others gives this concern its philosophical underpinning. Man, he implies, is always an integral part of the human context and cannot be understood in isolation.

There is a growing realization of the importance of "context," of interrelatedness and interaction. In various disciplines, and particularly in group work and systems-oriented therapies, "context" and "system" seem to me to have implications very similar to the existential notion of "being-in-the-world."

Rejection of the Object-subject Split

One of the consequences of proposing a mutual relation between myself and the world is that the world cannot be just an object for my observation: I always have to consider myself and the world together. The separation of subject from object on which traditional science is based cannot be maintained. (This is, of course, what puzzled atomic physicists — that the observer and the observed could not be separated.)

This has great relevance for psychotherapy. Freud thought that the therapist/observer, as long as he/she did not reveal anything about himself/herself, could receive an "objective" picture of the patient. Most therapists would now admit that, whatever technique they use, they can never eliminate themselves — their views and feelings — from the total therapeutic situation. A few years ago, the psychoanalyst Neville Symington wrote: "I think at one level the analyst and the patient together make a single system. Together they form an entity which we might call a corporate personality."[10] And what the psychotherapeutically oriented physician Victor von Weizsucker said about the relationship between doctor and patient, is perhaps particularly true of the psychotherapeutic situation: "It always seems to me important that in a comprehensive therapy the doctor lets himself be changed by the patient, that he allows himself to be affected by the wealth of impulses reaching him from the patient. . . . "[11]

As Medard Boss points out, what we call projection, identification, and transference are no more than "a tossing-out and carrying-over of psychic contents" unless they are understood as phenomena in a shared world, as a manifestation of "the primary, intrinsic being-together of all men in the same world."[12]

The Phenomenological Aspect

We have seen that the therapist cannot "observe" the patient like an object. The therapeutic situation is one of immediate mutual experience. This is its phenomenological aspect. What do we mean by that? Phenomenology is an approach to knowledge proposed and worked out by Edmund Husserl, a teacher of Heidegger. It stresses knowledge by experience rather than by explanation of causes and origins. As Robert C. Solomon puts it: "Husserl demands: Describe phenomena, don't superimpose theories on them and don't populate an imaginary 'behind-the-phenomena' stage with unknowable 'things-in-themselves.'"[13] Phenomenology's central question is: "how is it" rather than "why is it so?" A phenomenological approach has always been part of the existential view.

The relevance of psychotherapy becomes clear when we consider one of Freud's sayings in the Introductory Lectures on Psychoanalysis: "The phenomena perceived must yield in importance to the trends which are only hypothetical."[14] Psychoanalysis and psychoanalytic psychotherapies have tended to neglect what "meets the eye" in favor of digging for roots and causes (the word phenomenon means literally "the thing that appears"). An existential approach would be concerned with whatever showed itself in the meeting between therapist and patient where it is not only interested in the internal structure of disturbed behavior and its "psychodynamics," but also in the way it manifests itself, i.e., its "quality."

Embodiment

We have seen that our immediate experience is always one of being in the world with others. It is also one of being in a body. " . . . man's somatic aspect is inseparable from his being-in-the-world. Man . . . participates bodily in all his world-relationship."[3] Just as our understanding of "being-in-the-world" undercuts the object-subject split, the idea of man always being in a body undercuts the Cartesian dichotomy between the body and mind. Existential thinking considers this dichotomy an intellectual speculation that is not rooted in experience. Man's age-old efforts to bridge the gap between body and mind are doomed to fail, as they try to bring together what is not existentially separate.

The concept of "embodiment," of the body-liness of existence, is clearly of great relevance to psychotherapy, particularly in the area called "psychosomatic medicine." Within this area, causal connections are still assumed. This leads to difficult propositions of the kind that the repression of aggressive feelings "causes" high blood pressure. How such a jump from the emotional to the physiological sphere could come about remains quite unclear. An existential approach would propose that all existence reveals itself as both physical and mental (if I may use this word to cover both cognitive and emotional aspects), so that there is no gap to be bridged.

The Priority of Existence

The central importance of immediate experience was expressed by Sartre in his much-quoted and controversial sentence "Existence precedes essence."[15] What does this mean? There are black and brown pianos, uprights and grands, Steinways and Blüthners. But the "essence" of a piano is what all pianos have in common, what makes a piano a piano; its "definition." The definition of the piano in the Oxford Concise Dictionary is a "Musical instrument with metal strings struck by hammers worked by levers from a keyboard. . . . " There is a way in which I can say that the piano is "prior" to all the individual pianos that have been or could be made.

This, as Sartre saw it, was not so with man. There is, of course, a definition of man too. In the Oxford Concise Dictionary it reads: "Human being, individual of genus Homo, distinguished from other animals by superior mental development, power of articulate speech, and upright posture. . . . " But Sartre gave "priority" (chronologically and logically) to individually existing men/women and their immediate experience of themselves. Let me quote him more fully: "What do we mean by saying that existence precedes essence? We mean that man first of all exists, encounters himself, surges up in the world—and defines himself afterwards."[15] There is, in Sartre's radical view, no such thing as "the nature of man." Man defines herself/himself as she/he goes along.

Existence and Essence in Psychotherapy

Sartre's bold statement makes the psychotherapist face some difficult questions. What is "essence" in our patients, and what is "existence?" Has one "priority" over the other?

We can say that psychoanalytic theory (like all theory) has formulated certain "laws" which are assumed to underlie all human behavior. Examples of this are Freud's account of infantile sexuality and the Oedipus complex, or Melanie Klein's proposition of the move from the schizoid to the depressive position. To the extent to which these and other developmental phases are common to all men, they can be called "essential."

On the other hand, when we meet a patient, we meet that particular patient, different from any other, with his/her unique way of speaking, moving, being, and of affecting us as no other person has ever done or ever will. This is the existential aspect of therapy, and where we put the "priority" in our work, whether on the essential or existential aspects, will depend on our training and the kind of person we are. But the existential aspect is never entirely missing, I think, whether we call ourselves "existential" therapists or not.

The Problem of Choice

Another important question emerges from Sartre's proposition and concerns us as psychotherapists. Sartre says that man "defines" herself/himself, chooses what she/he is to become. But how much choice do our patients have? How far are they suffering from what they have not chosen — their genetic inheritance and the influences of background and upbringing? Is not the feeling that their ability to choose is crippled one of the reasons why they come to us for help?

Existential thinkers do not deny that we often find ourselves in situations which we have not chosen. What we can choose is our relation to the situations in which we find ourselves. "Man is always free within his situation to confer significance on that situation."[16] One could see it as an aim of psychotherapy to "free" the patient for a more fruitful engagement with the circumstances in which he/she finds himself/herself.

The question of choice touches on a paradox inherent in psychotherapy. The patient comes to us in the hope that we will help him/her to change his/her incapacity to change. If we could not assume that the patient has access to an area where choice is possible, no matter how limited this area may be, psychotherapy would be inconceivable.

Two Kinds of Anxiety

Making a choice means taking on a responsibility, and this generates anxiety. Anxiety is "the dizziness of freedom," in Kierkegaard's words,[17] and freedom is understood here as both opportunity and threat. Sartre puts it similarly: "Anguish is the reflexive apprehension of freedom itself."[18]

This is not the kind of anxiety psychotherapists expect to meet in their patients. The concept of anxiety which prevails in most schools of psychotherapy is the one formulated by Freud. Freud changed his view of anxiety in the course of his life. At first, he thought of it as "the universally current coinage for which any affective impulse is or can be exchanged if the idea-tional content attached to it is subjected to repression."[14] Later he saw it as "signaling" an external or internal danger. While in the beginning anxiety seemed to him a direct product of repression, he saw it later as a warning leading to repression.[19] By the time he had altered his view of anxiety, he had also formulated his concept of a "death instinct," so that the dangers against which anxiety is warning us are rooted in our aggression as much as in our sexuality.

The existential view of anxiety does not replace the psychoanalytic one; it explores a different aspect of this multifaceted affect. Man's capacity to choose his attitude to what is given, and the responsibility for his/her own life which this entails, may generate an anxiety which leads to a denial of this responsibility, of this freedom to choose. This denial, as all denial of our potentialities, has its own pathological manifestations. In Tillich's words, "Pathological anxiety leads to self-affirmation on a limited, fixed, and unrealistic basis and to a compulsory defense of this basis."[20] Neurotic symptoms are frequently a defense against the anxiety which the possibility of choice engenders.

Paul Tillich mentions yet another form of anxiety for which a Freudian explanation is insufficient — the anxiety rooted in a loss of meaning. "The anxiety of meaninglessness is anxiety about the loss of an ultimate concern, of a meaning which gives meaning to all meanings."[20] This anxiety too may manifest itself in mental disturbance.

Another kind of anxiety which is not covered by the Freudian concept and which is an aspect of existence itself is our fear of death. "The terror of death is ubiquitous and of such a magnitude that a considerable portion of one's life energy is consumed in the denial of death."[9] This denial also leads to disturbances of various kinds, and psychotherapists need to be attentive to this "repression" of a future event.

Perhaps we need to distinguish between two different kinds of anxiety — anxiety generated by the threats of our instinctual life ("neurotic anxiety") and anxiety produced by the threats of the very process of existence itself ("existential anxiety"). Freud seems to give us a hint of this twofold nature of anxiety by considering the "act of birth" as a "prototype" of all later anxie-ties, though he only sees the physiological and not the existential implica-tions of this.[14]

Two Kinds of Guilt

As we have seen, man's choice of taking responsibility for his own life, his existence, engenders anxiety. Avoidance of this choice engenders guilt. This is not the guilt psychotherapists usually talk about. As Tillich puts it: "Neurotic guilt is misplaced compulsory guilt feeling and not the existential experience of being guilty of a definite concrete act which expresses the general estrangement of our existence, an act for which responsibility cannot be denied. . . . "[21] The denial of our capacity to make choices and the denial of the limitation of our existence are examples of living "inauthentically" and may generate a feeling of having betrayed ourselves, a feeling of existential guilt.

Freud sees guilt as a reaction to the dictates of the superego which has absorbed parental aggression as well as the aggressive feelings of the child against the parents.[19] It is rooted in our relation to internalized convention and authority, and as such is a social phenomenon.

Freud does not distinguish between superego and conscience. Heidegger, however, believes in "the voice of conscience" as a "primordial phenomenon" which "has the character of an appeal to 'Dasein' (human existence) by calling it to its own most potentiality for Being-its-Self."[7] Conscience calls us back from denial and avoidance, from the lostness in inauthenticity.

"Existential guilt," says Martin Buber, "—that is guilt that a person has taken on himself as a person and in a personal situation—cannot be comprehended through such categories of analytical science as 'repression' and 'becoming conscious.'" As examples he mentions "the inner consequences of man's betrayal of his friend or his cause."[22]

The German word for "guilt" is "Schuld" which also means "debt." Boss refers to this when he says: "Man is aware of existential guilt when he hears the never-ending call of his conscience. This essential, inevitable being-in-debt is guilt, and not merely a subjective feeling of guilt."[3]

Existential and neurotic guilt are two facets of a complex phenomenon, and it is important to make a distinction between them. Neurotic guilt may need to be dissolved: existential guilt may need to be acknowledged. And sometimes neurotic guilt will be found to be a displacement of existential guilt.

Is There an Unconscious?

Psychotherapists with an existential orientation do not agree on whether to accept or reject Freud's concept of an unconscious. Medard Boss has no doubts about it: "One of the immeasurable advantages of the Daseinsanalytic understanding of man lies in its making superfluous the assumption of an unconscious. . . . Daseinsanalysis can elucidate without difficulty, on the basis of immediate experience alone, all those psychic phenomena that forced Freud to invent the unconscious."[3] He grants that there are "modes of being" of which we are not fully aware. What he opposes is the division of experience into two different realms with two different languages and the necessity to translate the language of the "unconscious" into that of consciousness in order to make it "valid." "All of the patient's modes of behavior—those openly carried out and those so far warded off—are considered autonomous by the therapist."[3] An example of Boss' view is his approach to dreams. He refuses to distinguish between content and meaning of a dream: the dream means what it says.[3]

Rollo May diverges from Boss' view. He admits "that the doctrine of the unconscious has played most notoriously into the contemporary tendencies to rationalize behavior, to avoid the reality of one's own experience, to act as if one were not himself doing the living."[6] He calls this the "cellar" view of the unconscious which he too rejects. But he proposes another way of looking at it. "Freud's great discovery . . . was to enlarge the sphere of the human personality . . . to include . . . the 'depths', that is, the irrational, the so-called repressed, hostile and unacceptable urges, the forgotten aspects of experience. . . . The symbol for this vast enlarging of the domain of the personality was 'the unconscious.'"[6] May suggests that the concept of the unconscious as a symbol for a "radical enlargement of being" should be retained.

Existential Aspects of Psychotherapy: A Summary

Existentialism as a Philosophical Orientation: Existentialism is not a school of philosophy but a philosophical orientation, with a particular way of viewing man in his/her relation to the world and to others. Its important aspects are:

1. Existence is seen as a process, man as "becoming."

2. Time is a dimension of existence whereby "now" always includes the past and points to the future.

3. Individual man has to be seen as part of the whole human context and cannot be understood apart from it.

4. In this context, individuals are in mutual relation to each other, and "objectivity" and "detachment" are not possible.

5. Immediate experience has priority over theoretical assumptions, and what "appears," the phenomenon, has to be taken seriously.

6. All experience is both mental and physical, and the body-mind dichotomy is an abstraction.

7. No matter in how many ways man is conditioned, we must assume that she/he has access to an area in which she/he is capable of choice, and moreover that she/he is responsible for this choice.

The Existential Tenets of Existential Psychotherapy: There is no "school" of existential psychotherapy, in the sense in which we talk of a Jungian or a Freudian school, but psychotherapists of most schools may stress the existential aspects of their work. This may affect the choice of their models and their techniques, but it does not create entirely new models and techniques. One could even say that the very process of psychotherapy implies certain existential tenets. What is the relation between these tenets and the psychotherapeutic process?

1. The view that existence is a process and that man is capable of change is fundamental to psychotherapy.

2. The existential view of time as a "now" containing the past and pointing towards the future is at the core of the therapeutic endeavor: the patient "presents" an unfinished past in the hope of creating a new future. The acceptance of death as an inevitable aspect of our future needs to be faced as an important element in the psychotherapeutic process.

3. We never meet just an individual patient, we also meet in that patient his/her "context," that is his/her family, other significant figures, etc.

4. The patient cannot be an "object" observed by a detached therapist: patient and therapist always affect each other mutually.

5. In any psychotherapy, it is important to be open to whatever the patient brings, verbally and nonverbally, and not to impose theoretical assumptions on the "phenomena."

6. So-called "psychosomatic" symptoms can be more easily comprehended if all experience is understood to manifest itself in both mind and body.

7. If we accept that man is capable of choice and is responsible for his/her choice, we need to introduce new dimensions of anxiety and guilt into our work as psychotherapists. For being confronted with choice engenders a kind of anxiety which is different from "neurotic" anxiety, and avoiding choice engenders a kind of guilt which is different from "neurotic" guilt feelings.

References

1. Freud S: Inhibitions, Symptoms and Anxiety, *Standard Edition*, Vol. XX, Hogarth Press, London, 1926.

2. Freud S: Psychoanalysis, *Standard Edition*, Vol. XVIII, Hogarth Press, London, 1922.

3. Boss M: *Psychoanalysis and Daseinsanalysis*, Basic Books, New York, 1963.

4. Maddi S: Existential psychotherapy. In Lynn SJ, Garske JP (Eds.): *Contemporary Psychotherapies*, Merrill, Columbus, 1985.

5. Onions CT: *Oxford Etymological Dictionary*, Clarendon Press, Oxford, 1969.

6. May R: Contributions of existential psychotherapy. In May R, Angel E, Ellenberger HF (Eds.): *Existence*, Basic Books, New York, 1958.

7. Heidegger M: *Being and Time* (1926). Transl. by J Macquarrie & E Robinson, Blackwell, Oxford, 1962.

8. Macquarrie J: *Existentialism*, Penguin, Harmondsworth, 1972.

9. Yalom I: *Existential Psychotherapy*, Basic Books, New York, 1980.

10. Symington N: The analyst's act of freedom as agent of therapeutic change. *Int Rev Psycho-Anal*, Vol. X, Balliere Tindall, London, 1983.

11. Weizsäker Vv: *Arzt and Kranker I*, Koehler, Stuttgart, 1949. (Translation of quoted passage by H. W. Cohn.)

12. Boss M: 'Daseinsanalysis' and Psychotherapy. In Ruitenbeck HM (Ed.): *Psychoanalysis and Existential Philosophy*, Dutton, New York, 1962.

13. Solomon RC: *Phenomenology and Existentialism*, University Press of America, Washington, 1972.

14. Freud S: Introductory Lectures on Psychoanalysis, *Standard Edition*, Vol. XV, Hogarth Press, London, 1916–1917.

15. Sartre JP: *Existentialism and Humanism* (1946). Transl. by P Mairet, Methuen, London, 1948.

16. Solomon RC: *From Rationalism to Existentialism*, Humanities Press, New York, 1970.

17. Kierkegaard S: *The Concept of Dread* (1844). Transl. by W Lowrie, Philadelphia University Press, Princeton, 1944.

18. Sartre JP: *Being and Nothingness* (1943). Transl. by H Barnes, Methuen, London, 1958.

19. Freud S: New Introductory Lectures on Psychoanalysis, *Standard Edition*, Vol. XXII, Hogarth Press, London, 1933.

20. Tillich P: *The Courage to Be*, Yale University Press, New Haven, 1952.

21. Tillich P: Existentialism and Psychotherapy. *Rev Existent Psychology and Psychiatry*, Vol. I, Seattle, 1961.

22. Buber M: *The Knowledge of Man*. Transl. by M Friedman & RG Smith, Harper & Bros., New York, 1964.

14

Dreams
Anthony Storr

EDITOR'S NOTE

In practice, therapists vary extensively with regard to the attention they pay to patients' dreams. In the strict psychoanalytic setting, dream analysis continues to be a serious focal point. In other settings, dream inquiries are more casually carried out, if at all.

In this chapter, the author briefly reviews the historical attitudes towards dreams. In ancient times, they were regarded as prophetic; nowadays, in sleep laboratories, they are considered phenomena associated with the REM (rapid eye movement) stage of sleep. Personality type appears to influence the degree to which we remember dreaming; we are more likely to remember them if we are encouraged to do so, as in the course of psychotherapy.

Freud and Jung emphasized the dream as a major source of understanding what was occurring within the unconscious mind, each in quite a different way. Departing from a rigid adherence to any particular way to interpret dreams, the author demonstrates how some dreams may reveal wish fulfillment, while others may carry on a process that has been going on in consciousness (such as anxiously working out the impact of a recent, traumatic event). Still others may indicate a subtle but powerful form of intuitive perception. Dreams also appear to have helped great minds crystallize their thinking into exciting, fresh solutions to issues, such as Kekulé's discovery of the benzene ring or Robert Louis Stevenson's creation of his character Dr. Jekyll and Mr. Hyde.

Definition

As defined in Chambers' Dictionary, a dream is "a train of thoughts and fancies during sleep." The dream is one of the most interesting of all mental phenomena. It can be demonstrated that all human beings dream, even if they are unable to remember their dreams; and there is also evidence to suggest that dreaming occurs in other animals. Yet the function of dreams is still a matter of controversy; and there is a great deal about them which we do not fully understand.

The Subjective Nature of Dreams

Until quite recently, scientists steered clear of dreams. This is not surprising as a dream is essentially a subjective experience depending upon one individual's report. Although the electroencephalograph can now tell us when a sleeping individual is likely to be dreaming, it cannot reveal what he is dreaming about. For that, we are entirely dependent upon the dreamer's power of recall, his honesty, and his willingness to cooperate. Science is predominantly concerned with events which can be repeated and which can also be scrutinized by a number of different observers. Dreams are not events of this kind and never can be. However, for the last 30 years, scientists working in sleep laboratories have been paying a great deal of attention to dreams, and, although we don't know all the answers, there is little doubt that dreaming is a significant mental activity.

The Two Kinds of Sleep

Before the invention of the electroencephalograph, it was thought that sleep was a uniform state of quiescence which remained much the same throughout the night. This proved not to be the case, much to the researchers' surprise. The fact that there are two quite different kinds of sleep was discovered in 1952 by Nathaniel Kleitman at the University of Chicago. He and his coworkers observed that, throughout the night, a regular cycle occurs. As people begin to relax and fall asleep, the fairly rapid electrical waves which are characteristic of the brain's waking activity are replaced by slower, more ample waves. These slower waves are accompanied by slow, rolling, involuntary eye movements which can easily be seen through the closed eyelids of the sleeper. It is possible to record these eye movements at the same time as the brain waves. When people first go to sleep, they fairly rapidly enter a stage of deep sleep from which it is difficult to arouse them. But, after about 30 or 40 minutes, they begin to sleep more lightly. The sleeper's breathing becomes faster and more irregular; there are some small twitches of his face and finger tips, and his eyes make rapid movements as if he was actually looking at things. This phase of rapid-eye-movement sleep, or REM sleep as it is now called, lasts about ten minutes. Then the subject goes back to sleeping more deeply. The whole cycle takes about 90 minutes.

Someone who sleeps for seven and a half hours generally spends one and a half to two hours in this lighter, REM phase of sleeping.

What is interesting is that a high proportion of people who are wakened during REM sleep recall a dream; whereas very few of those wakened during the deeper phases of sleep do so. In other words, it looks as if most people dream every night for short periods every 90 minutes or so.

The newborn human infant spends about half its sleeping time in the REM phase. This proportion gradually declines as the child develops until, in adulthood, only 15% of sleep is of the REM variety. REM sleep occurs in all species of mammals and marsupials so far studied, which supports the idea that dreaming must have some biological function.

Recall Varies with Temperament

Although, under laboratory conditions, a very high proportion of people can be made to recall dreams, the same is not true in ordinary conditions. Some people say that they never dream at all. Although this can be shown to be false, it is the case that some people habitually remember their dreams, whereas others hardly ever do. Liam Hudson, who is a professor of psychology at Brunel University, became interested in the differences between those who choose to specialize in arts subjects and those who choose to specialize in the sciences. As one might expect, these two types of person tend to be rather different from each other. In very general terms, those who choose the exact sciences tend to do well in ordinary intelligence tests, to pursue mechanical and technical hobbies in their spare time, to hold rather conventional attitudes, and to be more emotionally inhibited and less interested in people. Hudson calls this type of person a "converger." In contrast, those who choose arts subjects tend to be less conventional, more uninhibited, more interested in other people, and better at the kind of "open-ended" intelligence test in which there is no single clear-cut answer. Hudson calls this kind of person a "diverger." The convergers are better at logical, scientific thought, and tend to cut out imaginative and emotional material from their thinking. The divergers are less good at impersonal and disciplined thinking, but tend to be more intuitive and imaginative. Each type of person has advantages and disadvantages; but one of the interesting differences is that only about 50% of convergers recall their dreams when awakened from REM sleep, while nearly all the divergers do so.

REM sleep is more complex than it appeared to be at first. The rapid eye movements which gave it its name are intermittent. If individuals are awakened during the phase at which their eye movements are quickest, they tend to recall dreams consisting of images of a bizarre kind. If woken during the phase at which the eyes are moving less rapidly, they recall dreams which are much more rational, and which resemble conscious thought or coherent stories.

In ordinary waking life, as opposed to laboratory studies, I have found that some people who say they never dream start to remember their dreams if one suggests to them they might find them interesting. Patients in analysis generally become better at recalling their dreams because they have come to realize that they can be a valuable source of information and a way of gaining insight.

The Historical Background

In the course of history, dreams have been variously regarded. There are books of dream interpretation dating from antiquity, of which the most famous is that of Artemidorus, a Greek physician who practiced medicine in Asia Minor in the 2nd century A.D. In those days, dreams were chiefly thought of as portents; propositions about the future. Artemidorus gives many examples of dreams which he thought anticipated what was going to happen, or at least partially did so. For instance, a man dreamed that he died as a result of a stab wound in the stomach. In real life, he developed an abscess in his belly and was cured by surgery. At some periods, dreams have been thought of as being sent by God; at other times, the Devil has been held responsible. Although it has generally been recognized that dreams are hard to understand, it is only since the exact sciences came to dominate man's thinking that dreams have been regarded as unimportant. Francis Crick, one of the discoverers of the double-helix structure of DNA, has recently put forward a theory that dreams are ways of getting rid of thought patterns which the brain no longer needs, or which have proved faulty. Other scientists have said that dreams have no meaning, but are just "noise" in the complex networks of the brain's communication system.

Freud's Theory of Dreams

In modern times, it was Sigmund Freud who reinstated the dream as a phenomenon worth taking seriously. His book, *The Interpretation of Dreams*, was first published in November 1899, and may be said to herald the renewed interest in dreams which has continued and grown throughout the 20th century. Freud considered this book to be the most significant of all his writings. In the preface to the third edition, dated 1931, Freud wrote:

"This book, with the new contribution to psychology which surprised the world when it was published (1900), remains essentially unaltered. It contains, even according to my present-day judgement, the most valuable of all the discoveries it has been my good fortune to make. Insight such as this falls to one's lot but once in a life-time."

Freud even let himself imagine that a marble plaque would one day be fixed to the house in which he first studied dreams seriously. The inscription would read: "In This House on July 24th, 1895 the Secret of Dreams was Revealed to Dr. Sigm. Freud." This wishful fantasy of Freud's has since been fulfilled in reality.

Freud believed that dreams represented unfulfilled, and often unacceptable, wishes. Because these wishes were so often desires which the dreamer himself would not like to acknowledge, Freud believed that they appeared in dreams in disguised form. Hence, what the dreamer actually recalled was only the "manifest content" of the dream. The true meaning of the dream — the hidden or so-called "latent content" — could only be revealed when the dreamer's associations to the images in the dream had been subjected to trained psychoanalytical scrutiny and interpretation.

The unacceptable wishes, Freud believed, were mostly derived from the subject's early childhood, and referred to impulses of a sexual or aggressive kind which, if they occurred to the dreamer in undisguised form, would be likely to wake him up. Freud thought of the dream as a kind of outlet for such wishes, which not only provided expression for them, but also, because the dream disguised them, preserved sleep.

Although Freud was undoubtedly a genius, it is doubtful whether this theory of dreams can be considered his greatest discovery. Although dreams are not couched in the language of everyday speech, there is really no evidence that all dreams are concealing something unacceptable. Nor is there sufficient reason to believe that all dreams represent unfulfilled wishes, although this is certainly true of some. If dreams were all expressions of repressed impulses which found an indirect way past the censor, one would expect that the proportion of sleep spent in dreaming would increase with age. But, as we have seen, it is newborn infants who exhibit a greater proportion of REM sleep than adults.

Mastering Traumatic Experience

Freud himself recognized that one particular type of dream did not fit his theory satisfactorily. People who have been exposed to some "traumatic" incident like a railway accident, an air disaster, or an explosion, usually take quite a long time to recover from the shock. They often tend to bore their friends by telling the story of their escape over and over again. Some people who have had such things happen to them find that they have dreams in which the traumatic incident itself recurs in undisguised form. They are, as it were, reliving the experience in sleep just as they are when they tell others about it when awake. If one tells the same story sufficiently often, whether to one's friends during the day or to oneself during the night, the story tends to lose its emotional charge. Freud guessed that, in such cases, the dream might be a way of coming to terms with, or mastering, a disturbing stimulus. This way of looking at traumatic dreams involves no theory of infantile repression and suggests that the way the mind works in sleep is not very different from the way it works when the subject is awake.

Jung's View of Dreams

The Swiss psychiatrist, C. G. Jung, who collaborated with Freud during the early years of the 20th century, but who then parted company with him to found his own school, took a very different view of dreams. Jung did not consider that dreams were concealments, but rather that they were expressed in a symbolic language which, though it might be difficult to understand, was, in essence, a natural form of human expression. Poetry, for example, is another kind of human utterance in which symbols and metaphors play a predominant role. Some poetry is easily understood; some poetry is very difficult; but we don't usually think of poetry as willfully obscure or trying to hide something because we don't always immediately understand it. According to Jung, it is very much the same with dreams. Some dreams are easy to understand; some are very difficult. Others may not mean anything at all. Jung wrote: "The view that dreams are merely the imaginary fulfillment of repressed wishes is hopelessly out of date. There are, it is true, dreams which manifestly represent wishes or fears; but what about all the other things? Dreams may contain ineluctable truths, memories, plans, anticipations, irrational experiences, even telepathic visions, and heaven knows what besides."

Jung used dream analysis a great deal in his treatment of neurotic patients. In fact, he paid even more attention to dreams than did Freud. One idea which Jung contributed to the understanding of dreams is particularly important. Jung thought of the mind as a self-regulating system, very much as the body is. One of the ideas which 19th-century physiologists came up with was that of homeostasis; that is, there are all sorts of physiological systems which keep various aspects of the state of the body in balance. If the blood becomes too alkaline, the kidneys will excrete more alkali to get it back to normal. If the blood sugar drops, the liver will release some of the carbohydrate it keeps in store in order to put more sugar back into the circulation. The interactions between the various hormones are controlled by elaborate feedback systems which ensure that the glands which produce them put just the right amount into the bloodstream at the right time. Sometimes things go wrong; but, considering the complexity of the system, what is remarkable is that it works so well so much of the time.

If this idea of self-regulation is applied to the mind some interesting results follow. Dreams are spontaneous productions of the unconscious mind. It is difficult, though not unknown, to make oneself dream about anything particular. Mostly, dreams just happen without our playing any active part in their production. Jung thought that dreams often presented an opposite point of view to that consciously held by the dreamer, as a kind of compensatory mechanism. This was especially so if the consciously-held idea was extreme or one-sided. Let me give you an example.

Years ago I saw a young woman who was happily engaged to be married, but who, at almost the last moment, felt scared of leaving home and embarking on this new life. She was deeply attached to her mother, whom she described in terms of lyrical affection. Yet she told me the following nightmare. She was in her garden at home being pursued by a steamroller. As she reached the end of the garden and was just about to be overtaken and crushed, her mother appeared on the other side of the garden fence, laughing with hideous glee at the girl's dangerous predicament. What a very different picture of the mother the dream presents from the one which the girl's conscious mind had painted!

The explanation was as follows. When the girl was a young child, she suffered from a stricture of the esophagus which caused severe difficulty in swallowing. Feeding her had been a problem, and she had required a great deal of extra care and devoted attention from her mother. The mother had given this willingly. In fact, she had, as her daughter described, been a wonderfully good mother. But, as often happens in such cases, the fact that the daughter had been so much more dependent upon her mother than most children need to be had sapped her confidence. She was frightened that she would not be able to cope with marriage and the world on her own without her mother's support. Hence the dream presented the mother in an entirely different light: as a person who is acquiescing in the girl being crushed or "steamrollered" out of existence. Because the girl was so fond of her mother, she had not recognized that her independence and her individuality were being threatened. But something within her—call it the unconscious if you like—knew better.

It would be hard to interpret such a dream in terms of Freud's theory of wish-fulfillment, though I have little doubt that if Freud had been confronted with this dream he would have found some ingenious way of making it fit his theoretical scheme. But of course it is true that some dreams do represent

wishes; often wishes of the same erotic or ambitious kind that we are familiar with in day dreams. What Freud's theory fails to explain is why such
erotic and ambitious wishes sometimes appear undisguised and sometimes
in symbolic form. Dreams sometimes raise philosophical problems. In the
third century B.C. the Chinese sage Chuang-Tzu wrote: "One night I
dreamed I was a butterfly, fluttering hither and thither, content with my lot.
Suddenly I awoke and I was Chuang-Tzu again. Who am I in reality? A
butterfly dreaming that I am Chuang-Tzu, or Chuang-Tzu imagining he was
a butterfly?"

Dreams and the Future

I wrote earlier that the ancients thought of dreams as foretelling the future.
Unless you are a believer in extrasensory perception, you are unlikely to
think of dreams as prophetic. But dreams do sometimes make manifest
things we are hardly aware of. These are called subliminal perceptions. A
married friend of mine dreamed on several occasions that she was no longer
married. She work up in distress on each occasion because she was very fond
of her husband and certainly did not want to lose him. Within a few months
he unexpectedly died of cancer. I think it is reasonable to assume that she
had actually noticed something wrong with him, possibly some minimal
change which she didn't take seriously or didn't like to think about. In this
sense, her unconscious mind could be said to have been anticipating something which was going to happen.

Jung was once asked to see a girl of seventeen by another doctor. It was
not certain whether she was suffering from a neurological disease or from
hysteria. Jung asked her about her dreams. She answered that she had
terrible nightmares. One was as follows. "I am coming home at night.
Everything is as quiet as death. The door into the living room is half open,
and I see my mother hanging from the chandelier, swinging to and fro in the
cold wind that blows in through the open windows." Another dream was
that "A terrible noise broke out in the house at night. I get up and discover
that a frightened horse is tearing through the rooms. At last it finds the door
into the hall, and jumps through the hall window from the fourth floor into
the street below. I was terrified when I saw it lying there, all mangled." Jung
interpreted these gruesome dreams as indicating the destruction of life within the girl herself. The mother is the original source of life; the horse can be
interpreted as representing the animal life of the body. Both destroy themselves. The girl died shortly afterwards.

One odd instance of a dream which seems to have some connection in
time with an external event happened in Oxford. A lady had a frightening

dream in which she was about to be executed by decapitation. On the same night, one of the professors in Oxford committed suicide by putting his neck on a railway line in front of an oncoming train which did decapitate him. Probably this is no more than coincidence but comparable examples have been reported. When the philosopher Swedenborg had a vision of a fire raging in Stockholm, there was a real fire raging there at the same time. I can't explain this; but I think it may be worth recalling that some philosophers consider that our human categories of time and space are man-made, not absolute.

Recurrent Dreams

Recurrent dreams, especially those recollected from childhood, seem often to epitomize a series of difficulties which can be summarized under a single heading. One man remembered that, as a child, he had a recurrent nightmare. In the nightmare he was striving, entirely unsuccessfully, to unravel a complicated network in which pieces of string or wool formed an interlacing pattern of an irregular kind in which the threads were hopelessly tangled. He always woke up feeling ineffective and helpless. One could interpret this dream at various levels, but it really doesn't need any interpretation at all. It can be taken as a symbolic statement which reflects an attitude toward life. Why did this particular child have the feeling that he was recurrently confronted with something that was beyond his powers? Had too much been expected of him? Did life seem to him a series of knotty problems which he could never solve? The dream, with its vivid imagery, serves as a valuable starting point for psychological investigation, and also provides a vignette, which, like a miniature portrait, captures the essence of the dreamer within a small compass.

Here is another dream which I think reveals something about a person's character in a brief space. A man dreamed that he was looking into the window of a shop. Inside there was a statuette of a beautiful woman standing upon a square base. Both the statuette and its base were made of translucent material, and the dreamer could see that there were letters carved upon the underside of the base. He knew that this inscription was extremely important. In fact, he was sure that it contained what he called "the secret of life." But, because the letters were, from his viewpoint, upside down and the wrong way round, he could not read them.

The psychoanalyst, Charles Rycroft, published a book on dreams a few years ago. One dream he reported has a theme which is strikingly similar to the dream I have just quoted. A man dreamed that he was looking into the window of an antique shop. In it he saw an old book which he was sure contained "the truth." On inquiring inside the shop he was told that the book was the only known copy of an otherwise unknown work by the philosopher Immanuel Kant, but it was written in a language that no one could understand.

The themes of these two dreams are obviously similar, though they were dreamed by two quite separate people. I think they provide good illustrations of the language of dreams; the use of different forms of visual imagery to express an idea. These dreams raise interesting questions. Both dreamers are expressing the notion that there is some absolute truth, some secret answer to life. Most of us are content to rub along with partial explanations, uncertainties, and doubts. But some people seem to need a system of thought or a religious faith which provides them with a comprehensive pattern which attempts to explain everything. These are the kind of dreams dreamed by obsessional personalities who want to fit everything in life into one all-embracing scheme. Such an attitude is sometimes found among fundamentalist psychoanalysts of a type which, fortunately, is fast disappearing.

Dreams generally seem to raise questions rather than provide answers to them. But there are a few interesting examples of dreams offering solutions to problems which the individual's conscious mind could not unravel. One amusing example comes from the American golfer, Jack Nicklaus. He had been going through a bad patch in which there was something wrong with his game which he couldn't identify. Then he suddenly regained his championship form. He told a newspaper man:

I've been trying everything to find out what has been wrong. It was getting to a place where I figured a 76 was a pretty good round. But last Wednesday night I had a dream and it was about my golf swing. I was hitting them pretty good in the dream and all at once I realized I wasn't holding the club the way I've actually been holding it lately. I've been having trouble collapsing my right arm taking the club head away from the ball, but I was doing it perfectly in my sleep. So when I came to the course yesterday morning, I tried it the way I did it in my dream and it worked. I shot a 68 yesterday and a 65 today and believe me it's a lot more fun this way. I feel kind of foolish admitting it, but it really happened in a dream. All I had to do was change my grip a little.

Nicklaus's feeling that paying attention to his dream was in some way foolish may partially account for the fact that reporting problem solving in dreams is rather uncommon. Some authorities think it happens more often than is generally realized. Otto Loewi, who was awarded a Nobel prize for his discovery of the chemical transmission of nerve impulses, said that the crucial experiment which proved his theory originated in a dream. The best known example, which is quoted in virtually all books discussing creativity, was recorded by Friedrich August von Kekulé, Professor of Chemistry in

Ghent. One afternoon in 1865 he fell asleep. "I turned my chair to the fire and dozed," he relates.

Again the atoms were gambolling before my eyes. This time the smaller groups kept modestly in the background. My mental eye, rendered more acute by repeated visions of this kind, could now distinguish larger structures of manifold conformation; long rows, sometimes more closely fitted together; all twining and twisting in snake-like motion. But look! What was that? One of the snakes had seized hold of its own tail, and the form whirled mockingly before my eyes. As if by a flash of lightning I awoke . . . Let us learn to dream, gentlemen.

Kekulé's vision of the snake eating its own tail led to his discovery of the benzene ring; that is, to the notion that molecules of organic compounds can be arranged in closed rings rather than in open chains. His discovery has been described as one of the cornerstones of modern science.

Another remarkable dream was recorded by Hermann Hilprecht, a professor of Assyrian. In it, a priest appeared and told him the true translation of an inscribed tablet known as the Stone of Nebuchadnezzar. The translation later turned out to be correct.

Problem-solving dreams of this kind usually only occur to dreamers who have been consciously puzzling for years over knotty problems. In fact, most new ideas come to people when they are not actually asleep, but in a state of reverie, halfway, as it were, between full wakefulness and dreaming. But Robert Louis Stevenson said that the plot of Dr. Jekyll and Mr. Hyde came to him in a dream; and the composer Tartini recorded that the theme of his "Devil's Trill" violin sonata came to him from a dream in which he saw and heard the devil playing the violin.

There has been some experimental work on problem solving in dreams. At Stanford University, 500 undergraduates were each given a copy of a problem and a questionnaire. They were told not to look at the problem until 15 minutes before going to bed, but then to spend those fifteen minutes trying to solve it. In over a thousand experiments of this kind, the problem was solved in a dream in only seven instances. But one must remember that the problems posed were trivial, and that the students, unlike the men of genius already mentioned, were not strongly motivated to find solutions.

Dreams as Information Processing

An American psychologist, Stanley Palombo, has recently made the interesting suggestion that dreams are a way of processing information. During each day, every one of us is exposed to an enormous number of incoming stimuli and presented with a huge quantity of information. Only a very small proportion of this information will be remembered, even for a short time. We have to sort out the significant, which we need to store in our long-term memory, from the trivial, which needs only to be remembered briefly.

Human adaptation to the environment is connected with long-term memory. If we are to manage life effectively, we have to be able to compare our current experience with what has happened in the past, and the past is stored in the long-term memory. It is the unfamiliar which engages our attention, while we take the familiar for granted; but we can only recognize something as unfamiliar because we have a memory of what has gone before. Palombo thinks that dreams are one way in which the experience of the day is matched with the residues of previous experience before being assigned to the appropriate slot in the long-term memory.

This theory of dreams does explain one peculiar feature of them which everyone has noticed. Dreams are often a curious mixture of events of the previous day with memories from the past. In dreams, time often seems to have become dislocated, so that what happened yesterday and what happened in childhood seem to be going on together. If Palombo is right, some dreams are a kind of scanning process which tries to compare today with the past, perhaps selecting things which go together because they share a similar emotional tone rather than because they happened together in time.

Some such explanation might also account for why we seem to need dreams so much. Various types of drugs, including alcohol, have the effect of abolishing REM sleep. Laboratory studies have shown that when such drugs are discontinued, the sleeper, during the next few nights, dreams almost continuously, as if he had to catch up on what he had lost. Although we may not understand exactly what it is that dreams do for us, we evidently need them.

The 17th-century physician and writer, Sir Thomas Browne, best known for his book Religio Medici, also wrote a delightful essay on dreams which began as follows. "Half our days wee passe in the shadowe of the earth, and the brother of death exacteth a third part of our lives." He went on to consider the various ways of looking at dreams which were current in his day, together with examples from history. He came to the conclusion that, although some dreams can easily be interpreted, others cannot and said that "hee who should order his affayres by dreames, or make the night a rule unto the day, might bee ridiculously deluded." Nevertheless, he still thought that dreams were important, and went on: "However dreames may be fallacious concerning outward events, yet may they bee truly significant at home, & whereby wee may more sensibly understand ourselves. Men act in sleepe with some conformity unto their awaked sense, & consolations or discoureagments may bee drawne from dreames, which intimately tell us ourselves." Three hundred years later, it is difficult to improve on that statement about dreams.

Further Reading

Browne, Sir T: On dreams. In Patrides CA (Ed.): *The Major Works*, Penguin, Harmondsworth, 1977, pp. 473–479.

Dement WC: Some Must Watch While Some Must Sleep, *The Portable Stanford series*, W. H. Freeman, San Francisco, 1972.

Freud S: The Interpretation of Dreams, *Standard Edition*, Vols. IV and V, Hogarth Press, London, 1953.

Hudson L: *Night Life*, Weidenfeld & Nicolson, London, 1985.

Jung CG: The Practical Use of Dream-Analysis, *Collected Works,* Vol. 16, Routledge & Kegan Paul, London, 1954, pp. 139–161.

McKellar P: *Imagination and Thinking*, Cohen & West, London, 1957.

McKellar P: *Mindsplit*, J. M. Dent, London, 1979.

Palombo SR: *Dreaming and Memory*, Basic Books, New York, 1978.

Rycroft C: *The Innocence of Dreams*, Hogarth Press, London, 1979.

Storr A (Ed.): *The Essential Jung*, University Press, Princeton, 1983, pp. 168–189.

The Oxford Book of Dreams, (chosen by Stephen Brook), Oxford University Press, New York, 1983.

15

Current Developments in Group Psychotherapy
Henry I. Spitz

EDITOR'S NOTE

With the maturation of group therapy as a basic approach to dealing with psychiatric patients, certain trends have emerged that focus on the problems and opportunities group therapy efforts present. These include the increasing use of judicious self-disclosure by the group leader; the positioning of group process work within the framework of overall, integrated treatment planning; using them to educate and to encourage mastery of interpersonal skills, and to enhance insight-oriented approaches; varying leadership style; and growing emphasis on the importance of screening, diagnosis and patient preparation prior to beginning group work.

In this chapter, the author highlights the role of group therapy in the treatment of four specific clinical situations: the borderline personality, patients suffering with medical illnesses, the geriatric patient, and chronically ill psychiatric patients.

Introduction

The growth of the group-psychotherapy field over the past 30 years has resulted in expanded theoretical understanding, advanced technical expertise, and broader clinical applicability in dealing with diverse aspects of mental health and illness. In order to help conceptualize the "state of the art," one may examine major emerging trends as they reflect patterns of current practice. Six representative areas have been delineated in order to present a cross-sectional view of present efforts described with frequency and enthusiasm in the current group-psychotherapy literature.

Borderline and Narcissistic Disorders

The management of psychiatric patients diagnosed as having borderline or narcissistic personality disorders affords an opportunity to study the ways in which traditional group methods have been modified to meet the needs of a special patient population.

The importance of clinical diagnosis in considering borderline and narcissistic patients for group placement cannot be overemphasized. A comprehensive evaluation toward this end must take into account intrapsychic, interpersonal, and environmental variables. Before placement in group therapy, patients benefit from evaluation along the following parameters: ego structure, temperament, character traits, psychological-mindedness, and motivation. In addition, group leaders can utilize phenomenological, historical, and socioeconomic data to obtain a comprehensive picture of a prospective group member and then to make an informed appraisal of that person's likelihood of meshing or clashing with the proposed group membership and/or leadership. Most experienced group therapists advocate intensive pregroup evaluation and study to ward off inappropriate placement of borderline or narcissistic patients in groups.

Wong[1] conceptualizes the group work proper as having five focal considerations: clarity in defining the diagnostic criteria, the choice between supportive and reconstructive treatment, a decision on the value of simultaneous individual and group psychotherapy, homogeneity or heterogeneity in group composition (all borderline or groups of mixed diagnoses), and the possibility of more than one group experience. He favors combined individual and group therapy conducted by the same therapist and suggests that the groups be varied in diagnostic composition.

The expressed advantages of the combined treatment model over group or individual therapy alone include a greater sense of continuity of treatment focus and the ability to work on individual and interpersonal issues simultaneously. The options for management of troublesome transferential and countertransferential themes are increased. The borderline patient in individual therapy often has a stormy relationship with the therapist. The reality testing presented by other group members who share the therapist helps lessen extreme transference reactions. Group members function as interpersonal buffers for the borderline patient who is excessively anxious about being too close to the therapist. The group leader in the combined model can utilize the peer vector of the group to elucidate and resolve transferential roadblocks.

The recent literature on group therapy clearly calls for revision of older, rigid group models in order to make group therapy a viable treatment option for borderline and narcissistic patients. Careful attention to pregroup screening, diagnosis, member selection, and patient preparation reduces the chance of avoidable problems in group treatment. When these factors are effectively managed, the value of groups for the borderline population is considerable. Horwitz[2] has summarized this most clearly in enumerating the reasons why group therapy makes sense as part of the overall treatment plan. He cites the following seven advantages: (1) groups provide an opportunity for the dilution of transference by supplying several targets; (2) when necessary, patients can achieve greater social and emotional distance; (3) groups often tend to induce a greater reality orientation and to direct the patient toward appropriate social responses; (4) borderline patients who are schizoid and withdrawn benefit from the stimulation and activation of the group interaction; (5) borderline patients tend to have brittle controls over hostile impulses and may respond to peer pressure to control these emotions in a group more readily than in a dyadic relationship; (6) the opportunity for identification, not only with the therapist but also with other patients, may facilitate the consolidation of ego identity and more adaptive impulse-defense configurations; (7) the group interaction highlights certain maladaptive character traits — such as oral greed, inability to share, and pathological narcissism — and hence may effectively modify them.

While specific styles of intervention vary depending upon the group leader's theoretical orientation, consensus is growing that the combined individual and group therapy format has much to offer in the integrated psychotherapeutic management of borderline and narcissistic patients.

Medical Illness

A clear-cut track of group work that has gathered momentum in recent years tries to form psychotherapeutic group experiences for patients with a variety of medical conditions. The purpose of these groups is at least twofold: to help members comply with medical or surgical treatment plans and to define and treat psychological factors that contribute etiologically or are by-products of serious physical illness. Stress reduction and the acquisition of effective stress management skills form the mainstay of some of these groups.

The array of conditions and types of patients for which groups have been designed is impressive. Currently in progress is group work with dialysis patients; patients with coronary disease, multiple sclerosis, irritable bowel syndrome, cancer, type-A behavior, asthma, psoriasis, hypertension, epilepsy, chronic pain, arthritis, and other disorders; postoperative amputees; children with cerebral palsy and other neurological conditions; and kidney transplant patients. Despite the outwardly disparate nature of these groups, they share many common goals.

Groups for somatic conditions generally aim to provide an educational component for their memberships. The overwhelming majority of the groups described in the literature are composed homogeneously for an illness experienced by all members. This homogeneity both facilitates entry into the group and forms a building block for early group cohesiveness. Since all members are matched for common medical illness, it is easier to utilize common group themes to engage patients who might resist or resent defining themselves as being in need of psychological help. Such patients are at high risk to decline or drop out of psychotherapy. Consequently, one of the central goals of groups of this type is to offer a more palatable vehicle for patients to avail themselves of sorely needed treatment services.

A second overall goal is to help patients live more realistically and comfortably with their disease. The peer-support and staff-support elements of the group are important influences toward this end. Group membership helps counter feelings of uniqueness, freakishness, disfigurement, or social isolation and aims to preserve and build healthy self-esteem for the participants. In this process, another goal becomes clear: the importance of sensitizing the health-care staff to the emotional vulnerabilities and needs of the medical patient.

The effect of patients' debilitating or chronic diseases on individuals and families is a focal point for group discussion. Most groups make an organized effort to involve families and support systems in a constructive way. Encouragement of clear and open communication among patient, family, and members of the health-care team is an intrinsic element of these group approaches.

The group studies on coronary disease serve as a prototype for many of the current group designs in the field of general hospital psychiatry. These can be conceptualized as follows: (1) early intervention is highly valued; (2) spouses and significant figures in the life of the patient should be encouraged to participate in treatment plans; (3) therapists need not be physicians but should be informed about physical and psychological risk factors; (4) many physically ill patients are poorly suited to intensive, uncovering, insight-oriented, longer-term individual therapy and should be approached instead with methods that emphasize supportive, educative, and behavioral components.

Programs in some settings feature adjunctive groups that are focal, task-oriented, time-limited, and largely behavioral and are aimed at control or elimination of destructive habit patterns. In the case of coronary-prone patients, this would include group efforts to help members stop smoking, give up excessive use of alcohol, enhance efforts at weight reduction, or deal with specific concerns of the postcoronary patient—for example, resumption of work and concerns over aspects of sexuality.

Geriatric Patients

The problems of the elderly have been an area of increased interest and research. With the appreciation of the issues faced by aging people has come a significant body of group work tailored to meet some of the specific needs of this segment of the population.

Groups have become prominent in the psychosocial management of geriatric patients for many reasons. The constriction and attrition among the ranks of the natural groups surrounding the elderly increase with time. The resultant feelings of isolation, dysphoria, and loneliness can have a dramatic effect on the quality of life for older people. This, coupled with a growing concern about emotional or physical deterioration, places the geriatric patient at risk for the development of serious negative psychological sequelae.

These factors prompted the search for innovative and thoughtful group programs to help the elderly. Geriatric groups comprise the following categories: socialization, problem-solving, and competency groups; support groups; senior actualization and growth groups; interpersonal skill training; expressive psychotherapy; and resocialization groups.

The range of group services described encompasses preventive, therapeutic, supportive, and rehabilitative goals. Many centers utilize groups in conjunction with other critical services for geriatric patients: crisis intervention, appropriate placement services, home visits, family therapy, transitional residential care, and inpatient treatment.

A representative survey of different group formats used to accomplish positive therapeutic results reveals an increasing affinity for structured, often behaviorally oriented, and supportive group types. The work of Lesser and colleagues[3] represents an example of an innovative format used with psychotic geriatric patients. "Reminiscence group therapy" differs from traditional group therapy by being structured and theme-oriented. Members are requested to discuss a historical topic—their first day at school, first date, etc. This serves as a catalyst for group interaction and provides a constructive matrix through which geriatric group members may become engaged. Group silences were noted to diminish, and questions about non-group-related issues were markedly reduced, as were pseudoconfusion and group lateness and absences. Direct intermember confrontation increased, and the earlier sense of passivity and apathy, so commonly felt in these groups, was replaced by a more animated group climate.

The literature also shows modification of behavioral therapies to address the problems of the elderly. Structured behavioral therapy to promote group participation by elderly depressed patients is commonplace today. Behavioral groups are often felt to be advantageous in stimulating group interaction, lessening awareness of depressed feelings, and providing members with greater overall treatment satisfaction.

The loss of a spouse is another stress that frequently befalls the elderly. Group experiences for widows are discussed in the group literature in two major forms: self-help groups (often leaderless) and groups conducted by mental health professionals. In self-help programs, peers receive training and function as contacts to conduct community-based educational programs to help women through the bereavement process.

In groups of another type, there is often a special place for a group facilitator. Usually this is a woman who has experienced the loss of her husband and has made a successful life adjustment. The facilitator serves at least two purposes: as a role model, she indicates that successful adaptation is possible, and she serves an educational function by being better able to identify for recently widowed women the expected stages of the grief and mourning process.

Problems faced by older widows emerge as core-group themes. The issues that occur with regularity and are confronted in older widows' groups are difficulty managing guilt and anger; the changing relationship with adult, independent children; problems of decision making, financial management, and legal arrangements; fears of being alone; and struggles in overcoming depression. Stress management, health maintenance, disease prevention, education, support in mobilizing psychological resources, sharing of tasks, cognitive guidance in handling life crises, and promoting a sense of personal responsibility and self-control are the central goals of group efforts aimed at geriatric populations.

The Chronic Psychiatric Patient

For many years, group therapy has been a discipline concerned with the treatment of the chronic and severely impaired psychiatric patient. Today this emphasis is as strong as ever, and it has resulted in a multiplicity of articles devoted to aspects of dealing with psychotic inpatients and outpatients in groups.

The literature suggests that groups are particularly useful for the patient who has had more than one psychotic break and for whom the rehabilitative process is difficult. This is most clearly manifest in the areas of difficulty with interpersonal skills, resolving family problems, and effectively utilizing community support options. Groups are also helpful in providing a vehicle for regular opportunities to socialize in a safe and controlled setting. In addition, groups offer a medium for problem sharing and serve as an outlet for the expression of tensions stemming from work and the vicissitudes of daily life for discharged patients.

Keith and Matthews[4] make some cogent observations with respect to the pros and cons of group therapy as a form of psychosocial treatment of patients with schizophrenia. First they note favorable factors, such as the economy of professional staff time and the cost efficiency that group therapy in general affords. They also acknowledge the ability to adopt other techniques for use in the group setting. At the same time, however, they advise caution in several key areas, especially concerning the issue of timing of group intervention. Evidence indicates that groups work best after the resolution of florid psychotic symptoms. Furthermore, there is reason to suspect that groups, especially those of a more traditional and uncovering nature, may be deleterious during the acute phase of a psychotic episode. The milieu-therapy literature and the studies on the emotionally charged nature of schizophrenic families attest to the need for a stimulus-reducing environment, especially in the acute phase of the illness. Lastly, what is called "group therapy" is loosely defined. Often groups are given lower status on inpatient services or in outpatient departments and may be led by less highly trained professional—factors that may foster negative pretherapy expectations on the part of patients or staff.

While agreement exists in principle concerning the general usefulness of groups for chronic patients, there is considerable divergence in the literature with regard to the array of techniques advanced to realize the goals. Mosher[5] conceptualizes the focus of therapy as encompassing seven distinct areas in order to be useful for schizophrenic patients: (1) discussion of day-to-day problems; (2) the sharing of relevant experiences; (3) learning to listen and thus becoming more sensitive to the needs and feelings of others; (4) offering new perspectives on situations being discussed; (5) asking questions; (6) expressing contrary opinions without fear of criticism; and (7) keeping a topic in focus until a conclusion is reached.

From an analysis of the varied points of view expressed in the group literature, the clinician can extract valuable general principles referrable to the group climate and leadership style felt to be most advantageous for the chronic patient. Gentle confrontation, high support elements, active leadership (especially around structuring and defining the group norms), liberalization of group standards based upon acceptance of realistic limitations of patients, and an avoidance of dwelling on delusional material are a few factors common to many of the approaches. Cotherapy or multiple leadership and an evenhanded leadership style that avoids extremes of behavior (charismatic or passive) are considered the most conducive to beneficial change.

The abilities to define modest and realistic goals, to identify and work with patient's strengths, to offer some immediate reward, to emphasize skill acquisitions, and to use groups to monitor pharmacological, interpersonal, and individual needs are other variables that contribute to the utilitarian aspect of groups.

The mounting awareness of the role of social networks and support systems as they affect mental health in general, and schizophrenia in particular, has resulted in therapeutic efforts that involve the natural groups surrounding the chronic patient. The group-therapy version of this theme is evident in the recent surge of interest in multiple-family group therapy. Multiple-family groups may be viewed as intermediate between a psychotherapeutic and self-help group model, often employing team leadership, with careful selection and matching of families, as well as attention to the early group focus and the need for the leaders to effectively channel and direct the group process.

Tucker and Maxmen[6] originally categorized the great potential of multiple-family groups for psychiatric inpatients. The principles they delineated are useful in explaining current clinical enthusiasm for multiple-family groups with the chronic patient. The 11 general functions served by these groups are: (1) deisolation, (2) socialization and support, (3) imparting of information, (4) catharsis, (5) problem solving, (6) therapeutic competence, (7) instillation of hope, (8) patient support, (9) interfamily learning, (10) facilitation of group therapy, and (11) data source. This conceptual scheme is clinically useful in understanding the goals and methods employed by those who advocate the multiple-family approach as a treatment option for chronic patients.

Also noteworthy is the work with affective disorders and groups. Long-term homogeneous outpatient group treatment of patients with manic-depressive illness is another popular approach in use today. Groups of this type are conducted in conjunction with lithium maintenance treatment and are aimed at getting patients to better comply with pharmacotherapy regimens. Advocates of groups for patients with bipolar affective disorders feel that they offer stability of treatment with a patient population notorious for poor compliance. Early research findings on outcome suggest that rehospitalization rates may be reduced significantly by use of combined lithium maintenance and outpatient group therapy.

In principle, the group treatment of chronic patients, schizophrenics, or manic-depressives parallels Keith and Matthews' observation about psychosocial treatment of schizophrenia in general—that group therapy works best in "ameliorating negative symptoms or in improving social competence, not at alleviating positive symptoms" of the primary conditions.

Pretraining, Patient Selection, and Group Dropout Prevention

A wealth of new material is designed to improve meaningful group entry and participation and to reduce the likelihood of adverse responses either in the form of premature dropouts or in outright psychiatric casualties directly traceable to group events. This portion of the group literature deals with the prevention of avoidable "mistakes" owing to leadership deficiencies.

Pretraining as it relates to groups in terms of process, outcome, attendance, and remaining in therapy is a focus of current research. Over the years, studies have shown that pretrained members tend to do better along these lines than do members who have not been pretrained.

Pretraining appears in the literature in varied forms. Pretherapy formats of shorter or longer term are useful for various patient populations. There is a major school of thought that employs pretraining to facilitate group experiences for patients who are ordinarily regarded as difficult prospective group members. Much of this work was historically done with schizophrenic patients, but in the past few years there have been reports of successful use of pretherapy with other patient populations. Adolescent groups are an area of new work utilizing pretherapy training. These models deal with the special problems in group structure and preparation that are most commonly encountered in this age group. Several methods utilize behavioral contracting, establishment of clear guidelines, and programmed pretraining to foster development of verbal and interpersonal skills. The specific advantages that result include a more rapid development of group cohesion, increased positive expectancies for treatment, reduced time spent in irrelevant group discussion, decreased concerns about confidentiality, and a facilitation of participants' skills in giving and receiving verbal feedback.

The factors that increase the chance of patients' dropping out of groups represent another critical area of group research. This problem is addressed from three prevailing points of view: studies of curative factors inherent in groups; analysis of the role of therapist, patient, and environmental variables; and treatment expectations and interpersonal behaviors that influence outcome in group therapy.

The theme of therapist error appears in several studies. Inability to handle problem patients (help-rejecting complainers, group monopolists, etc.), the difficulty adjusting from a dyadic model to a group model, and issues that reflect technical errors or countertransferential problems constitute the most difficult leadership issues for beginning group therapists. Negative effects of self-disclosure in certain group members and by group leaders are another source of growing concern. The detrimental effects of indiscriminate insistence of therapists on high degrees of self-disclosure, especially with lower-functioning patients, is noted in many circles.

Observations regarding the size of groups afford a specific illustration of the type of concern evident in the aforementioned research. Group size as a factor in therapeutic outcome is considered crucial, especially when groups shrink to four or few members. When this happens, group members tend to become frustrated and disappointed with group therapy. Undesirable group norms are likely to develop, characterized by conflict avoidance, equal time for each member, therapist activity and patient passivity, obligatory as opposed to spontaneous intermember feedback, and a leader-centeredness in which group members abdicate their responsibility for determining the direction of the group. Group image—the group parallel of self-image in individual psychotherapy—is strikingly negative in groups of insufficient size.

Optimum size for an outpatient interactional group is five to nine people when one leader is present, or a maximum of 12 people with two leaders present.

The general research described in this section is noteworthy because it reflects a major trend in the field of group psychotherapy: a departure from a literature that was largely anecdotally based and the appearance of better-controlled, more scientifically oriented efforts aimed at documenting the specific elements that have contributed to clinical favor for groups over the years.

Sexual and Marital Problems

The growing interface between group and family therapy is reflected in a body of work that addresses the treatment of dyadic relationship issues in the context of group psychotherapy. The two most prominent examples of this are group approaches to sexual dysfunction and group methods for the treatment of marital problems.

The group types most commonly in use to treat sexual difficulties are same-sex groups without partners, as in an all male group for premature-ejaculation problems, and mixed male-female groups composed, for example, of sexually dysfunctional married couples. Along with group composition, group leadership style is a significant variable. Groups that are homogeneously composed with respect to specific sexual symptoms tend to be led more behaviorally, with structured, time-limited group formats including out-of-session "homework" and a large educational component. Heterogeneous groups of sexually dysfunctional members gravitate toward more traditional interactional group psychotherapeutic models in conjunction with specific behavioral elements; intrapsychic and interpersonal themes are incorporated into the goals of the latter group type.

Dominant themes in the work reported over the past few years center around the expanded use of men's and women's groups designed to help with specific elements of sexual dysfunction. Women's groups have gained favor in the treatment of primary anorgasmia and more recently with women who are situationally organismic.

The sentiment expressed earlier about the need for "comprehensive assessments" of both the applicants for treatment and the treatment process itself, in order to be more specific in defining those who would benefit and not suffer from groups of this nature, holds equally true for all group approaches to sexual problems.

Treatment of couples in groups when sexual dysfunction is not the primary complaint is another practical and widespread therapy form. Elsewhere, Spitz[7] has reviewed the subjects of couples group therapy and the use of cotherapy in the small-group milieu of conjoint therapy for marital problems. In many ways, the results of couples group therapy parallel what the outcome research on marital therapy in general reveals: that the (1) behavioral group methods are the clearest in terms of describing actual technique and in assessing their methods of treatment and (2) shorter-term, focal (as opposed to global) treatment goals with some form of structured communication training conducted by leaders, whose relationship skills appear to be more effective than their theoretical orientation, is the set of variables most helpful on the basis of current research data.

Summary

The tendencies in groups today may be interpreted as (1) encouraging activity and judicious use of self-disclosure on the part of group leaders; (2) endorsing groups as part of integrated treatment models; (3) renewing the interest in groups as a vehicle for education both in the acquiring of concrete information and the mastery of specific interpersonal skills; (4) reinforcing the value of psychodynamic groups approaches and expanding them to include elements that enhance insight-oriented approaches and yield more technically eclectic leadership styles; (5) insisting on more systematic and scientific evaluation of advantageous versus deleterious group models; and (6) paying more attention to aspects of the pregroup period—namely, screening, diagnosis, and patient preparation.

References

1. Wong N: Focal issues in group psychotherapy of borderline and narcissistic patients. In Wolberg C, Aronson M (Eds.): *Group and Family Therapy*, Brunner/Mazel, 1980, pp. 134–147.

2. Horwitz L: Group psychotherapy for borderline and narcissistic patients. *Bull. Menninger Clin.* 44:181–200, 1980.

3. Lesser J, Lazarus LW, Frankel R, et al.: Reminiscence group therapy with psychotic geriatric inpatients. *Gerontologist* 21:291–296, 1981.

4. Keith SJ, Matthews SM: Group, family and milieu therapy and psychosocial

rehabilitation in the treatment of schizophrenic disorders. In Greenspoon L (ed.): *Psychiatry, 1982*, American Psychiatric Association Press, Washington, D.C., 1982, pp. 166–178.

5. Mosher LR: A psychosocial approach to returning schizophrenia. *The Schizophrenic Outpatient* 1:1–11, 1982.

6. Tucker GJ, Maxmen JS: Multiple family group therapy in a psychiatric hospital. *J. Psychoanal. Groups* 4:21–34, 1972.

7. Spitz HI: Group approaches to treating marital problems. *Psychiatr. Ann.* 9:318–330, 1979.

16

The Psychotherapy
of Psychiatrists
Robert L. Stewart

EDITOR'S NOTE

One of the most difficult areas of treatment, for both therapist and patient, is when the patient is a psychiatrist. Not only it is obviously difficult for the doctor to assume the patient's role, but, when he does, we often regard him as "special," thereby running the risk of not bringing to bear on his behalf our full therapeutic skill and, in a sense, denying him the right to be a patient. In psychoanalytic institutes the idea that the psychiatrist's analysis is only a training experience and not really aimed at treating problem areas in his life and personality is often a camouflage to protect the subject from embarrassment and the therapist from having to see, in one of his colleagues, difficulties that may disturb his own sense of intactness and self-esteem.

Psychiatrists can experience the same psychopathology that any other physician can experience, although two conditions may be a bit more prevalent among psychiatrists: depression and self-pathology. Understandably, psychiatric work often does not provide as strong support for one's self-esteem as certain other forms of work; when this, plus the impact of regularly dealing with emotionally disturbed patients, falls on a substrate of early childhood deprivation, the consequent depressive feelings can be particularly problematic. Ironically, depression in a parent — particularly a mother — may be one of the motivating forces in the choice of psychiatry as a career.

Depression in a psychiatrist is obviously quite amenable to treatment in most cases, if only the doctor can admit his condition and reach out for help. Self-pathology or narcissistic disorders are far more difficult to deal with, since the vulnerable psychiatrist may be highly successful in spite of his lack of genuine empathy for people and patients — a deficiency that, at times, can reach a point of arrogance.

The author highlights some of the specific problems associated with the treatment of psychiatrists and special issues that must be taken into account if therapy is to be successful. Most disturbing of all his comments — although not surprising — is the observation that even psychiatrists may stigmatize their colleagues if they learn of their emotional difficulties, so that even the recovered psychiatrist risks professional and personal complications for having suffered with a condition that he and his colleagues are supposed to understand and about which they presumably assume public leadership to help create broad acceptance.

The Psychiatrist as Patient

"Just like a psychiatrist, you are constituted differently," remarked a surgeon during an operation. The operation was a ligation of a femoral vein, and the surgeon had just encountered a vascular anomaly. The patient was psychiatrist Frederic Wertham.[1] The surgeon's remark, Wertham recalled, was not unfriendly. Martin Grotjahn,[2] a psychoanalyst, wrote: "My complaints [stabbing pain in the back and hematuria] were taken as the typical behavior of a psychoanalyst who always sees the psychogenic mote in his brother's eye, but never the hysterical beam in his own."

It is a commonplace that physicians often have a hard time arranging for suitable medical care for themselves. Sometimes they neglect their health because of counterdependent attitudes, however well rationalized they may be. Also, they may dread getting into a genuinely difficult position. When a physician does seek care, he is often quickly categorized as a "special" patient, either at his own instigation or through some attitude of the treating physician, maybe by both. The two fragmentary anecdotes suggest that psychiatrists, being "constituted differently," may be at greater risk of being treated as special patients than their nonpsychiatrist colleagues—and not necessarily in a beneficial way. Incidentally, psychiatrists' bland acceptance of the trivializing epithet "shrink" doesn't help matters much.

Medicine has its own version of Murphy's Law: "It always happens to a doctor!" Whether or not that dour perspective is justified could be debated; but it is clear that a physician, being better informed about medical matters than most other patients, is more likely to know about it when something does go wrong. Then indeed he does become a special patient. Unfortunately, if the patient and the doctor are both psychiatrists, when something does go wrong (it doesn't always) the problems may be so subtle that neither the patient nor the doctor may be fully aware of them.

The purpose of this lesson is to consider what happens when a psychiatrist seeks treatment from another psychiatrist. The notion of the "special" patient is just as applicable, but there are often some additional twists in the treatment situation that pose problems not usually as important in nonpsychiatric medicine. Psychiatrists, both as patients and as therapists, live in a fish bowl, like members of other specialty groups. This circumstance—the "small world" phenomenon—is of the utmost importance in the treatment of a psychiatrist by a psychiatrist. This lesson will focus on some of the potential relationships between being a special patient and being a member of a small world in the psychiatric treatment of psychiatrists.

The literature on the psychiatric treatment of psychiatrists is surprisingly thin. Aside from some studies on training analysis, only a few papers deal with the subject as the main topic; studies of impaired physicians deal with psychiatrists only as a small part of the whole, and seem to emphasize the problems involved in encouraging the psychiatrically impaired non-psychiatrist to seek treatment. The psychiatrists whose treatment is considered in this lesson tend to seek treatment on their own, and only rarely would be regarded as "impaired physicians."

Idealization of Psychiatry and Psychiatrists

Recent discussions with advanced psychiatric residents about to go into private practice showed that a common concern is treating their "first mental-health professional." For residents, the experience that comes closest to the treatment of a mental-health professional is the psychotherapy of medical students. It is there that what one resident labeled the *"sheesh!"* phenomenon emerges: psychopathology that wouldn't cause a turned hair if it were observed in a clinic patient produces astonishment and dismay when it occurs in a medical student. To what can this be attributed? Some sort of idealization seems to have taken place that dictates that medical students — the physicians of the future — are, or at least should be, free of gross psychopathology. This process occurs in residents who may themselves be in psychotherapy or psychoanalysis for subjectively distressing symptoms. There is an obvious conflict or dissonance between the resident's self perception and his idealized view of his chosen specialty and what he would like himself to be. A physician's tendency to deny the presence of pathology in himself and other physicians is one way of resolving the discrepancy between ideals and realistic perceptions.

When denial begins to break down, another possible resolution for the resident is to assume that psychiatric training hasn't worked very well for him; but maybe it is his own fault. If only he had worked harder to overcome some flaw within himself, the discrepancy and his perceptions of the difficulties of the specialty would fade away. If a resident has not had any significant psychotherapeutic successes during his residency (and some do not) he may consider either his training or perhaps his own learning effort to be at fault. One answer is more training, and he may attend every available workshop or conference about often irrelevant topics. Or he may apply to an institute for psychoanalytic training. This is an important point of entry into

personal therapy, but here the leading motivation may be more for validation and integration of training than for treatment. If this conflict does not
proceed toward some realistic acceptance of life's ironies at this point in his
career, the psychiatrist could find himself in a serious depression later in
life.

The Range of Pathology

The range of psychopathology in psychiatrists isn't much different from
that seen in physicians generally. There is probably some weighting in the
areas of depression and self-pathology; but almost every kind of psychopathology, from the most mild to the most severe, can be found in psychiatrists. The incidence of psychopathology, however, may possibly differ in
various specialty groups. A longitudinal study of Swiss army conscriptees
found that at age nineteen, even before receiving specialty training, the
group of conscriptees that would eventually become psychiatrists showed
more mental disorders and psychomatic disturbances than the group that
eventually became internists and surgeons. The future internists tended to
have more constitutional problems and fewer emotional problems.[3]

Oddly enough, one condition that amounts to a limiting neurosis is "nor-
mality," something that we do not often think of as an illness but that can
lead to a major functional impairment in a psychiatrist. It is possible that if
a "normal" person has chosen psychiatry for his specialty, there could be a
substrate of narcissistic pathology, well defended. The "normal" person is
notoriously difficult to treat and may not be treatable at all, even though the
treating psychiatrist may encounter considerable pathology.

Another phenomenon that is sometimes seen in psychiatrists (although
psychiatry has no monopoly here) is one developing from being intellectually gifted. Keiser[12] described a group of patients whose comprehension of
family events was not inaccurate, distorted, or even repressed. Often these
patients were subjected to premature stimulation, perhaps by primal scenes
or their variants and later by reading material far beyond their years. Regulation and control of stimulation became a major concern, putting their
pathology somewhere within the narcissistic spectrum. Their high intellectual endowment, however, permits significant but uneasy achievement, along
with some intolerance for failure. These patients may become excellent
though anxious psychiatrists: they may require careful treatment, usually
analysis.

Although the range of pathology in psychiatrists is wide and its occurrence relatively frequent, this lesson will focus primarily on two clusters of
findings: depression and self-pathology.

Depression in Psychiatrists

Probably the most common complaint of psychiatrists is depression. Depression, of course, is not a symptom with a simple, single constellation of dynamic or genetic factors as its cause. In the psychiatric treatment of psychiatrists, a wide range of causative forces can be identified. There are depressions that are obviously neurotic and reactive and in which an important structural conflict can be delineated. There are the midlife depressions,[5,6] which have a more existential coloring; these may arise from chronic feelings of being a failure and a misfit—cognitive dissonance catches up with the psychiatrist. Then there are what have come to be known as "depletion" depressions, which in theory are seen to be a consequence of early environmental failures; growth-promoting affirmations of one's own worth were not forthcoming in childhood because of an unempathic, narcissistic, or possibly psychotic parent, or maybe only a worried parent. The depression of the midlife crisis could sometimes be a variant of this. Certainly the practice of psychiatry often provides at best only an uncertain affirmation of one's self.

Not to be ignored in any consideration of depressive states in psychiatrists is depression linked to biological genetic factors. A careful history may disclose a high incidence of suicide, depression, manic traits, and alcoholism in the family tree. Here the therapist is confronted with a problem that is not unique to the treatment of psychiatrists: if one or both of the parents were depressed because of biological factors, the offspring are in double jeopardy not only from the genetic inheritance but also from the psychological difficulties inherent in being brought up by more or less chronically depressed parents. This is a serious problem, often calling for some sort of approach to treatment that combines both medication and intensive psychotherapy or analysis.

The presence of depressive pathology in the parents, especially the mother, seems at times to have played a part in the career choice of psychiatrists. Psychiatrist-patients may repeat in the transference some aspect of a painful childhood accommodation to a depressed parent. They may be unusually sensitive to variations of the therapist's mood, seeing him as depressed when he isn't. It is as though they began their psychiatric practices in early childhood, and their first patients were their mothers. Sometimes these psychiatrists are very effective in their treatment of depressed women. (Major parental pathology need not be limited to the depressive spectrum.)

Suicide among psychiatrists is not rare. Although the validity of some of the statistical studies has been challenged, it seems likely that the suicide rate among psychiatrists is significantly higher than that in other specialty groups. Rich and Pitts[6] observed that "physicians with a preference for psychiatric practice kill themselves much more frequently [*sic*] than expected and the statistical likelihood is less than 1 in 10,000 that this is a random finding. . . . " They noted that "the occurrence of suicides by psychiatrists is quite constant year-to-year, indicating a relatively stable over-supply of depressed psychiatrists from which the suicides are produced." They suggested that "physicians with affective disorder tend to select psychiatry as a specialty."

In 1978, Olin[5] surveyed psychoanalytic societies and institutes affiliated with the American Psychoanalytic Association to study suicide among analysts and candidates in training. His findings do not support any statistical generalizations except that suicides do occur in that group. Sixteen analysts and ten candidates had killed themselves in the 18 years before his study. Since not all societies and institutes responded to his questionnaire, the actual number of suicides was almost certainly higher. There were, in addition, several unsuccessful suicide attempts by both candidates and analysts. It would be impossible to say how many candidates and analysts would have been included in Olin's data base; but the number of active members of the American Psychoanalytic Association, not including the various candidate members and analytic graduates, is currently only about 1500. Olin thought that he was able to detect a link between suicide and midlife crisis from his data. Career dissatisfaction seems to loom large in studies of depression in psychiatrists.

Self-Pathology in Psychiatrists

Fashions in diagnosis change, but that does not necessarily mean that the psychopathology is much different. Today, almost every psychiatrist who comes for therapy or analysis talks sooner or later about his "narcissistic personality disorder" and his need for "empathic affirmation" along with his hunger to be "understood"; 30 years ago, he would have talked about his "pseudoneurotic schizophrenia." But without much question, young psychiatrists who come into treatment today have lived through one of this country's most significant periods of social change and upheaval, and this may be reflected in their pathology.[8] Moreover, our knowledge of early childhood development has grown at an almost explosive rate in the past two decades. The work of Jacobson, Kernberg, Kohut, and Mahler, to name only a few of the investigators, has alerted us to the possibilities of real environmental deficiencies in early childhood that produce rather characteristic disturbances in adult life.

To recapitulate briefly, the psychiatrist-patients under consideration often appear to others to be successful and to function very well, although inwardly they may feel empty, dissatisfied, and ill-at-ease; and they may show a deficiency of empathy for others to the point of arrogance. They demonstrate a degree of incapacity to relate to others as real persons in their own right. Rather, they tend to form "self-object transferences"—that is, they experience and treat others as though they were more like parts of themselves than separate people.[9]

The term "self-psychology" refers to the theories and the techniques based on those theories that have been developed in recent years by Kohut and his co-workers. Self-psychology emphasizes the importance of environmental forces on human development, both normal and flawed; intrapsychic conflict is assigned a role of secondary importance in contrast to its position in classical psychoanalysis and in ego psychology. The "self" is a rather elusive term to define, partly because most psychiatrists have an intuitive, if imprecise, grasp of its meaning. It is not synonymous with "ego," which Kohut[9] regarded as too mechanistic a concept; it is not the same thing as Erikson's "identity," which Kohut saw as "the point of convergence between the developed self and the sociocultural position of the individual." Rather, Kohut wrote of a programmed "core self consisting of nuclear ambitions, nuclear skills and talents, and nuclear idealized goals . . . [all] poised toward the future." The role of the environment in the development of the self was emphasized by Goldberg,[11] one of Kohut's co-workers:

Over and over in the narcissistic personality disorders, we see the failing of these patients' parents in the arena of their inability to comprehend empathically the need of the child to have a reliable self-object to promote one or another form of structuralization. Various combinations of parental intrusiveness and parental neglect fail to provide the proper and fitting availability of the parent as part of the patient's narcissistic matrix.

Others, of course, have been concerning themselves with the study of the same developmental phenomena but have taken different theoretical stances. Otto Kernberg,[12] for instance, emphasizes the role of primitive aggression and intrapsychic conflict instead of a centrally important unempathic parent.

In 1980, Kohut wrote: "I believe the great majority of analytic candidates suffer not from classical transference neuroses but from self pathology." Kohut based his conclusion on his experience doing second analyses of analysts. Since many of those analysts probably sought out Kohut because of his preeminence in the study of narcissism, there was probably some degree of self-selection into the group, with an accompanying feeling of "inness," itself a narcissistic gratification. Some caution in interpreting Kohut's statement is warranted. But Kohut, like others, does point to treatment failures, especially the failure to deal adequately with negative and with narcissistic transferences, as one cause of the cliques, schisms, and idealizations that are so readily observable in psychoanalysis and in psychiatry in general.

A patient's desire to be "understood" may at times be a wish for unconditional approval and license rather than for insight. A theoretical orientation that is too strongly focused on the "enemy without" may lead to a sort of psychotherapeutic witch hunt, and significant oedipal and structural pathology—the "enemy within"—may be almost untouched. In some instances, a psychiatrist's overenthusiastic embrace of some aspects of narcissistic theory functions as a resistance toward the recognition of his own hostile impulses and represents a wish to maintain an image of himself as an innocent and mistreated child. The goal is to sanitize dynamics (and perhaps to maintain a masochistic, self-righteous orientation toward the rest of the world). This is not to say that real narcissistic problems do not occur in a psychiatrist—they do; but they probably are only a part of the picture, albeit an important part.

Recognition of Physical Illness

The psychiatrist is occasionally in an unusually favorable position to contribute to the diagnosis of physical ailments in his psychiatrist-patients. Because of his prolonged and intimate acquaintance with his patients' psychopathology, he may know preconsciously that a patient is not hysterically producing symptoms even when a nonpsychiatrist physician believes the diagnosis to be a functional disorder. There may simply be no plausible psychological cause, say, for a serious neurological problem, and the treating psychiatrist may be the first physician to recognize the nonfunctional nature of his patient's pathological processes. The psychiatrist's non-psychiatrist physician may be too inclined to dismiss a psychiatrist's valid physical complaint as being "all in his head," especially if he knows the patient is in psychotherapy. Grotjahn's[2] encounter with very real kidney stones, mentioned in the introduction to this lesson, is a good example of this problem.

The Small World

The small world of psychiatrists and their psychiatrist-patients is one of collegiality and cliques, of idealization and hostility, of information and misinformation, of competition and collaboration. It is a world that includes spouses and families, multiplying greatly the possibilities of extratherapeutic interaction and the risks of misunderstanding. It is a world where gossip travels fast, where it is difficult to keep personal secrets. It is a world where, if there are no secrets that need keeping, some will be invented by a fertile mind. In the small world, the psychiatrist comes to know a great deal more about his colleagues, and maybe his best friends, than he wants to know. Fortunately, though, most psychiatrists eventually train themselves to leave confidential information in the office where it belongs. It would simply be too difficult to function in the real world if they did not do so.

The small world affects every aspect of the treatment process when the patient is a psychiatrist — the transference, the countertransference, the beginning, the middle, and the termination of therapy, and even life after therapy. While some of the effects of the small world arise from "real" circumstances, however, most originate in unconscious sources. The influence of the small-world environment, whether it is grossly obvious or subtle and insidious, leads to many an unrecognized and undiagnosed transference jam and to the ultimate failure of many psychotherapies. It is in such a small world that the psychiatrist-patient and his psychiatrist-therapist must find each other and begin their work.

The single most important rule for the therapist to observe must surely be: Don't do anything that deprives the patient of his right to be a patient. And becoming a "special" patient of any kind does deprive a patient of a piece of his most basic right. The psychiatrist-patient and his therapist, being members of the same small world, often find it hard to resist the temptation to make the patient special; and the atmosphere of the treatment may become too collegial, too friendly, too free of productive tension, or maybe too competitive, and so on. Does it really make any difference that the patient is a psychiatrist? Are the patient and his therapist really "constituted differently"? The answer is both yes and no. Yes, in that the psychiatrist brings to the treatment a more crystallized set of transference expectations than does a nonpsychiatrist — some based on factual knowledge, some based on misinformation and fantasy. Also, without quite knowing it, the therapist may listen to his patient in a little different way. No, in that transference is transference wherever it may occur, either in the patient or in the therapist; and it differs only in its content and not in its dynamics when it occurs in the psychotherapy of a psychiatrist.

The second principle of treatment that can be compromised in the small world is that the therapist should do nothing that interferes with his serving as a day residue for the formation of transferences,[13] provided that the treatment plan calls for the exploration of transference reactions (something else may be needed!). Just as the day residue is in itself often only an unimportant detail that is taken over by unconscious impulses in the formation of a dream, the day-residue function of the therapist requires that he maintain a relatively low profile in his relations with his patients so that his real behavior does not interfere with the formation of intelligible transferences but instead makes them possible. This presents a problem to a therapist who takes pleasure in being a celebrity or a public figure. In the small world of psychiatry, if the therapist must simultaneously relate to his patient in some important administrative capacity, for example, transferences will inevitably occur, but they become more difficult to sort out and to demonstrate to the patient. These points will be considered in connection with two small worlds: a psychoanalytic institute and a large department of psychiatry.

Therapy in a Psychoanalytic Institute Setting

For the treating analyst or psychiatrist, there are few challenges as great as maintaining a genuinely therapeutic frame in the treatment of his psychiatrist-patients. The proper management of the therapeutic frame and of his real relationship with his patient may make the difference between success and failure in the therapy. In a psychoanalytic institute, the most obvious problem bearing on the psychiatric treatment of a psychiatrist—in this instance, the training analysis of the analytic candidate—is that the therapist is often in a variety of relationships with his patient. The analyst may, for example, serve on the institute's admissions committee; he may be on the progression committee and the education committee; he may be a classroom teacher of his patient; and he is usually a supervisor, not of his own patient but probably of some of his classmates. The strict observance of confidentiality applies to the analyst but not to his patients, so in the everyday exchange of gossip between candidates information about the analyst-as-supervisor (tough, easy, good, bad, etc.) eventually is incorporated into the candidate's knowledge of the analyst-as-therapist. And all of this is filtered through several transference screens.

Institutes are either "reporting" or "nonreporting," which means simply that the training analyst may or may not report to the education committee on his patient's progress, depending on local custom. Even though there may be an institute policy about reporting, to report or not to report is the decision of the training analyst. Most institutes are nonreporting and try to protect the confidentiality that is so necessary to the analytic situation. Those institutes also have a policy that the training analyst should not participate in any administrative decision-making about his patients, but it is questionable whether such a policy can be strictly observed. A lifted eyebrow in a committee meeting can be very telling.

How do candidates react to this complicated situation? A lot depends on the pathology of the candidate and the shape of his transference neurosis. The question of the evaluating function of the training analyst comes up in almost every training analysis, and it can become a strong resistance in some. Even though the treating analyst does everything he can to preserve the confidentiality of the analyst and scrupulously avoids taking part in any decisions about his patient, a candidate can use the possibility of a crossover of function as a building block in his transference neurosis, possibly repeating something about fantasized collusion between his parents or lending some substance to his feeling that his training analyst wants to hold him back just as he once felt his parents did. This last fantasy can come from a wish that an omnipotent parent protect the analysand from the dangers of the grownup world and from his own repressed drives.

The term "training analysis" is itself a contradiction. Reviewing her nearly 40 years' experience as a training analyst, Therese Benedek[14] observed that near the end of her career she had become more concerned about what kind of analyst her patient was going to become. This involves a valuative function that can detract from, rather than augment, the therapeutic function of the analysis of the candidate. A training analysis certainly has a training aspect, in that any patient learns something about analysis by being a participant in the process. But that is not the primary goal of a training analysis, although many believe that it is in a training analysis that an analyst learns how to analyze others. Some such term as "personal" or "preparatory" analysis avoids this bit of obfuscation, and attempts to restore at least a measure of the future analyst's right to be a patient.

There are pitfalls for the treating analyst in the institute setting, most of them arising from the analyst's vulnerability. To some extent, the analyst's reputation is on the line, and he wants to do well in his work. Future referrals can to some extent depend on his continuing good reputation. But if the analyst lets himself get caught in his psychiatrist-patient's transference game, the integrity of the analysis will be threatened. Idealizations and negative transferences will not be sufficiently analyzed, and can come back to haunt everyone in the form of public dissension and discontent, as Kohut and others have observed. The therapist needs to have a steady hand on his own narcissism to ride out a colleague-patient's negative transference and his often accurate criticisms of his technique, of his teaching, even of his very life, if he is to do justice to his patients.

A further difficulty with analysis of the psychiatrist comes with the termination of the analysis. Ideally, there should be a period of time away from the analyst after the formal termination during which the patient can consolidate his gains, including his self-analytic function, and mourn the loss of his analyst as a real person as well as a transference figure. In the institute setting, however, the patient often becomes an instant colleague of his analyst, sometimes taking a place on the institute faculty. An important step of the analytic process may be bypassed altogether. A training analysis usually is not a "normal" analysis, but the difficulties are not insuperable.

Therapy in a Psychiatric Departmental Setting

In the second example of the small world, a large department of psychiatry, the interferences in the psychiatrist's personal treatment may be more rampant, but will probably not be as sharply focused as in the institute setting. To illustrate, a patient may go directly to a therapy session from a teaching presentation given by his therapist. He may even have been involved in some sharp public exchange with his analyst or therapist. The occasions for extratherapeutic contact are numerous: patient and therapist may meet on the elevator, in the parking garage, in the hallways, in the library, in the washroom or at the symphony, theater, baseball game, or even at the Parents' Association meeting at their children's school. If the therapist or a member of his family has to be hospitalized for some physical illness, he may discover that his patients have had access to his hospital records. A "No Visitors" sign on the door may not seem to apply to his psychiatrist-patients, who are, after all, on the same hospital staff.

All grist for the mill? Perhaps, but the sheer volume of the extratherapeutic interaction will more likely dull the sensitivity of both the therapist and the patient to the potential for using the material therapeutically. Then the result is apt to be a mutual acting-out, a collusion between patient and therapist not to notice what is really going on. If the treatment is an analysis, the transference neurosis may fail to develop because so much of the instinctual life of the patient is being directed into acting-out and other forms of gratification. A negative transference may be split off from a more positive transference and be redirected toward other members of the department, perhaps the therapist of peers. This can take the form of malicious gossip that gives expression to aggressive transference feelings in a displaced form while preserving the positive transference to the therapist. The director of some essential rotation or perhaps a supervisor may become a target of this kind of displaced transference.

One complication arises from the fact that some of the persons being talked about by the psychiatrist-patient are often well known to the therapist and may even be personal friends of his. It is hoped that the therapist's view of those who appear frequently in his patient's material is tempered by his own personal experiences and objectivity. Otherwise, the narcissism of the therapist can lead to an almost unanalyzable transference situation in which neither the negative transference to the therapist nor its derivative and displaced forms in the hostile, rebellious, or other feelings toward another person can be analyzed. It is especially in this way that a therapist gets to know more about his colleagues than he really wants to know. He will hear from his patients about behavior that sounds irrational, and those reports will receive consensual validation from the reports of other patients. The therapist's job is to remain as objective as he can about the transference to himself. He needs to recognize that the patient's reality testing is not at fault, but he should insist on a strict analysis of the transference determinants of the reports. Realistic or not, the appearance of such reports in the patient's associations is often strongly determined by transferences that really belong in the treatment, not in the extratherapeutic world.

An interesting form of resistance that arises only because the patient is himself a therapist is the attempt to turn his treatment into a supervision. If the treating psychiatrist feels that supervision is necessary, he should, after exploring the transference significance of this development, suggest to his patient that he seek supervision with someone else. Although this sets the stage for a split transference, the risk is usually offset by the possibility of keeping the treatment situation relatively clean. This situation calls for a careful monitoring of the countertransference, and the therapist may find himself in competition with the supervisor. This can be very illuminating for the understanding of the transference-countertransference interaction.

Hospitalization

Although most of the psychiatric treatment of psychiatrists is conducted on an outpatient basis, it occasionally becomes necessary to persuade the patient to enter the hospital. In the author's experience with this problem, the results have often been disappointing; perhaps other psychiatrists have had more encouraging results. The reasons for poor outcomes are at least three: the nature of the disorder itself, the small-world context within which hospitalization must take place, and the "special patient" status of the psychiatrist. Erwin,[15] a psychiatrist, pseudonymously described his struggles with a manic-depressive illness. The cycles eventually recurred with such frequency that he was no longer able to sustain a psychiatric practice. (Erwin's account was before the development of effective psychotropic medications.) The practice of psychiatry differs from some other specialties in that if the psyche is too disarrayed, the psychiatrist's capacity to use himself diagnostically and therapeutically may be seriously compromised. This is not true of some other specialties. A cardiologist, for example, might have heart disease; but as long as he is not physically incapacitated, he may continue to practice excellent cardiology, since the heart is not the perceptive and executive tool of the cardiologist in the same way that the self or ego is the perceptive and executive tool of the psychiatrist.

The second problem area in the hospitalization of psychiatrists arises from the fact that the details of the illness tend to become public, at least within the professional community. It is a good idea to arrange for hospitalization outside the psychiatrist's home community, if possible. In that way, the psychiatric community can do less second-guessing about what the treating psychiatrist should or should not have done (often without any valid information about the treatment). It is quite possible that there is a double standard at work here: hospitalization of a psychiatrist is regarded as a much more serious event than hospitalization of a nonpsychiatrist. Although this could be based on the likelihood that hospitalization is generally undertaken only with more serious disorders, it is probable that some irrational elements enter into this attitude. Even though the psychiatrist might be able to return to his work at his former level of performance — or even at a higher level — knowledge of his hospitalization will not soon be forgotten by his professional colleagues, and his career could be damaged. This is unfortunate, since it is precisely in the post-hospitalization period that the psychiatrist is in the greatest need of his colleagues' support and understanding.

Two Recommendations

Probably the most sensitive element in the therapeutic system is the therapist's narcissism. The amount of narcissistic gratification can be great, but it can become a counterresistance. Or the therapist's sense of narcissistic vulnerability, which is often put to a severe test, can lead him to avoid doing some of the things that he should be doing for his patient.

Two important recommendations can be made to the therapist of psychiatrists. First, he should honestly try to answer the question: "Why, of all the psychiatrists available, is this patient coming to me, now, for treatment? Why not someone else?" The answer can be revealing. Second, a therapist of psychiatrists is to do nothing that deprives his patient of his right to be a patient. He may be a gifted and unusual patient, to be sure, but his right to good therapy — and his need for it — must at all times be protected from the intrusions of the therapist's narcissism and from intrusion from the outside. Only in that way can the important difficulties be overcome.

References

1. Wertham F: A psychosomatic study of myself. In Pinner M, Miller BF (Eds.) *When Doctors Are Patients*, W. W. Norton & Company, New York, 1952, pp. 102–118.

2. Grotjahn M: A psychoanalyst passes a small stone with big troubles. In Pinner M, Miller BF (Eds.): *When Doctors Are Patients*, W. W. Norton & Company, New York, 1952, pp. 89–95.

3. Willi J: Higher incidence of physical and mental ailments in future psychiatrists as compared with future surgeons and internal medical specialists at military conscription. *Social Psychiatry* 18:69–72, 1983.

4. Knutsen EJ: On the emotional well-being of psychiatrists: Overview and rationale. *Am. J. Psychoanal.* 32:123–128, 1977.

5. Olin HS: Survey of suicide among psychoanalysts and candidates. *Psychoanal. Rev.* 65:641–647, 1978.

6. Rich CL, Pitts FN Jr: Suicide by psychiatrists: A study of medical specialists among 18,730 consecutive physician deaths during a five-year period, 1967–72. *J. Clin. Psychiatry* 41:261–263, 1980.

7. Lasch C: *The Culture of Narcissism: American Life in an Age of Diminishing Expectations*, W. W. Norton & Company, New York, 1978.

8. Kohut H: *The Analysis of the Self*, International Universities Press, New York, 1972.

9. Kohut H: Reflections on *Advances in Self Psychology*. In Goldberg A (Ed.) *Advances in Self Psychology*, International Universities Press, New York, 1980, pp. 473–554.

10. Goldberg A (Ed.): *The Psychology of the Self: A Casebook*, International Universities Press, New York, 1978.

11. Kernberg O: Further contributions to the treatment of the narcissistic personality. *Int. J. Psychoanal.* 55:215–240, 1974.

12. Keiser S: Superior intelligence: Its contribution to neurogenesis. *J. Am. Psychoanal. Assoc.* 17:452–473, 1969.

13. Kohut H, Seitz PFD: Psychoanalytic theory of personality. In Wepman JM, Heine RW (Eds.) *Concepts of Personality*, Aldine Publishing Company, Chicago, 1963, pp. 113–141.

14. Benedek T: Training analysis — Past, present and future. *Int. J. Psychoanal.* 50:437–445, 1969.

15. Erwin W: A look into another world (manic-depressive psychosis). In Pinner M, Miller BF (Eds.): *When Doctors Are Patients*, W. W. Norton & Company, New York, 1952, pp. 211–220.

17

Terminating Psychotherapy
Leon Salzman

EDITOR'S NOTE

The conditions under which the average medical patient terminates treatment or modifies the nature of his contact with his physician are reasonably clearcut, in contrast to those which optimize the ending of psychiatric treatment and psychotherapy in particular. Should psychotherapy end when the patient feels better? Should it continue until personality changes have been accomplished that will permit the patient to function more effectively and hopefully prevent recurrences of illness? If the patient comes with a particular complaint — about his or her marriage or sex life or difficulty at work — should therapy continue after the specific problem has been attended to and, if so, on what basis? Should the decision to terminate originate with the patient or should the therapist initiate it under various circumstances?

These are but a few of the issues that the author highlights in this chapter as he defines the conditions for termination in general, while cautioning that these conditions are specific in each individual patient. In some, excessive expectations must be modified first; in others, constricted expectations must be expanded. The therapist must be careful not to impose his own, often perfectionistic standards on patients. Many patients are reluctant to terminate treatment. Some fear the possibility of failure. Others have strong dependency needs fulfilled in the doctor-patient relationship. Still others want to avoid expressing feelings of independence that they fear the therapist might interpret as rejection of or dissatisfaction with him. It is equally possible that reluctance to terminate may stem from conscious or unconscious motives within the psychiatrist. Financial considerations, the preference for working with a familiar patient rather than a new and unknown one, perfectionistic attitudes, giving up a valued friendship — these are a few of the more obvious ones.

When termination is being considered, it should be discussed, not acted on impulsively. A resurgence of symptoms at the time may indicate the patient's reluctance to terminate at a time when termination is indicated or it may reflect unresolved issues in need of further work. The psychiatrist must be skilled at distinguishing one from the other. Finally, rather than giving the patient the sense that the end of treatment is a final, irreversible step, it is generally better to offer an open door policy so that he or she can, if desired or needed, return for brief visits to clarify new conflicts or obtain support for dealing with life stresses on a preventive basis.

The Challenge of Terminating Treatment

Generally, a patient's goal in therapy is to achieve a state of anxiety-free living without having to change his personality. For therapy to be effective, the patient must recognize the nature of his unrealistic demands, since it is the excessive neurotic trends in his personality that prevent him from expanding his living and produce his anxiety. Termination is possible when he can accept some limitations of his expectations and can achieve some balance and compromise in his goals and behavior.

The criteria for termination are therefore dependent on a number of issues but are determined primarily by the degree to which the patient has achieved some understanding of his problems and has increased his capacity to deal with them. This should not necessarily mean that the patient's anxiety has disappeared or that he no longer has any difficulties in his living. Such unrealistic demands may be made by the patient. The therapist must recognize that adequate functioning for the patient is a reasonable goal, especially when the patient has come into therapy with marked incapacities for functioning interpersonally and is beset by severe anxieties.

The therapist must not impose his own set of standards and goals on the patient. He should be flexible and not bring his own perfectionistic expectations to bear by requiring a perfect or total resolution of the problem before considering termination. Such a goal is never possible, and the struggle to achieve it betrays the therapist's compulsive demands.

The criteria for termination are different in each case, since the problems of each patient require a variable set of goals and expectations. If the problems are specific and limited—for example, the patient who has marital problems and wants to limit his therapeutic involvement to improve his relationship with his partner—treatment can be terminated when it is evident that the communication and the interaction of the couple have noticeably changed. On the other hand, the marital problems may represent only a minor symptom of a pervasive depression that has consequences in many areas of the person's life. Then treatment would not be terminated until some understanding and alternation of the depressive problems had been achieved.

The criteria for termination will therefore be determined by the nature of the problem, the patient's goals, and the therapist's ability to see these goals as valid and reasonable. At times, the therapist will try to expand the patient's goals by helping him recognize that more pressing personality problems are the issues, rather than some symptom that may be troublesome. Insomnia can be alleviated by drugs, but the anxious, obsessive ruminations that impeded sleep need to be recognized and treated.

At other times, the therapist must make the goals more realistic when the patient's expectations are perfectionistic and extreme. This is especially true with obsessional patients, who want perfect solutions and life without anxiety. Their expectations of magical amelioration and total relief from symptomatic distress require extensive clarification before termination of therapy can be considered. They must recognize and acknowledge that these demands are part of their disorder. Only when they can accept some imperfections and uncertainties that acknowledge their humanness can termination be considered. An awareness of fallibility and an acceptance of some deficiencies and incapacities to manage and control all the elements in their living will remove the need for the obsessions and compulsions, the purpose of which is to give the person a false sense of security and control. Then it is possible for the person to face new challenges and take risks which are an intrinsic part of nonneurotic functioning. A significant reduction of these unrealistic expectations will be the signal for considering termination. It may also be manifested in the patient's increasing ability to tolerate anxiety without the impatient and impetuous resort to all sorts of anxiety and distracting or relieving ritualistic behavior.

Patient Resistance to Termination

A noticeable alteration of the patient's previously neurotic behavior, manifested in his world and personal life, often precedes his request to consider termination. However, the initiative may come not from the patient but from the therapist. While there may be some pressure from the patient to terminate therapy, there may also be great reluctance to give up the comfortable world of talk and move into the real world of action until he is certain that he can handle his affairs. Again, the matter of risk and rejection or failure to fulfill preconceptions or distorted goals interferes with the pursuit of change in spite of an abundance of understanding.

To prevent the expected anxiety, the patient may avoid situations that might test his emerging self-esteem and assertiveness. Thus, the gains manifested on the analytic couch would not be tested in the real world, and the rewards of the newly developed achievements would not be experienced and serve as an impetus for further growth. It is at this time that the therapist must share the patient's uneasiness and reassure him against possible rejection and failure, encouraging him to try his new skills. The possibility of failure must be acknowledged—especially since the anxiety will prejudice the outcome as it did at the height of the patient's illness. Now, however, the anxiety has been reduced and a renewed self-awareness has emerged, permitting the occasion to be experienced with a greater potential for success. To win a race, one must compete—which means that one must risk the possibility of losing. However, maximum training (understanding) will enhance one's prospects and encourage further participation if one does not win on the first try. This metaphor is apt in encouraging the patient to try out newly discovered insights and emerging skills.

A passive, timid, and insecure lawyer came to treatment for his inability to assert his clients' claims in a contentious atmosphere. He was eager to change his behavior. The therapeutic work clarified the dynamics of his timidity and uncertainty in his interpersonal relationships. In the course of our work, he faced a situation in which he needed to confront an opposing, aggressive attorney. Even though he felt justified in his position, he was extremely hesitant, fearing he would appear inept to his client as well as to the other attorney. By accepting the possibility of failure, he did manage to assert his position mildly and, to his surprise, he won the motion. This experience permitted him to take more risks and achieve more success, which raised the issue of his terminating treatment. This request enabled us to examine the intricacies of the characterological underpinnings of his timid behavior and produced more meaningful insights and changes that made the request for termination more valid.

The lonely and uneasy patient whose difficulty in establishing relations with the opposite sex brought him to therapy must be encouraged to pursue such relations when the possibility of success has increased. Premature pressures would guarantee failure, while moderate success would be an impetus for further efforts. Termination in such cases can be considered when the capacity to tolerate some rejection does not prevent further efforts and when the patient is able to recognize that not all rejections are due to his ineptness or undesirability.

A patient will often insist on remaining in therapy, pleading too much anxiety without it. At such times, the therapist may need to prod and push him into the world. Termination plans, therefore, cannot be left entirely in the patient's hands. Some patients—namely, obsessionals—cannot be relied on to raise the question or to press for termination on their own. These patients require perfect performance and absolute freedom from anxiety, and so never feel ready to stop. With each new understanding come the uncertainty and doubt about whether it is the "whole answer"; therefore, work must proceed further before they can try their mettle in the outside world. This is also very clear with the phobic patient who, despite understanding the roots and patterns of his avoidances, requires active assistance from the therapist in trying to deal with the situations of his phobia. The therapist may need to get into the elevator with the patient to overcome the initial resistance to trying something new. This understanding has produced a burgeoning of phobia clinics, where this simple notion claims to have magical consequences. Agoraphobias, particularly, benefit from such behavioral modification efforts. But premature attempts at modification of behavior may have negative consequences; this modality, which is applicable in one's private practice, requires a sensitivity to the patient's readiness to accept new challenges. Termination at this time implies not a total absence of anxiety but a readiness to accept some discomfort in performing hitherto phobic tasks or entering into previously avoided situations.

Difficulty terminating may also be expected in very dependent patients, who are so uneasy about their incapacities in dealing with life with competence and success that they hang on to the therapy and therapist for fear of failure even after demonstrating their ability to function independently. Here, too, the therapist must be firm, energetic, and empathic and must promote independent action with reassurances and active support. Others postpone the question of termination for the very reason that brought them into therapy; i.e., their passivity, low self-esteem, timidity, and fear of displeasing the therapist.

Overall, there is a tendency for the patient to resist termination in spite of the evident beneficial growth and maturation experienced in the therapeutic process. The feeling of security in the relationship, feelings of gratitude toward the therapist and concern about losing a friend, as well as the uncertainty that characterizes their problems, which are never wholly overcome, necessitate a clear and determined therapist who sees the patient's attitude as the major determinant for terminating therapy.

Therapist Reluctance

Termination may also be a problem for the therapist, who must deal with his own resistance to change and separation. This factor must always be taken into account when the patient raises the question and the therapist immediately reacts with some distress and resistance. While such a reaction can be justified on clinical grounds, the lack of definitive criteria permits the therapist's own neurotic tendencies to distort the needs of the patient.

There are practical and realistic issues that involve professional as well as personal problems. There is always some reluctance to terminate a patient's therapy without finding a replacement, or to terminate care for a well-understood patient and begin again with a new, untried and uncertain one. In the face of patient shortage, this may be especially difficult. Many rationalizations may be offered to hold on to a patient, and some are more reasonable than others. Some longterm patients become part of the therapist's family, and terminating is like giving up an old friend. These factors must constantly be kept in mind in appraising the therapeutic validity of terminating or continuing with a patient.

Termination Tactics

The criteria for termination can be established only in specific cases, depending on the patient's idiosyncratic symptoms, anxieties, dependency needs, and readiness to go it alone. In all cases, however, when termination is achieved, it is important to maintain an open door if there is a need for the patient to return. The patient and therapist should part as friends and collaborators who can meet again if need be. Expressions of gratitude, whether in words or in material gifts, should be graciously acknowledged and accepted without interpretation and with thanks. Before termination, the therapist should review the work done and also what has been left undone. Introspection, not preoccupation, should be encouraged, and a closing statement of the history of treatment and assessment of progress should be made before the therapeutic relationship is brought to an end.

Termination should be gradual and rarely absolute. Nor should it be done at the moment the issue is raised either by the patient or by the therapist. The topic should first be considered, evaluated, and discussed. It should be done not to discourage the suggestion but to clarify the patient's decision (if it is his). Relevant consideration should include the questions how and why the issue arose when it did, what progress justifies the decision, how the patient assesses his present style of functioning, as well as what his future plans might be in the context of the problems that brought him into therapy. Have there been clear and demonstrable changes in behavior as well as verbalizations in the office setting? Can the patient identify any characterological alterations as a result of therapy? The last requirement is extremely difficult to assess, and too often it becomes the therapist's justification for an interminable therapeutic arrangement.

If termination is agreed upon, the frequency of sessions should be reduced over a reasonable period of time. This will help both patient and therapist to arrive at a date more comfortably. The therapist's criteria for reducing the frequency of sessions should be: (1) when the patient becomes more comfortable about accepting some reverses in living that heretofore would have stimulated panic and anxiety; (2) when there is a reduction of tension in many areas of his living, coupled with a greater emotional involvement in all his relationships; and (3) when there is evidence of reduction of the distressing symptoms and an increased capacity for the patient to enjoy life without having to fulfill certain demands all the time.

However, the criteria listed above should be flexible, and one need not wait until all have been fulfilled. Often, when a termination date has been set or agreed upon, there is a resurgence of symptoms, or a situation develops that poses a great difficulty for the patient; the patient may then insist that his agreement to terminate was premature and may try to persuade the therapist to abandon the program. While the situation may be a valid challenge and the presenting symptoms may be surfacing again, it may represent the uncertainties and uneasiness in facing new experiences that characterized the initial neurotic process. This should not necessarily be viewed as regressive, as it may be an anxiety response to the threat of separation and independent functioning. Such a reaction does not imply that the decision to terminate was incorrect. It should be expected and needs to be dealt with in the closing phase of therapy. The therapist should not be trapped into postponing or abandoning his plans to terminate because the patient experiences renewed anxiety. It should be clearly understood by both patient and therapist that anxiety attacks will occur throughout the patient's life and that therapy is not a permanent guarantee against disturbed living. Some uneasiness is inevitable when any new development occurs. Thus, if anxiety does occur, the therapist should not be stampeded into changing his arrangements.

The decision to terminate cannot be made in terms of the fate of some particular symptom, especially in the case of psychosomatic symptoms. Gastrointestinal disorders, cardiovascular problems, and symptoms of all sorts may clear up in the course of therapy without any particular emphasis being placed upon them. Some symptoms, however, may continue no matter how successful the therapy is. If somatic problems have continued for too long, they may be irreversible and may continue after many other characterological problems have been resolved. Therefore their status should not, in general, determine the decision for termination. The patient should know that after a formal termination there will be ample opportunities for occasional visits and brief contacts at times of particular crisis. While it is hoped that the patient will have developed sufficient skills in introspection during the process of therapy, new problems may require occasional contacts or the resumption of formal therapy.

The timing of the termination discussion is a key issue, and it is the therapist's responsibility to be attuned to the process. As evidence of altered behavior or an increased capacity to understand and objectively review one's anxiety reactions begins to appear, the therapist should begin to consider termination. As indicated above, consideration of termination should not wait for the patient's initiative, as the patient is often reluctant and uneasy about suggesting it. He may be concerned that the therapist will view his request as evidence of dissatisfaction or as an escape from emerging disturbing material. Because of a past habit of derogating his worth or distrusting his assets, he may have difficulty viewing his wish to terminate as an index of growth and maturity. With this in mind, the therapist must view such a request not necessarily as evidence of continuing neurosis but as a possible measure of maturity that may or may not indicate the time has come for termination of treatment. It should not be viewed as evidence of the patient's inability to accept his own inadequacies or automatically characterized as a "flight into health." While the patient's wish to terminate may be premature or an evasion of the discomforts of further exploration and investigation of his neurotic trends, it may also be valid and should not automatically be viewed as another defensive tactic. A faulty handling of this sort may discourage the patient and force a postponement longer than might be therapeutically constructive.

However, the patient's insistent desire to terminate can be the initial impetus for the therapist to consider it in a serious way. A fear of becoming too dependent on the therapist or the process can be the incentive to terminate. The issue must be confronted, since there may be partly realistic and partly neurotic factors to be considered. While the therapist's goal is to enable the patient to function independently of the therapist, the patient should be able to experience dependency on supportive and concerned partners. Such patients are frightened by their awareness of minimal dependency and see it as total dependency; they want to escape from the process. Others may see therapy as a lifetime dependency: they cannot allow anyone else in their living. Under these circumstances, termination must be considered when they seem to be settling in for a long-term dependency.

Selected Reading

Alexander F: The voice of the intellect is soft. *Psychoanal. Rev.* 28:12–29, 1941.

Salzman L: Chapter on Termination. In *The Obsessive Personality*, Jason Aronson Press, New York, 1968.

Weigert E: Contributions to the problem of terminating analysis. *Psychoanal. Q.* 21:465–480, 1952.

Index

CREATED